Lessons from the Hill

Lessons from the Hill

The Legislative Journey of an Education Program

Janet M. Martin
Bowdoin College

St. Martin's Press
New York

For my mother,
Mary Martin

Executive editor: Don Reisman
Managing editor: Patricia Mansfield-Phelan
Project editor: Alda Trabucchi
Production supervisor: Alan Fischer
Art director: Sheree Goodman
Cover design/art: Ed Smith Design

For information, write:
St. Martin's Press, Inc.
175 Fifth Avenue
New York, NY 10010

ISBN: 0-312-07933-8 (paperback)
         0-312-10685-8 (cloth)

Foreword

The United States Congress reflects the virtues and imperfections of the American people. That is as it should be, since in the eyes of many we are a uniquely enduring democracy. Those of us elected by our fellow citizens to serve as their national representatives attach great importance to what our constituents want from government. Professor Martin delivers an insightful, timely account of the processes that largely determine whether an idea becomes law. In a very real sense, the effect of legislation approved by Congress and the consequences realized when the body does not act are measurements of whether members of Congress live up to these expectations.

The primary topic of Professor Martin's case study, legislation designed to continue funding of a national dropout prevention program, offers an instructive step-by-step view of how an idea becomes law. The book describes the emotional and intellectual vacillations experienced by those involved in a legislative initiative. Most importantly, *Lessons from the Hill* is an excellent discourse in civics both for people who consider themselves well versed in this procedure and for the uninitiated. I commend it to students, teachers, and the increasing number of Americans who have decided to take a more active role in how their national legislature works.

The year 1990 was a difficult legislative year. In June President Bush publicly acknowledged that the federal fiscal condition had so deteriorated that additional revenue, along with spending reductions, were required. This ushered in five months of negotiation that culminated in a bipartisan budget agreement. The year also held midyear elections for members of the House of Representatives and some senators. Although these larger issues dominated the press, numerous important issues of less media appeal were introduced, debated, and acted upon by the Congress. The School Dropout Assistance Act is an example of meaningful legislation passed that year while other bills of equal or lesser magnitude received more attention.

The latest wave of education reform began in the early 1980s. This rebirth of interest in the learning outcomes of children led to a reexamination of the efficacy of American elementary and secondary schools. Parents, educators, public policymakers, and businesspeople increasingly recognized that, in effect, writing off one-fifth of students would eventually severely hamper national economic productivity. More compellingly, they began to accept a moral responsibility to combat the dropout phenomenon.

The dropout legislation Professor Martin uses to illustrate the work of Congress was designed to help determine what type of services would help disparate schools made up of students from different backgrounds reduce national dropout rates. She gives voice to the story as only an insider could. This book accurately characterizes the creativity, persistence, and compassion required of staff as they assist elected officials.

Constructive representation for members of Congress often involves compromise as negotiation helps move the legislative process closer to one's original objective. The stress engendered by the give-and-take required sometimes leads honorable people from their mission. Fortunately, that was not the case for the members who labored to pass a dropout prevention bill in the last year of the One Hundred and First Congress.

Readers will live through private constituent meetings, speeches, committee hearings, and markups, and finally the complex web of rules that govern legislative procedures on the floor of the U.S. House of Representatives and the Senate.

Lessons from the Hill illuminates the best this institution can be when enough of its members understand what is in the best interest of the United States and its citizens and decide to act on that now more than 200-year-old ideal.

George J. Mitchell
U.S. Senate Majority Leader

Preface

In the spring of 1989 when I was awarded a congressional fellowship to spend a year as a participant-observer on the Hill, I began to think about what I might learn that year and could share with my students and fellow political scientists. One project that was always in the back of my mind was that perhaps I would be able to trace a bill through Congress and tell a story of the legislative process that would enable others, especially my students, to find the same fascination in Congress that I have found. In February 1990, as Senator Herb Kohl's office (where I was working) began to become more involved in the issue of school dropouts, I realized that I might be in the middle of just such a legislative tale. At that point I had no way of knowing the outcome, but as each day went on I found myself observing firsthand many of the things I teach my students. I began to keep notes and ask questions (endless questions that were patiently answered by many of those acknowledged below). The issue was a small one, like most that Congress faces every day.

As Congress-bashing became a popular theme throughout 1992, not only by the media, but also by President Bush and members of Congress itself, and as my students indicated more and more disgust with "Congress," I wrote faster.

Lessons from the Hill reflects much of what I find to be positive about the institution and its members. Congress is a responsive institution and a fundamental part of an enduring and workable system of government.

As I write this in January 1993, a sense of hope and optimism greets the new Democratic administration from an American public that seems willing to give the national government a chance to work and that wants to join in as participants in that process. Lately, I have not heard the same bashing of Congress as strongly as I did throughout much of 1992. Perhaps this has to do with the new tone set by President Bill Clinton. He is reaching out to all members of Congress—the leadership, new members, Democrats, Republicans, and Independents—to end the gridlock that was caused by twelve years of split-party control of the White House and Congress. I hope this book will contribute to a better understanding of the role of Congress in this process.

This book is a very personal account of the efforts made to retain the funding for a federal school dropout prevention program. The book reflects my perspective as political scientist, student of Congress, and staff member in the U.S. Senate. However, the book has benefited from the input of many people, acknowledged below.

I would like to thank Don Reisman, executive editor at St. Martin's Press, who early on shared in my vision, and helped keep the project on target, as well as Frances Jones for her valuable suggestions and prompt assistance and response to all inquiries, and Alda Trabucchi, who guided this through to completion.

I am certain this book has profited from my students of Congress, both at Gettysburg College and Bowdoin College. Not only did their questions force me to constantly work on doing a better job in explaining, but also they shared their experiences with me as they returned from a semester on the Hill in a Washington Semester program or as they caught "Potomac Fever" and began a career on the Hill. Some students and former students also helped in the research that followed my year on the Hill while others shared insights gained from their vantage point on the Hill, including Michelle Chaffee, Deirdre Griffin, Chuin Ming Lee, Torben Pastore, John Dougherty, and Dave Wilby. In addition, Sarah Jensen, Jini Linkovich, and John Calabrese of the Government Department of Bowdoin College gave me valuable assistance in meeting my deadlines.

I must also thank the American Political Science Association for giving me the opportunity to spend a year on the Hill as a congressional fellow, and the congressional fellowship class of 1989–90 who spent that year on the Hill with me. While I benefited from conversations with many, Kristin Huckshorn, Sharon Basso, Lisa Pullen, and Chris Bailey shared many insights gleaned from their experiences, some of which were very helpful to me.

All the members of Senator Herb Kohl's staff, both in 1989–90 and in subsequent years, have proven to be excellent teachers, including Bob Seltzer, Sherry Hayes, Marsha Renwanz, Mike McCarthy, Tom Stubbs, Kate Sparks, Bev Anthony, Cris Coffin, Jon Leibowitz, Arlene Branca, Lynn Becker, David Ward, Tom Mullooly, Katey Schoenecker, Kris Sandine, Tracy Hahn, Michelle Albers, Kristy Schantz, John Zobeck, Jackie Dickens, Harry Nathanson, Eva Malecki, and the late Keenen Peck.

Kim Wallace and Pat Sarcone of Senator George Mitchell's staff have been most generous of their time in helping me on this project. Jeanie Bowles provided exceptional help in tracking down key documents necessary in fully understanding the legislative history of the school dropout program.

Others on the Hill and in Washington to whom I owe a debt of gratitude include Ann Young, David Evans, Amanda Broun, Mike Casserly, and Jeff Simering; and in Wisconsin, Maureen Coffey and Joe Pellegrin.

I would finally like to thank Senator Herb Kohl and Majority Leader George Mitchell, both of whom found a place for me to work on the Hill and shared with me their insights which have greatly added to my understanding of Congress. I will always remember and appreciate their support both in Washington and upon my return to academic life in Maine.

The book has greatly benefited from the suggestions of those who critically reviewed the manuscript, including Michael Berkman, Pennsylvania State University; John F. Bibby, University of Wisconsin—Milwaukee; Christopher J. Bosso, Northeastern University; Barbara C. Burrell, University of Wisconsin—Madison; Roger H. Davidson, University of Maryland; John J. Pitney, Jr., Claremont McKenna College; Brad Mitchell, Ohio State University; Morris S. Ogul, University of Pittsburgh; Bruce I. Oppenheimer, University of Houston; Samuel C. Patterson, Ohio State University; James P. Pfiffner, George Mason University; Randall B. Ripley, Ohio State University; and June Speakman, Claremont McKenna College. They will recognize where their suggestions improved the manuscript and also where I, perhaps stubbornly, persisted in telling the story the way I thought best.

Finally, my mother, Mary Martin, and my sisters, Jean T. Martin and Judy Ann Bromberek, have supported all of my endeavors. That support has kept this project going, as has the support of John Winship, a good friend, and an astute and diligent critic, whose painstaking readings of the manuscript and frank criticisms have helped in ways that only we will know.

Janet M. Martin

Contents

Introduction

The United States Congress is a fascinating institution, serving as a legislative model for democracies around the world. Each year foreign governmental officials and scholars come to the United States to study Congress, joining, among others, American journalists, doctors, health care administrators, and scientists who spend a year or two as participant-observers on the Hill. These observers have all discovered that the best way to gain an understanding of Congress is to immerse oneself in daily life on Capitol Hill. However, since this immersion is an opportunity available to relatively few people, the inner workings of the U.S. Congress remain unknown.

In the past few years Americans have been given a snapshot of Congress through the eyes of the C-SPAN cameras as viewers watch hearings, floor debates, and even stump speeches on the campaign trail. Yet such a snapshot captures only a fragment of activity. The viewer sees only one vote or one hearing at a time when on any given day twenty hearings may be taking place. The reason why so few hearings are televised is that C-SPAN may only have enough television crews to cover three hearings.[1] What the viewer sees on television is also deceptively simple. The viewer may tune in to a hearing on health insurance reform and several months later see four hours of debate, climaxed by the final vote on passage of the health care financing bill. What the television audience will not see is the months, if not years, of learning, discussion, debate, and negotiation that have taken place among members of Congress on that topic. In almost all cases, these discussions extend beyond the House and Senate chambers to include staffs of members, interest group lobbyists, executive branch personnel, and even constituents in town hall meetings.

Congress may be the least appreciated of the three branches of government, perhaps because it is also the least known of the three to the American public. Even in a time when public opinion polls are finding that fewer Americans are approving the way Congress generally is doing its job, Americans are more approving of the way their own representative is doing her or his job.[2]

I have been one of the fortunate few who has been able to learn about Congress firsthand by immersing myself in life on the Hill. I was in Washington, D.C., from November 1989 to August 1990 as an American Political Science Association (APSA) congressional fellow on sabbatical leave from my job as an assistant professor of government at Bowdoin College in Brunswick, Maine. I worked first in the office of Senator Herb Kohl (D-Wis.) and then in the office of Senator George Mitchell (D-Me.).

What follows is a case study involving a federal school dropout prevention program. Although it is a very small piece of legislation, it has had a tremendous impact on the lives of many Americans. The case study involves congressional efforts to create a federal dropout prevention program which originally funded eighty-nine program sites in thirty-one states and the District of Columbia for two years. In particular, this is the story of the hard-fought battle to continue the funding for a third year in 1990, the year I was on the Hill. During my stay, I was able to play a small part in helping move the funding request through the legislative process.

To provide some perspective on the size of the dropout prevention program, of a total federal budget of over $1 trillion the program consumed only $19.945 million for the continuation of the eighty-nine projects.[3] Like so many other federal programs, it was indeed a small one. Preliminary evaluations by the Department of Education indicated that the projects were effective in increasing high school graduation rates. Yet in the politics of the federal budget even effective programs do not have guaranteed funding, and in January 1990 it was almost assured that no funding would be forthcoming. There was a particular irony in this poor prospect, for 1990 had been dubbed the "Year of the Dropout," owing to the public rhetoric proclaiming the importance of this issue.[4] However, by May of that year, funding for this program had been approved, and the projects, after being labeled a "dire emergency," were able to continue.

This story will be told in part from the perspective of my firsthand experiences of the legislative process. I will also draw upon a wide range of sources since congressional involvement in school dropout legislation was long established by the time I arrived on the scene.

This case study is important for a number of reasons. First, because this study provides a good example of many aspects of the legislative process, it will enable the reader to gain an understanding of Congress—the members, staffs, its complexity, and its responsiveness as a representative legislative body.

Second, the reader will come to realize that much of what goes on in Congress is not linear. Flowcharts (reproduced in every American Government textbook) of how a bill is introduced in Congress and then ultimately signed by the president are far too simplistic. Perhaps they even do a disservice to the student of American Government by failing to convey the fluidity and openness of the process (see Figure 1). Unlike the president, Congress is not a unitary actor. Congress is confusion, chaos, complexity. To understand that complexity is to understand the beauty of the United States Congress and its representative nature which attracts so many foreign observers to study how and why it works. Congress is responsive, but there are many clashing and divergent interests to which it must respond—constituents, party leaders, the president, emerging democracies around the world, and even a member's own conscience.

Third, this story will illustrate that there are important brakes on congressional responsiveness. It must be remembered that Congress is but one of three coequal branches of government, with the president and Supreme Court able to check congressional action. In the 1990s, members of Congress, along with many others, have had to come to terms with the

Figure 1   How a Bill Becomes a Law

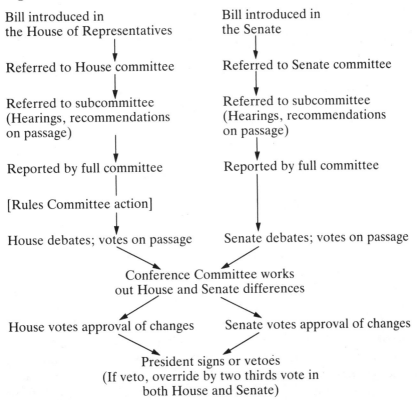

Bill introduced in
the House of Representatives

Bill introduced in
the Senate

Referred to House committee

Referred to Senate committee

Referred to subcommittee
(Hearings, recommendations
on passage)

Referred to subcommittee
(Hearings, recommendations
on passage)

Reported by full committee

Reported by full committee

[Rules Committee action]

House debates; votes on passage

Senate debates; votes on passage

Conference Committee works
out House and Senate differences

House votes approval of changes

Senate votes approval of changes

President signs or vetoes
(If veto, override by two thirds vote in
both House and Senate)

tremendous national debt that has accumulated and the budgetary limitations that have resulted. Securing funds for programs many would feel are worthwhile is not as easy as it once was.

Fourth, the case study will give the reader a sense that the victories or "wins" one side or another experiences in Congress are often small and incremental. Change comes slowly. However, for most participants—whether they be constituents, members, interest groups, or congressional staff—a little triumph is all that is needed to reaffirm a belief that the system works. I have always had an optimistic enthusiasm for Congress, and while representative democracy may be frustrating, whatever one's political goals, it is still possible to achieve legislative success in those areas we feel are important. At times some cases may succeed even in the face of insurmountable odds. As this book will illustrate, Congress provided money for one particular domestic program even in a time of fiscal austerity when the rules of the game were weighted heavily against funding for domestic, nonentitlement programs.[5] Most legislative proposals die in any given year, but this particular effort succeeded. This book focuses on this successful story not only because it is inherently interesting and appealing, but also because it can more fully inform the reader of the legislative process from beginning to end.

Finally, congressional staff have taken on important roles, and some would argue too large a role. Staff members enable Congress to be responsive by providing access to a wider range of citizens, groups, and organizations. They also expand the information base available to members of Congress and they augment the legislators' capacity to engage in legislative activity—that is, the bargaining and negotiating between members on the Hill, organizations, and executive branch personnel.[6] Yet there are differences in the backgrounds, role, perspective, and use of staff. This case study will illustrate some of the variations and, in particular in this example, the greater role played by staff on the Senate side, with the members of the House taking on more of the deliberative and negotiating role some fear has been lost in Congress.[7]

Before turning to the narrative of how Congress became involved in the policy area of school dropouts, I want to give the reader a brief introduction to how I came to be involved with the issue of school dropouts during my first week on the Hill. I also want to share my impressions of these first days—a time when I found myself quickly becoming immersed in a way of life an outsider only sees in glimpses. By sharing some of these first experiences and observations, I hope to make Congress come alive to my reader. While a few of my experiences may be unique, they have enough in common with those of the thousands of others who have come to work on the Hill that the "institution" of Congress in all of its complexity may be better understood.

CHAPTER 1

A New World: First Days on the Hill

For as long as I can remember, I have had a deep interest in American government and the political process. I received a doctorate in political science from Ohio State University and since 1983 have taught courses on Congress and American Politics to undergraduate students, first at Gettysburg College and then at Bowdoin College. And so when I came to Washington, I had some familiarity with the institution of Congress—including committee and leadership structure as well as congressional procedures—and with the members most frequently in the news. When I was awarded a congressional fellowship from the American Political Science Association (APSA) in 1989, through which I would work as a legislative assistant on Capitol Hill for a year, I couldn't have been happier or more eager to immerse myself in the experience. And not surprisingly, at the end of my year, I found that however well prepared I had been in an academic sense, I had attained an understanding of Congress at work that no textbook could have taught me.

THE APSA CONGRESSIONAL FELLOWSHIP PROGRAM

The American Political Science Association first began sponsoring political scientists and journalists as participant-observers of Congress in 1953. Some of the more prominent scholars of Congress have come through this program, as well as some who decided to stay in Washington and take a nonacademic career path.[1] Students of Congress have long benefited from the experience of those fellows who have returned to academic life, whose writings have become classics on Congress in the modern era.[2]

In the 1960s federal civil servants representing many departments and agencies in the executive branch (from the Department of Agriculture to the CIA and the Nuclear Regulatory Commission) began to participate in this program, and worked for a year on the Hill. "According to Frank Duggan, 'Jack Kennedy got the federal employees involved because he wanted them to realize the role of Congress in their agencies rather than to think of Congress as an interruption in their day.' "[3] Over the years this program has expanded to include anthropologists, historians, German and French fellows, Robert Wood Johnson Health Policy fellows, and Asia Foundation fellows.[4]

An Orientation to the Hill

Before the new fellows go to the Hill, they attend an orientation program that provides information and insight into the workings of Congress, Hill personalities, the major issues before Congress, and the relationship of Congress to the outside world, including interest groups. In addition to a series of speakers, the orientation includes a workshop by the Congressional Research Service (CRS), which presents an overview of Congress, CRS's research services for members of Congress and their staff, and information on committees, procedures, and rules.[5] As any staff member soon learns, the CRS is an invaluable resource that provides not only quick turnaround to requests for items such as statistical data but also in-depth research on a wide range of topics. Our orientation to Congress was complete when we were given a tour of the U.S. Capitol by Cornelius Heine, the executive secretary of the Capitol Historical Society. He regaled the group with enough anecdotal material to impress any friend or family member who should visit the nation's Capitol in the future.

Fortunately for me, by the time I would begin work on the Hill I had already developed an extensive network of friends and acquaintances throughout the House and Senate by virtue of the fellowship program and its month-long orientation program. This network would prove invaluable to me later when I needed to identify the right staff member to call in an office or learn why a particular representative or senator had taken a particular position.

The Search for a Job on the Hill

In the midst of their orientation, the Fellows begin a search for a position on the Hill in November. Even a newcomer soon understands why Congress is often referred to as Capitol Hill. Not only is the Capitol itself situated on the top of a hill, but also members of Congress and the congressional staff work in a number of different buildings surrounding the Capitol itself. In fact, except for the party leaders who have their offices in the Capitol, most senators and representatives spend very little time in the Capitol itself. An elaborate underground subway system connects the Russell, Dirksen, and Hart Senate Office buildings with the Capitol. A similar subway system connects the Rayburn Building on the House side to the Capitol. This subway system allows members to zip in and out of the Capitol and only spend as much time as they need to participate in debate on the floor, cast a vote, or attend committee meetings or receptions held in the Capitol. It is in these buildings that members of Congress and their staffs are most likely to be found engaged in the work they have been elected to do.[6]

After a few days on the Hill, I became adept at using the vast network of underground tunnels that reduce the time it takes to get from one side of the Hill to the other. I discovered that the fastest way to locate a member's office is to ask directions of members of the Capitol police force stationed at the entrances of each building. They can quickly direct you to any one of the 535 offices, usually without even checking the directory.

In one's first days on the Hill, it soon becomes apparent that each office has its own unique organization. Some offices, for example, are organized hierarchically, with a chief of staff or administrative assistant in the top post, and a legislative director to coordinate the policy work of the office one rung below. In these offices below the legislative director come the legislative assistants and legislative correspondents, each covering several policy areas.[7]

In some offices there may be a co-sharing of top responsibilities between an administrative assistant and legislative director. Other offices may combine the job of legislative assistant with that of legislative correspondent, a pattern found more frequently on the House side than on the Senate side. The chief of staff or administrative assistant may choose to locate his or her desk in the center of activity in the office, or have an office secluded from the rest of the staff. Some chiefs of staff in the Senate even have a separate office down the hall from the senator's main office.

The size of House and Senate offices also varies a great deal, with some staff in the House forced into areas far too small for the number of people in the office. The huge increase in staff size over the last thirty years, about which we all heard in the 1992 presidential campaign, has created a space crunch (see Table 1-1). In many of these offices, bathrooms and closets have been converted into additional office space. Desk space is such a serious problem on the House side that House members often cannot avail themselves of the free labor of fellows. In contrast, the Senate has much larger offices, with an entire section of one or two floors assigned to one senator.

All senate offices have "member's doors," in addition to front doors.

Table 1-1 Congressional Staff
Size

	House	*Senate*
1957	2441	1115
1967	4055	1749
1977	6942	3554
1987	7584	4075

Source: Norman J. Ornstein, Thomas E.
Mann, and Michael J. Malbin, *Vital Statistics on Congress 1991–92* (Washington, D.C.: Congressional Quarterly,
1992), p. 126.

Designed for fast entrances and exits, these doors come in handy when
an office is located far from the Senate floor and the senator has only a
brief period of time to get to the floor for a vote. In this way, senators
can avoid the potential awkwardness inherent in having to tell constituents that they have no time to chat. In addition, the most senior members of the House and the Senate also have "hideaway offices" located in
the Capitol Building.[8]

On the House side, most staffs in Washington consist of an administrative assistant, press secretary, and eight to ten staffers, with legislative
staff handling both constituent mail and legislative policy—that is, recommending which bills to co-sponsor, how to vote on an upcoming bill, and
drafting legislation.[9]

On the Senate side, the staff is larger and so a greater differentiation
in roles is possible. The entry-level legislative correspondent positions
often go to recent college graduates, who draft replies to constituent mail
and also assist in research in legislative areas as time permits. The legislative assistants are responsible for several different policy areas (e.g., defense and foreign policy, or health, education, and labor) and oversee the
correspondence drafted by the legislative correspondents. They are primarily responsible, however, for the legislative positions a senator will
take and the legislation he or she will sponsor and support. As soon as a
senator has been in the Senate for a year or so, and especially if he or she
is in the majority party, the number of staff begins to expand. Most senators in the majority party become chairs of subcommittees within the first
two or three years of being in the Senate, and through that post they are
able to hire additional staff. As seniority accumulates, the size of the staff
grows, until some senators have control over 100 positions or more.

When a congressional fellow seeks a position with a representative or senator, a number of criteria must be considered, including the senator or representative's ideological leanings and partisan identification. In addition, some thought must be given to whether the approach of the member and staff is pragmatic and flexible, or if they possess a rigidity that may prove troublesome to the fellow's own ideology. Basically, is this an office the fellow can work in, and are these people he or she can get along with? It is also important to determine whether there is a good fit between the fellow's own background and experiences and those of the legislator. A good fit will be invaluable when the fellow has to deal with the needs and problems of a state or congressional district. Having lived in a state may also be a criterion in deciding which applicant gets a position. Other important factors are the style and ambience of the office (e.g., does an office manager run a tight ship with all staff needing to check in at 9 A.M. and out at 6 P.M., with lunch hours to be taken only from 12 to 1, with no provisions for flex-time?); the availability of desk space; and the location of the desk (will the new hire be working in an office of the representative or in one of the House Annex buildings far removed from any interaction with the member of Congress and principal staff?).

In addition to an assignment on the personal staff, fellows have opportunities on committees. Since the 1940s, committees have routinely hired professional staff, who usually work for the chair or ranking minority member of the committee and bring with them appropriate training and experience. For example, lawyers work on the Judiciary Committee; those with experience in state departments of education or education associations in Washington may serve on the education committees.[10]

The fellowship program provided us with a list of representatives and senators, their staff contacts, and office staffing needs (e.g., policy areas, press), which helped to narrow down the search process. In 1989 twenty senators or senate committees and forty offices on the House side were seeking the service of a fellow. Based on this information and on research I had done on members and their areas of interest and ideological positions, I narrowed my choice to eleven offices. From interviews with staff in these offices (and experiences in attempts even to schedule an interview) I began to fully understand the individualistic nature of Congress. Constituent interests, ideological preferences, seniority, committee assignments, personality, and election concerns were among the many factors influencing a member's own agenda and use of staff.

I also became aware of the vast differences between the House and Senate. Since most members of the House have only half the number of staff of even the most junior member in the Senate, there is little differentiation in roles among House staff members. Correspondence with constituents, as well as the coverage of a number of diverse policy areas, was expected of all. The size of the House of Representatives allows members to specialize in just a few areas, yet their staff do not have the luxury of a well-defined, narrow role. Conversely, with only 100 members, senators tend to be generalists in order to cover a heavier committee workload per member. But the large number of staff per member enables the staff to take on more differentiated roles. Given the differences in the House and Senate, I had hoped to spend half of the year on the House side and the other half on the Senate side. Because of the House's space problems however, I ended up exclusively in the Senate.

I observed the tremendous space crunch on the House side first-hand. Given my own interest in education policy, I met with the administrative assistant for Representative Pat Williams (D-Montana). Williams, a former public school teacher, was chair of the Post-Secondary Education Subcommittee of the Education and Labor Committee. A brief tour of his office suite revealed a lack of space for even one additional staff member. Desks, chairs, and bookcases were all wedged into a space far too small to adequately provide workspace for his staff.

This pattern was repeated in many House offices. Next, I tried a member with more seniority with the expectation that greater seniority would mean more generous office space. Because of my interest in women in politics, I met with a member of Representative Pat Schroeder's (D-Colo.) staff. Elected in 1972, Schroeder was one of the most senior members on the Armed Services Committee. However, while her office space was larger than that of Williams, she already had a fellow from another program who would be working until April. Again there was no room.

After several other tries on the House side, I went over to the Senate side, where I found space to be less of a problem, though still an issue. For example, Senator Paul Simon (D-Illinois) and Majority Leader George Mitchell (D-Maine) had fellows from other programs and no desk space available at that time for additional staff. Senator Al Gore's (D-Tennessee) office had space, but really needed a scientist who could be of assistance to the senator in global environmental issues as well as national health care policy and technological issues in health care, such as genetic engineering. His chief of staff, Roy Neel, did give me good advice: work for a junior member of the House or Senate, with a small staff, in order to have an opportunity to work with the member; also, seek out a position in the most active office possible. As it turned out, I followed Neel's advice.

After visiting with legislative and administrative assistants in several offices in both the House and Senate, I found that the best match for my interests (and available desk space!) was in the office of Senator Herb Kohl (D-Wis.), who was looking for someone to work on health or education policy. As a Wisconsin native, I would, of course, be familiar with the state, which would be an advantage in any work I might do with the senator's constituents and their issues of concern. Kohl, first elected in 1988, was one of the most junior senators and one of only a few Democrats who was not even the chair of a subcommittee. He had never held any kind of political office, but his staff had many years of experience on the Hill, having been drawn from the offices of Senators Simon, Leahy, Metzenbaum, Dodd, Glenn, and Adams. His staff was clearly working on defining a policy agenda for the upcoming session that would help create a legislative record. The issue of education was to be prominent on that agenda, since it had been a campaign commitment. Kohl's business background made him acutely aware of the need for gains in basic literacy and in math and science skills at all levels of education, beginning with elementary and middle school students.

SENATOR HERB KOHL

A relatively low-profile senator with a noncollegial style, Kohl has not won critical acclaim from either his colleagues in Congress or congressional observers. Nonetheless, he appears to be effective in representing the interests of his Wisconsin constituents, despite a style different from that of most senators. Kohl came to Washington in 1989 as a nonpolitician. His most visible role in Wisconsin had been as owner of the Milwaukee Bucks basketball team. One Wisconsin newspaper compared the neophyte Kohl to the political naif played by Jimmy Stewart in the classic film *Mr. Smith Goes to Washington.*[11] Kohl came under fire in the 1988 campaign for spending over $7 million to win the election, much of it his own money. At the same time, he took no money from political action committees (PACs), and in a campaign that foreshadowed Ross Perot's bid for the presidency in 1992, he ran with the slogan, "nobody's senator but yours."[12]

Kohl's parents, who came from Eastern Europe, had no formal education but had a deep respect for cultural values. Their lives were difficult as new immigrants, especially given a lack of knowledge of English. His parents spoke Yiddish at home until Kohl was about 6 or 7, and they struggled to learn English and use it in dealing with the customers in the small store they ran. Like so many immigrants in America's history, Kohl's parents insisted that their children go to school, get good grades, and excel scholastically. It was expected that all four children in the family would go on to college, and in fact all four not only graduated from college but also went on for advanced degrees. Unlike many politicians who give lip service to the educational issue, making it part of their platform to win election or stay in office, Kohl genuinely believes in the importance of education for both individual betterment and national excellence:

> When I was young, high school graduates were guaranteed good jobs. Now, in a competitive world, students need more skills—a high school diploma is not enough. What I sensed about education when I was young has come to the forefront like gangbusters. Now we all know and talk of the importance of education. It enlarges life, one's universe. Education allows you to get out in the world and meet interesting people, opening to all possibilities and enjoyments in life. If we in the United States want to be the best by the year 2010, 2020, or 2030, then a good education for all must be a priority.[13]

Kohl has even used his own financial resources to demonstrate his commitment to education. In 1990, for example, he began an annual program of $1000 awards to 100 students, 100 teachers, and 100 schools in the state of Wisconsin. Scholarships are awarded to students recognized for "academic achievement, leadership, citizenship, community service, honesty, integrity, and special talents"; Kohl Teaching Fellowships are awarded "to teachers who have inspired a love of learning in their students, inspired and motivated others, provided outstanding service within and outside the classroom, or helped improve the morale and status of their profession"; and grants go to the schools of the winning teaching fellows to be used for "an innovative educational project." Kohl gives out the awards in person each year, which gives him the opportunity to meet and talk with the students, their parents, and the teachers and their principals and colleagues. In announcing this award program, Kohl stated that "Our state's future is directly tied to the quality of education we give our children. In this small way I hope to say to our young people and our teachers if you do your best and work hard you will be rewarded."[14]

The more cynical among us might argue that Kohl came up with the program simply to enhance his visibility and to gain support among voters. But refuting this argument is the fact that the program is kept totally separate from his congressional office and work. As a philanthropist, he has decided to devote a substantial portion of his immense fortune to education. Because of his low profile in Washington, few outside of his home state are aware of his personal commitment to education. Yet it is clear that this dedication would remain even if he were not in the Senate.

Incredibly, for over a year, Kohl had no press secretary. This position rarely remains unfilled very long in any office in Congress, since visibility and "credit claiming" are usually considered essential for any U.S. senator, especially if he or she wants to be reelected. But getting reelected is obviously not a motivating factor for Kohl, which makes him something of an anomaly on the Hill and, also, a little bit difficult to get to know. It can also cause some consternation and frustration among his staff, for although staff cannot take any direct credit for the successes of their boss, they at least want to see him honored and taking the bows when he deserves them.

Kohl's staff has more experience than that of most newly elected senators and has come to develop a deep loyalty to him and his programs. Part of that loyalty can be attributed to his tendency to treat his staff like family and to display thoughtfulness and kindness to everyone around him. During the time I worked there he made a point of greeting not only each staff member every morning, but also all of the Capitol Hill workforce, from subway operators and the police force to the staff of other members. (Only a staff who felt a particular closeness to their boss would have given a United States senator a birthday lunch of peanut butter and jelly sandwiches accompanied with chocolate- and strawberry-flavored milk. After all he does represent Wisconsin, the dairy state!)

Kohl's staff, like most on the Hill, works long and hard hours. In the middle of a session, when Congress is meeting far into the evening hours, it is not unusual to walk through the buildings and see as many lights on and staff at their desks at 8 P.M. as at 4 P.M. In fact, it was a midnight hour when I received a phone call from Sherry Hayes, a legislative assistant to Senator Kohl, offering me the job in his office. The late hour of the call stunned me at the time but seemed not at all extraordinary once I joined the staff. This first call was my introduction to routine Senate "overtime."

In many House and Senate offices, hiring may be done based on the recommendation of the legislative director or administrative assistant, but the final decision is up to the particular representative or senator. When I met Senator Kohl for the first time, I discovered that we had both attended the same public grade school (Sherman Elementary School) in Milwaukee. What is more, my family had always done our grocery shopping at Kohl's family's grocery stores; probably many years before, he had bagged my mother's groceries while learning the family business from the bottom up.

THE WORK BEGINS

I met with Sherry on Tuesday, December 5, for an orientation to the office. Rather than gradually work in a new staff member, Sherry believed it was best to plunge right in. So even before I had a desk, phone, and computer, which today constitute the basic necessities of any staff aide, she gave me a folder full of information to read. She also gave me the name and phone number of a staff member on the Senate Subcommittee on Education, Arts and Humanities whom I was to call in an effort to resolve a problem facing one of Kohl's Wisconsin constituents. I immediately got the feeling most newcomers to the Hill get: I felt totally overwhelmed. How would I be able to quickly digest and fully understand the particulars of this case in order to help these constituents?

The problem concerned funding for school dropout programs in a vocational education bill that was then before Congress. I made the phone call to Ann Young, a staff member of Senator Claiborne Pell's (D-R.I.) Subcommittee on Education, Arts and Humanities, on Monday, December 11, and got my first taste of a number of experiences that would shape the rest of my year on the Hill. The next day Ann returned my call, and as I spoke with her I began to realize the value of committee staff and the help they provide constituents with problems. With this phone call, I was also beginning to build ties with staff outside of Senator Kohl's office. These contacts, as I would soon learn, would be invaluable to Senator Kohl's efforts to continue funding for another school dropout program.

On my first day in the office, I was given the grand tour and introduced to all the other staff members, the location of the photocopy machine, fax, office mailbox, and autopen of Senator Kohl's signature, all of which would become part of daily routine. I was amused to discover that the old wooden desk I inherited had popcorn in most of the drawers. I soon learned that Senate staff live on popcorn as the late afternoon snack, some of which had made its way into that desk. If you walk the underground corridor connecting the Hart and Dirksen Senate Office buildings, especially as a scheduled recess period draws closer and the Senate is staying in late over the course of several days to complete work on several bills before the recess, you may see a trail of popcorn leading from the snack bar down the corridor to the elevators. Some offices have even installed their own popcorn machines (e.g., Senator Tom Harkin of Iowa), especially when the promotion of corn helps constituent farmers back home.

When I finally started work in December, Congress was in recess until the new session began in January. This lull gave me the perfect opportunity to get a feel for what lay ahead and to gain the skills I would need as a legislative assistant.

Aside from a steady supply of popcorn, a computer terminal is a staple of every legislative assistant. Every Senate and House office has its own computer system, with any one of several different operating languages. This has led to the creation of the job of computer systems operator and technician in each office. I had expected all the Senate offices to have the same system, with similar equipment and brands, given the cost savings involved. However, each office, on both the Senate and House side, has its own system, perhaps reflecting the fierce sense of independence and individuality prevalent on the Hill. Staff members who move from one office to another must be quick to adapt to the new operating language and word processing system in place in the new office. As a further example of the individuality of the offices, even phone messages are handled differently from office to office. Some still rely on the tried and true pink slips, while others have a completely computerized system for phone messages.

The Senate offers a series of ongoing computer workshops to cover the different operating systems and word processing systems found throughout the Senate. I took several of these workshops and found that the requisite skills are quickly gained, especially if you have had prior computer experience. Being adept at using computers and adapting to different computer systems is essential. Within each office, in addition to phone messages being sent via computer, most memos, and drafts of memos, speeches, and bills are edited as they circulate among several staff members. In the ten months that I worked on the Hill, I used three different operating systems, four different word processing systems, and several online databases.

In addition to the computer workshops, the Congressional Research Service (CRS) conducts a series of workshops on a wide range of topics from congressional procedures to study of substantive policy areas. These workshops are especially beneficial to new staff or to staff moving into new positions, providing quick knowledge of a particular topic and an introduction to the analysts in CRS who can provide future assistance in many different policy areas. I attended several workshops on education issues that would be on the agenda during the upcoming second session of the One Hundred and First Congress.

There are few "secretaries" on the Hill, and the few who could be classified as executive secretaries primarily handle the representative or senator's personal correspondence and scheduling and are more likely to have the title of executive assistant or scheduler. (One of the fellows who participated in our program was a midcareer civil servant who had always had access to a typist in his jobs in the executive branch. He soon discovered that the biggest change he would experience in shifting to the legislative branch was that he would have to do his own typing. He spent the first few weeks learning how to type.)

In no time at all, the press of work becomes great. The luxury of not having much on your desk in the first few days on the job quickly fades away, as does the time available to take advantage of these workshops. Throughout the year I would be involved with a number of different aspects of the legislative process—from drafting language in bills to protect Wisconsin programs, to briefing Senator Kohl, to preparing press releases for the assistant press secretary, to writing floor speeches, and making recommendations as to which bills to join in as a cosponsor, and even suggesting ideas for legislation the senator should introduce.

My first task on the Hill was an appropriate one: to intercede on behalf of a Wisconsin constituent, the Milwaukee Area Technical College, and make the phone call mentioned above to Ann Young in order to let the subcommittee know how language changes in the vocational education bill would affect the Milwaukee dropout program. The efforts to continue funding for the demonstration dropout programs and the involvement of Senator Kohl and his staff began with that first phone call. However, before going any further, I had to acquire a full background on the issue of dropouts and the different federal programs dealing with dropouts. I was soon to learn a great deal about the legislative history of the demonstration dropout program, as well as the complexities of the congressional budget process. Thus, in December, the stage was being set for Senator Kohl's involvement in the effort to continue funding for the demonstration dropout programs.

As with most issues before Congress, there is a long, ongoing debate that involves many different actors at any given point in time. Issues become redefined, and the membership of Congress and committees changes. Congressional attention to the high school dropout problem began years before Senator Kohl was even elected to the Senate. Moreover, while the subject of the separation of powers is ever present in any discussion of the U.S. system of government, the constitutional separation is often less apparent when we examine the actual policy process more closely. Indeed, a subgovernment phenomenon exists in a number of policy areas. "Subgovernments are clusters of individuals that effectively make most of the routine decisions in a given substantive area of policy."[15] The individuals in a subgovernment typically include the members of House and Senate committees with jurisdiction in a particular policy area, the congressional staff of these members, bureau chiefs and their aides, and lobbyists representing private sector organizations and groups. These different sets of people both inside and outside of government frequently interact. At times a symbiotic relationship may develop among them, with congressional staff and the members for whom they work dependent on a lobbyist for drafting the language for a bill, for organizing the support of members in the opposite chamber, and for grass-roots lobbying.

At the same time, only a member of Congress can actually introduce a bill and personally intercede with other members to support a bill; otherwise, the White House and interest groups would see no federal program or funding. In addition, the support of administration personnel is needed to see that a program is implemented in accordance with congressional intent. However, many congressional staffs are also dependent on bureaucrats to find out if programs are working, whether funding can be justified, and what impact the particular language in a bill will have on a program.

Throughout this book, the interdependence of members of Congress, congressional staff, interest groups, and, in this case, program directors in the Department of Education will clearly demonstrate this symbiotic system, with its web of assistance, guidance, and help in working to obtain funding for the continuation of the dropout projects. At the same time we will see how a parallel, opposing network attempted to apply the brakes to this forward movement.

So, while Senator Kohl and his staff first enter the discussion in December 1989, we need to go back in time not only to see how this issue first came on the Congress's agenda, but also how the issue of dropouts came to be an ongoing agenda item for Congress in the 1990s. Chapter 2 explores how dropouts moved onto the congressional agenda, and Chapter 3 begins to tell the legislative tale of congressional involvement in setting up a demonstration dropout prevention program. Subsequent chapters explain how the junior senator from Wisconsin and his staff were inextricably drawn into the web of staff, constituents, interest groups, and executive branch personnel that work together on a program. Many individuals eventually played a role, since the success of any legislative initiative is rarely, if ever, the result of just one person or one office.

CHAPTER 2

Agenda Setting

> At the age of nine, my mother took me out of school, which meant she
> no longer sent me to school. I became, in a sense, a mother figure for
> my [six] brothers. I started cooking, cleaning, and taking care of them.
> Now that I think back on it, my question is how come no one ever
> knocked on my mother's door and asked, "How come your child is not
> going to school?" But I guess it wasn't important.
>
> Maria Garcia, New York City[1]

Today the issue of school dropouts is firmly on the nation's policy
agenda, but for many of the nation's dropouts, like Maria Garcia, it may be
too late. During the 1980s a movement began in which serious attention was
given to the extent and nature of the school dropout problem in the United
States. Educators, school administrators, students, parents, education
groups, bureaucrats, and politicians at many locations throughout the country began to push for help in resolving the intractable problem of dropouts.

By 1990 the nation's governors set a national goal that the high school
graduation rate be increased to 90 percent by the year 2000, and President
George Bush reiterated the same goal in his State of the Union Message to
Congress in January 1990. Yet in that same year the only federal program
targeted specifically to address the school dropout problem came close to
losing its funding.

This chapter examines how issues become identified and how they
work their way onto the national agenda, with subsequent chapters show-
ing how the policy process nearly brought funding to a halt.

AGENDA SETTING IN CONGRESS

It is simplistic but no less true to say that before an issue can become
part of the public policy debate and move on to the national agenda, an
awareness of a problem must exist. While members of Congress are already familiar with certain issues, such as smoking bans on airplanes or

14

airplane safety since they are, after all, frequent flyers, other issues on which they have less firsthand knowledge, especially those affecting the poor, have to be brought to their attention. For example, the president may include a list of programs he or she would like to see passed as part of an Annual State of the Union Message to Congress. Or a cabinet secretary testifying before a congressional committee may indicate the need for congressional legislation in a particular area. The agenda may also be shaped by proposals interest groups and other private sector organizations present to congressional staff or a congressional committee; by the media, especially through editorials and op-ed pieces; by research institutions and think tanks through their commissions and reports; or even by constituents who may ask their representatives in Washington to provide help in some way. This list is not exhaustive; it merely suggests that issues may come to the attention of members of Congress in a variety of ways.

Issues that affect individuals who are not organized in society cannot easily get on the congressional agenda. In this case, "agenda setting is facilitated through issue expansion—by involving other individual groups," or by expanding the size of the audience by identifying how others may be directly or indirectly affected by the issue.[2] Issue expansion will occur if an issue is perceived to be of "social significance."[3] In addition, an issue that appears to have staying power and to affect other areas has a greater chance of expanding to a larger audience. Once the scope of an issue is enlarged, "a multitude of new resources . . . becomes available; solutions inconceivable at a lower level may be worked out at a higher level."[4]

The dropout issue is an issue that primarily affects the unorganized—the economically disadvantaged, especially the young, economically disadvantaged minority populations. The issue reached the congressional legislative agenda and national agenda only after it was redefined as having significant and long-lasting implications for society. With an expansion of the groups concerned with the problem and a broader audience looking at the problem, dropouts finally became an agenda item for Congress. However, in the case of school dropouts, once the issue attained national prominence as a federal public problem, the spillover effects kept the issue in the private sector as well.

Broadening the Scope of Education Policy

Education as a policy area has long been in the domain of local governments, but throughout this century the states have gradually taken on more of the funding responsibilities. Consequently, the states have become increasingly active in setting education policy and in overseeing local school districts (see Table 2-1).[5]

Table 2-1   Revenue Sources for Public Elementary and
Secondary Schools

School Year Ending	Percentage of Revenue from Government Sources		
	Local	State	Federal
1920	83.2	16.5	0.3
1930	82.7	16.9	0.4
1940	68.0	30.3	1.8
1950	57.3	39.8	2.9
1960	56.5	39.1	4.4
1970	52.1	39.9	8.0
1974	50.1	41.4	8.5
1978	47.6	43.0	9.4
1982	45.0	47.6	7.4
1986	43.9	49.4	6.7
1988	44.1	49.5	6.3

Source: U.S. Department of Education, National Center for Education Statistics, *Digest of Education Statistics, 1988,* reprinted in Laurence T. Ogle, ed., *The Condition of Education, 1990, Vol. 1: Elementary and Secondary Education* (Washington, D.C.: U.S. Government Printing Office), p. 168.

One of the reasons states began to take on more responsibility for education in the late 1970s was due to the link made between quality education and economic competitiveness: ". . . high quality education would help ensure a highly trained and motivated labor force, a necessity in an increasingly technological world. . . . [and] the presence of good schools would attract new industries and would help keep old ones." These were important considerations for states hoping to attract new industries.[6] This was especially true for the states in the Southeast where the governors of Florida, Virginia, Mississippi, Arkansas, North Carolina, South Carolina, and Tennessee were pushing for education reform and an increase in spending in states traditionally ranked low in per pupil education funding.[7] In this way they hoped to attract new industries and increase economic competitiveness in their states.[8]

At the same time that education was becoming a focal point of discussion at the state level, the bipartisan National Commission on Excellence in Education established by Secretary of Education Terrel Bell in 1981[9] issued its report, "A Nation at Risk," in 1983 and "called for a nationwide effort to halt what it called the 'rising tide of mediocrity' in the public school system."[10] This report, which proved a catalyst in the nation's discussion of education, emphasized ways to improve the quality of education in public schools.

In fact, the report triggered a new round of discussion which would shift the focus from excellence in education to those "at risk" of being left out of the system. Following the release of the report and the subsequent push for reform, some people also began to discuss those "at risk" in the nation's public schools, and those who had dropped out of the school system, who had problems that were not being addressed by this reform movement. Governor Lamar Alexander of Tennessee (who would later serve as President Bush's secretary of education) observed in January 1984: "We can no longer afford a situation where one-quarter of our ninth-grade students cannot pass a seventh-grade test and where one-third of our high school freshmen never graduate."[11]

Some critics suggested that the education reform movement might lead to "unwanted consequences." For example, a task force report of the Association for Supervision and Curriculum Development, based in Alexandria, Virginia, noted that some states had increased their requirements for high school graduation since the report "A Nation at Risk" had come out in 1983. More mandatory courses were now required of students, and they had fewer electives available. The task force warned that "low-achieving students 'may drop out of school earlier and in greater numbers' when forced to take more academic and fewer elective courses."[12]

Once the dropout problem was identified on a number of different levels, the whole issue became part of the national public agenda. A movement was emerging which would bring together a wide range of individuals—members of Congress, elementary school teachers, school dropouts and their families—who would work together to resolve the problem of school dropouts through appropriate policies. The problem came to the forefront at the state and local level at about the same time as it attained national status, but several years would elapse before linkages between the different individuals working in this area began to be made. The federal dropout prevention program would become a mechanism for facilitating these linkages, but the program was also the result of some of these early linkages. Once the issue was on the national agenda, the second stage of the policy process—formulating policy—began.

Policy Formulation

During the policy formulation stage, an issue is "discussed and potential solutions [are] explored."[13] Members of Congress and their staffs contribute to this process by holding committee hearings and issuing written reports. As a part of this process, Congress turns to policy specialists from a wide range of areas, including executive departments and agencies, interest groups, think tanks, businesses, universities and colleges, and labor unions, for guidance in shaping legislative proposals. This stage of the policy process, as is true of agenda setting, may last several years and even decades as support for a given proposal or solution gains strength.[14]

In the spring of 1983, a bipartisan group of twenty-five senators formed the Senate Children's Caucus. A caucus is one of the numerous informal organizations that have long served the legislative needs of members. These groups can provide research and analysis for members, facilitate the formation of strategic voting coalitions, protect regional interests, lend campaign assistance, and give a minority group a forum in which to address issues that are not on the agenda of the majority.[15] The Children's Caucus became a mechanism for more liberal members of the Senate to pursue an agenda addressing social concerns: Since the Republicans controlled the Senate in the early 1980s, the Democrats could no longer control committee resources or set committee agendas. The Caucus sponsored a series of forums and hearings on such topics as the needs of latchkey children, and gifted and talented children. For each topic outside experts were brought in to brief congressional staff.[16]

In 1983 the Senate Children's Caucus heard testimony that provided wide-ranging causes and explanations for the nation's high dropout rate. Senator Christopher J. Dodd (D-Conn.) later reported these findings in a speech on the floor of the Senate: "One of every five high school dropouts is a gifted student who has not been adequately challenged. Other students drop out for failing to master basic skills. Yet others find that high schools are just not meeting their special needs, whether it be child care for teenage parents or rehabilitation programs for alcohol and drug abusers."[17]

In that speech, Dodd also raised concern that "the debate on education has focused on increasing excellence and standards in schools. But virtually no attention has centered on those students who, for many good reasons, fail to meet the standards already set. . . . until we address the educational crisis posed by high school dropouts, we will remain a nation at risk."[18] This was a direct attack on the excessive attention the report, "A Nation at Risk," gave to those who were already succeeding in the educational system at the expense of students who were not succeeding or not likely to stay in school.[19]

In January 1984, the Caucus, under the leadership of Senators Dodd and Bill Bradley (D-N.J.), sponsored a forum in New York on the subject of school dropouts. The forum, which was held in a high school in New York City, discussed, among other topics, the approaches being tried by schools, community service organizations, and private sector organizations to reduce the number of school dropouts. They met with teachers, dropouts, near-dropouts, and school officials to learn more about what Dodd termed a "national problem that has reached 'epidemic proportions.' " The focus was on the reasons for the nation's high dropout rates. The forum participants cited numerous factors, including boring classes, pregnancy, and the lack of money to support services that would help kids stay in school. The Chancellor of the New York City Public Schools, Anthony J. Alvarado, compared federal high school funding to elementary school funding and noted that secondary schools had received cutbacks in federal funding. Students at risk of dropping out needed support services that were too costly for local school districts to provide. "It's strange," he said, "we know what to do, we just don't do it."[20] Part of the problem was funding, especially the lack of federal money in education. George E. Altomare, vice president for high schools of the United Federation of Teachers, stated that "New York City schools have $135 million less in Federal funds, taking inflation into account, than they did in 1981."[21]

Although the participants easily identified contributing factors to the dropout problem, they could reach no consensus on the extent or nature of the problem. At this point there was also no consensus as to whether this problem should be handled at the federal level. In 1984, when the Department of Education released figures that showed the dropout rate had risen in the ten-year period from 1972 to 1982, Secretary of Education Bell stated: "I think we ought to move to the point where not more than 10 percent are dropping out of school." Interestingly, the reporter covering this story noted that Bell "did not say how local officials should meet that goal."[22] No one apparently expected this issue to be addressed by national officials.

Problems in Definition and Measurement

Part of the problem in finding a solution to the dropout dilemma is that we have never had a consistent definition of a dropout or a consistent measurement of the problem. In 1984 the Hispanic Policy Development Project, a nonprofit citizens group based in Washington, D.C., sponsored a report by the National Commission on Secondary Schooling for Hispanics to examine why Hispanics were not staying in school. One discussant of the report noted that "figures on dropouts are considered among the least reliable statistical areas by educators because of wide discrepancies in the way records are kept."[23]

The difficulties in defining the problem have not been overcome to this day. In testifying before a House subcommittee, William J. Gainer, associate director of human resources in the General Accounting Office (GAO), reported that "data on the number of school dropouts are inconclusive. National estimates of the rate at which youth drop out of school range from about 13 to 25 percent. The differences result from factors such as varying definitions, data collection methods and the group of youth studied."[24]

Estimating the extent of the problem is complicated by the matter of what is counted. For example, students may drop out and yet still attain a GED (General Educational Development) certificate. Should they be included in dropout figures? Some school districts and states may track a particular class from the sophomore year on to see who graduates two years later, and therefore not include students who may graduate a year or two later than their class when computing graduation rates. Or in the case of home schooling, are students educated at home included as dropouts? What of military enlistees? To give some sense of the variation in definitions and data collection, in a study done by the Council of Chief State School Officers in 1986, 34 states include military enlistees in the definition of a dropout, 21 states include those who have received GED certificates, and 8 states include students educated through home schooling. In addition, 12 states report dropouts for grades 9 through 12, 15 states report dropouts for grades 7 through 12, while other states may include dropouts from kindergarten through grade 12.[25]

In the 1980s the debate centered on the economically disadvantaged, but a widening perception on the extent of the problem was emerging. A study done in Houston in the mid-1980s, for example, found that "twenty-five percent of the dropouts were in the top quarter of their classes in reading and mathematics."[26] This group of potentially high achievers has been labeled the "new dropouts." These students should not necessarily be handled in the same way as low-achieving dropouts. For these, job-training programs are not the answer, and in some cases, day care for the children of teenage mothers and more personal attention are needed. "Listening to them and letting them take some responsibility for improving the direction of their lives might well produce surprising results," according to Margaret LeCompte, who was director of Research and Evaluation in the Houston school district at the time of the study.[27] Thus, the dropout problem will probably remain and be reformulated as time goes on.

A Broadening of Concern

The degree of attention that this issue received in Congress was equal to the attention a number of other groups were also giving to this issue. In 1984 several corporations began sponsoring programs to help reduce the dropout rate, usually targeting students from economically disadvantaged and minority backgrounds.[28] Programs by such corporations as Coca-Cola, Pepsi-Cola, and the Standard Oil Company of Ohio were undertaken throughout the 1980s to help improve graduation rates by giving students incentives to stay in school.[29] The Hodgkinson report served as the catalyst for some important members of the education community to encourage public officials to respond to the dropout problem. The report, "All One System: Demographics of Education—Kindergarten through Graduate School," released by Harold L. Hodgkinson of the Institute for Educational Leadership in 1985, vividly presented data that made the link between economic development in states and high school retention:[30]

> In a state that retains a high percentage of its youth to high school graduation, almost every young person becomes a "net gain" to the state—with a high school diploma, there is a high probability of that person getting a job and repaying the state for the cost of his/her education, through taxable income, many times over. However, in a state with a poor record of retention to high school graduation, many youth are a "net loss" to the state, in that without a high school diploma, the chances of that student getting work, and thus repaying the state for that person's education, are very small indeed. Additionally, that young person is unlikely to leave the state, becoming a permanent economic burden to that state's economy.[31]

This study also noted that, although many states had enacted reforms to call for higher standards in education, little was done to provide remedial assistance. The result was potentially high dropout rates with more serious economic costs for states.[32]

In the 1980s some states launched aggressive programs to combat the dropout problem. One program, "Operation Success," was geared for at-risk students in five public schools in New York City and was a state-financed experiment run by a nonprofit agency. One early study indicated that 93 percent of the students in the program either completed high school or were remaining in school. The program offered "special counseling, individual attention, job training, jobs, [and] help for their families."[33]

In June 1985 the state of Georgia and the Appalachian Regional Commission (ARC) organized a workshop on school dropouts for over 200 educators and community leaders. Although a school dropout problem is usually thought to be a concern primarily for the inner cities of the nation's largest urban areas, it is actually an even greater problem for rural America: "Appalachia . . . has more students dropping out of high school proportionally than the rest of the United States."[34] The seriousness of the problem in the Appalachian states was an influence on governors such as Alexander of Tennessee, Joe Frank Harris of Georgia, and James B. Hunt of North Carolina. At that workshop, the federal co-chair of the ARC, Winifred A. Pizzano, discussed the problem of dropouts from an emerging perspective—in terms not only of equal opportunity for students, but also the economic consequences for the United States:

> There are two ways to look at the economic consequences of school dropouts. From the standpoint of the student, we know that dropouts will find fewer opportunities for employment and job advancement than students who complete their high school educations. We also know that, as a group, those dropouts will earn some $237 billion less during their lifetimes than if they had stayed in school.
>
> On the other hand, in terms of our national interest, we know that America has already begun to pay a staggering price for dropouts—both here at home and in the world marketplace.
> . . .
> As the demand for highly skilled workers increases, the supply of jobs suitable for those with inadequate education and training shrinks. For example, of the more than 100,000 new jobs created each year in New York City, fewer than 10 percent will be for the standard dropout jobs, such as messengers, janitors, busboys, and maids. Less than 10 percent. And yet, just last month, the New York Stock Exchange released a report predicting that 38.4 percent of all New York high school students in the next four years will drop out without graduating.[35]

Students were also trying to get at the problem. For example, high school students in Chicago, with funding from the Joyce Foundation, put out their own report on the problem and found that students were dropping out because "schools lack a sense of community," which in turn leads to alienation among the students.[36]

In 1985 the National Education Association (NEA), with 1.7 million members, decided to use one dollar from the dues of each member to help set up a permanent endowment and start an anti-dropout effort—the Dropout Prevention Initiative. The projects were to be designed by local organizations. Part of the driving force behind this move was the experience of the president of the NEA, Mary Futrell, who as a junior high school teacher in a dropout prevention program in Alexandria, Virginia, knew firsthand about the problem and possible solutions. The NEA hoped to inspire other groups, for example the PTA, to adopt the same plan.[37] (The NEA's Dropout Prevention Initiative has been extremely successful, targeting students at risk of dropping out in elementary and middle schools, as well as in high schools. More than 86 programs have been assisted through the initiative, with 80 percent of the programs now institutionalized in these school districts.) However, some still did not believe that the dropout issue warranted federal involvement. At the time the NEA program was announced, Secretary of Education William Bennett stood on the sidelines: "We don't know precisely what the NEA has in mind. We will watch with interest the reaction of other educational groups."[38]

While Congress was drawing on the expertise of the education community in considering strategies for combatting the dropout problem, the education community was also coming together to share their resources and energies to address the problem. A number of studies, including the Hodgkinson report, published in the early 1980s began to provide data on dropouts.[39] These studies led many around the country to begin looking at their own students.

Nancy Peck, working in Florida, a state that targeted its resources for dropouts as early as 1984, as the Director of the Dropout Prevention Center at the University of Miami, called every state Department of Education to learn what each state was doing for dropouts and found that few other states were so involved. However, she began to make contact with other educators, who were working with dropouts and until then had experienced the same isolation that she had felt, unaware that many others shared their interest. This group of concerned educators first met informally in Washington, D.C., in 1985, and held subsequent meetings both in Washington and at various state and regional meetings in the following years. The Washington location allowed the involvement of the National School Boards Association, the National Association of Secondary School Principals, and other education interest groups in the Washington area. A formal National Dropout Prevention Network would soon follow, established primarily for practitioners—principals and teachers. Slowly, a "little revolution" began, and in time the network would grow to over 3000 members.

By 1985 a variety of task forces had published their reports, all of which seemed to indicate the criteria of programs that were successful in improving graduation rates: providing job opportunities, coordinating social services for families, and intervening at an early age, that is, in the elementary grades or in programs such as Head Start.[40] These strategies were identified as effective because "the causes of dropping out were [found to be] wide-ranging . . . some were school related, such as poor grades, inadequate counseling or student-teacher difficulties. Other reasons cited were the need to earn money, poor health, pregnancy or a disrupted home life."[41]

While these studies were being reported, some opinion leaders still maintained that no clear consensus existed as to the nature of the problem. The following editorial raised the issue of individual responsibility:

Perhaps high school graduation rates illustrate a paradox concerning individual responsibility. As long as it was mainly the responsibility of the students and their families to see that they persevered through 12 years of school, graduation rates improved. But in the 1960s the balance shifted, and it became increasingly the responsibility of the school and society in general to see that everyone got through. That's also the period in which graduation rates ceased to improve. Possibly there's a relationship.
. . .

It would follow that the most promising way to get the drop-out rate down would be to pay less attention to the drop-out rate and instead convey more forcefully to students the thought that earning a diploma is up to them.[42]

Two years later, the struggle to define the issue continued as the *New York Times* reported that "The consensus of funding sources is that the dropout problem is so complex and ingrained that it cannot be solved by a single institution. Some of the funds now come from the United States Department of Education, the Ford Foundation, the Exxon Education Fund, the Prudential Foundation, the Carnegie Corporation and the National Foundation for the Improvement of Education, created by the NEA [National Education Association]."[43]

A CONGRESSIONAL RESPONSE

The groundwork for specific federal involvement in the dropout problem was clearly being laid as both staff and senators became educated as to the nature of this policy area. In the testimony of at least one witness at the forum in 1984, the national government was challenged to involve itself in efforts that were already under way in many communities, by both public and private sector organizations.

We must learn to identify those seed projects that have the potential to serve as models and build on them and refine them and perhaps find more efficient and effective ways to replicate them. This nation and its government and voluntary agencies must rethink our project mentality of designing, funding and implementing a project for one, two, or three years, issuing a report and going on to the next project. . . . It is Congress through its oversight and legislative committee hearings that can identify that which works in our nation. It is Congress through its committee structure such as this one here today that can assure that future funding is legislated so that it is utilized to expand and build on those successful model programs that will help to provide the highest quality of service at the lowest cost per unit while meeting the education, economic, social and human needs and objectives of our nation.[44]

The nation's governors were beginning to call attention to the matter, and a national movement of educators interested in the dropout problem was taking form.

Several federal education programs operative during the 1980s allowed funds to be used for dropouts. For example, under the Elementary and Secondary Education Act, Chapter 1 programs provided financial assistance to improve the basic academic skills of disadvantaged children. Chapter 2 block grants to states could be used in a broad range of areas, including programs for students who were failing or dropping out of school. Under the Higher Education Act, the Migrant High School Equivalency Program provided financial assistance to enable adult migrant and seasonal farm workers to obtain a high school diploma or equivalency certificate. This Act also authorized a Talent Search which provided funds for programs that identified academically talented disadvantaged children and encouraged them to earn a diploma and then go on to continue their education in a postsecondary program. The Job Training Partnership Act provided funding for several programs, such as the Job Corps and Summer Youth Employment, as well as training grants for job training programs, along with supportive services such as literacy training and other remedial educational programs that might assist dropouts.[45]

None of these programs, however, specifically targeted funds for dropouts. Nor did they guarantee that states or local school districts would use the program funds for programs to increase the high school graduation rate, although in some instances the funds were clearly being used for dropouts.[46] For example, in Boston the Boston Private Industry Council (PIC) in collaboration with the Boston public schools had created the Compact Ventures program. This program was designed to improve academic achievement and lower dropout rates through support services to the schools (e.g., tutoring, teaching assistants); programs to let teachers and administrators see the needs of business; and the creation of incentives for kids to stay in school and achieve an academic record to qualify for college (e.g., summer jobs, work-study, career opportunities).[47] In Cabell County, West Virginia, Chapter 2 funds were being used to support a countywide public school dropout prevention program that was successful in reducing the percentage of dropouts. Based on the success of that program, Representative Nick Rahall (D-W.V.), speaking on the floor of the House, urged his "colleagues to review any legislative measures which would address" as he called it, a "national dilemma."[48] While the funding of dropout programs was allowed with a number of these federal programs, the funds could be used in a broad range of areas. Therefore, some members of Congress felt the need for a special program with funding specifically targeted at dropouts.

In the spring of 1984, Senators Bradley and Dodd followed up on the 1983 hearing with the introduction of a bill to "provide a program of planning grants, demonstration grants, and formula grants to assist local educational agencies to improve the basic skills of economically disadvantaged secondary school students."[49] As was true of several other programs, the bill did not necessarily target school dropouts, nor did it focus on programs to specifically address their needs. The intent of the legislation was to improve the basic skills of economically disadvantaged high school students in such areas as reading, writing, and mathematics. With an improvement in the educational performance of students, it was expected that school dropout rates would decrease. When Senator Bradley introduced the bill, he expressed his concern over the lack of basic skills as a factor contributing to high-dropout rates:

> I am convinced that one of the reasons students drop out of high school is that they lack basic skills. They are—to use the current jargon— "functionally illiterate" and they cannot even get to first base with the high school academic curriculum. Considering the frustration, discouragement, and humiliation that many of these students must experience, it is not surprising that leaving school seems like an appealing alternative.
> . . .
> So far, most of the important educational reforms that are being implemented across the country have not addressed directly the problems of the high school student who has not mastered basic skills. Many states, including my own State of New Jersey, have increased academic course requirements for graduation. . . .
> I strongly support setting high standards for our students. But I am also concerned that without sufficient support, the higher standards will discourage the educational involvement of some students, rather than inspire their greater effort. We could see an even greater rise in the number of students who drop out of schools because they consider their prospects for meeting the standards too remote to keep trying.[50]

The First Dropout Bill Fails to Become Law

Although a bill similar to the Bradley bill was introduced in the House several months later by Representative Pat Williams (D-Mont.), legislation would fail to become law in the Ninety-eighth Congress for several reasons. First, the time was not yet ripe for congressional action, for the movement addressing the dropout problem was still in a nascent stage and had not yet developed a national audience. At a time when "excellence" in education was being discussed, dropouts were not the highest priority in education, although many were interested in the problem.[51]

Second, while Representative Williams was on the House Committee on Education and Labor, neither Senator Bradley nor Senator Dodd was on the Senate Labor and Human Resources Committee which had jurisdiction over education bills in the Senate. If he was a member of the committee, he could give his legislative proposal extra prodding. Although Bradley had a high profile on education issues, he lacked the structural position that would enable him to get his bill consideration by the Senate committee. In fact, with Republican control of the Senate and its committees, and with conservative senators such as Jeremiah Denton (R-Ala.) pushing for an agenda that was more focused on prayer in school and the problem of teenage pregnancy, new spending for a domestic social program would not receive the support it needed.[52]

Finally, since the bill had been introduced so late in the Ninety-eighth Congress, in the middle of the second session, the bill would not likely see the light of day in this Congress. There would be little time remaining in either the House or the Senate in which to schedule subcommittee and committee hearings to complete the work needed on this bill. However, the introduction of the bill in the Ninety-eighth Congress would help move the issue of dropouts to the forefront of the active congressional agenda in the next Congress. The Ninety-eighth Congress, then, would be a time of "policy incubation" until broader support and a more favorable partisan lineup could be obtained in a later Congress.[53]

On the House side, where the bill had been introduced by Representative Williams, it got a more favorable reception. The House Subcommittee on Elementary, Secondary, and Vocational Education held hearings in Washington, D.C., on June 12 and 13, 1984. Senator Bradley, who had introduced the companion bill in the Senate in March, was among those testifying in support of the bill. He reemphasized some of the same points made in the 1983 hearing, in particular that the educational reform movement had "not addressed directly the problems of the high school student who has not mastered basic skills."[54] Bradley went on to say that: "Considering the frustration, discouragement, and humiliation that many students who cannot read experience, it's not a surprise to me that leaving school seems like an appealing alternative."[55]

Bradley noted the effectiveness of Chapter 1 funding, which provides federal funds primarily for elementary schools to improve the students' basic skills. The legislation Senator Bradley and Representative Williams were sponsoring would create a parallel program to meet the needs of high school students. The result of a program of federal funding for elementary students but not continued for secondary school students was that "the disparity between the test scores between minority and white elementary school children was cut nearly in half in the 1970s, but gains in basic skills among high school, low-income minority youth have been minimal at best."[56]

While an identifiable problem—increasing high school dropout rates— was clearly evident, the solution was not. Bradley and Williams proposed that money be provided to support and encourage new, "innovative approaches" to deal with remedial education for high school students, with evaluation as to which models were effective.[57]

The hearing included the testimony and written letters of support of many members of the education community, including a school principal and representatives of different education associations.[58] One letter came from Michael Casserly of the Council of the Great City Schools, who wrote a letter of support for the legislation to Representative Williams. Casserly

---

Box 2-1

DEFINING THE PROBLEM

To give a sense of the numbers of individuals who might benefit from dropout prevention programs, "nearly 350,000 students withdraw from grades 10 through 12 each year," while "several hundred thousand others probably leave from earlier grades." In addition, nearly 3.8 million sixteen to twenty-four year olds not attending school have never completed high school or passed a general equivalency exam.[59]

Marian Wright Edelman, president of the Children's Defense Fund, has noted the depth of the problem this tremendous number of dropouts presents for society: "A national investment in education will . . . save our society money in the long term. One recent study estimates the total lifetime earning loss for the dropouts in the high school class of 1981 alone is a staggering $228 billion, with an approximate loss of tax revenue of $68.4 billion."[60] A study that tracked the paths of 100,000 students in Chicago schools in the early 1980s identified how the costs to society add up: "Dropouts disproportionately receive welfare and unemployment transfer payments, are significantly more involved in the high cost of crime and, because of reduced lifetime earnings, contribute significantly lower taxes to Federal, State, and local governments." The lifetime social costs of nearly 13,000 dropouts from one class were estimated "at over $2.5 billion in transfer payments, crime costs, and lost taxes," with many of these individuals becoming a part of "a permanent underclass."[61]

would be instrumental in framing the dropout legislation that would emerge in the next Congress. In the course of the testimony of these representatives of the education community, much statistical data on the number of high school dropouts and skills level of students were included, as were examples of models of successful high school programs that were working to improve basic skills levels and the high school graduation rate of students.

One co-sponsor of the Williams bill was Representative Charles A. Hayes (D-Ill.) As a member of the Subcommittee on Elementary, Secondary, and Vocational Education, Hayes, along with his staff, was learning about one aspect of the dropout problem in the United States. One of the jobs of a legislative assistant is to acquire information—through hearings, meetings with constituents, floor debate, contact with interest groups, research done by the Congressional Research Service or the General Accounting Office, and other committees and offices on the Hill. Files are created, which may include bills that have died in a prior Congress, along with ideas, facts, and *Congressional Record* entries, which may be useful at a future time. If a representative or senator then has an idea for a bill, a legislative assistant can turn to an appropriate file and have sufficient information to get the legislative process going. In addition, through hearings, constituents and representatives of interest groups are not only contributing information, but also gaining information—factual information, a sense of how representatives and senators view a particular issue, as well as who might be potential allies in the future on similar issues.

Throughout the hearing only brief mention was made of the need to stem the increasing high school dropout rate and to ensure that graduates achieved basic skills in terms of the United States' economic needs.[62] However, the next level of argument, that in order for the United States to be economically competitive the dropout rate must be lowered while improving skills levels, was yet to be made.

When the Ninety-eighth Congress came to an end, the dropout issue had been identified and discussed, but no legislation had been passed. Following up on the forums, Senators Bradley and Dodd had introduced a bill in the Senate that was far reaching in scope and would provide funds for economically disadvantaged secondary school students (The Secondary Schools Basic Skills Act) in order to improve the basic skills of low-achieving students. Representative Williams introduced the companion bill in the House. However, the work and research done on the issue of school dropouts as part of the effort to build support for a broad bill covering federal assistance for disadvantaged secondary students laid the groundwork for the legislative process to follow. Congressional staff, lobbyists, educators, and researchers in education associations would add to their files the information on dropouts.

Spillover Effects—Implications for Society

The dropout issue reached the congressional agenda in part because it began to be addressed in terms of spillover effects and broader implications for society. Whereas in 1984 the discussion had focused on equal opportunities for successfully moving from school to employment opportunities, by 1985 it began to be recast in terms of economic competitiveness and the loss of human resources.[63]

At a Senate hearing in 1985, in reference to the overall 25 percent dropout rate, 50 percent dropout rate in urban areas, and 70 percent dropout rate for some minority populations, Senator Pell observed that

> In human terms, dropping out of school all but extinguishes the chance that each child has to make it in our competitive economy. In economic terms, the sharp loss in productivity and generated taxes, as well as the prices of incarceration, unemployment, and welfare assistance, inflicts a heavy drain on our economy. It is sadly true that what we fail to invest in dropout prevention, we will be forced to pay many times over in social costs.[64]

Senator Lawton Chiles (D-Fla.) commented that

> Many high school dropouts will become our next generation of illiterates. In his book, "Illiterate America," Jonathan Kozol estimates that adult illiteracy costs the Government $120 billion per year. Our population of 23 million adults who are functionally illiterate puts us 49th out of the 159 members of the United Nations in illiteracy. That results in 85 percent of juveniles who come before the courts being unable to read; 22 percent of adults being unable to write a check so a bank will take it; and an illiteracy rate among black youths that will rise to 50 percent by 1990. We simply cannot afford this waste of human resources.[65]

The American public expressed strong support for doing something about school dropouts and those at risk. A Gallup Poll in 1986 found that 72 percent of Americans favored setting up remedial programs in high schools to help students meet graduation requirements, with only 19 percent preferring the awarding of a lesser diploma to those unable to meet the standard requirements. In addition, by an almost 2–1 margin, the public supported a remedial program *funded by taxes* rather than through tuition paid by those in the program.[66]

SCHOOL DROPOUTS: A NATION'S PROBLEM

At a Senate hearing in 1985, Keith Geiger, vice president of the NEA, stated: "If I had one wish, I would again create the kind of atmosphere in this country in which public education is an issue that the Federal Government has to be concerned about, the State government has to be concerned about. It is a sharing of responsibilities."[67]

While Congress might not have initiated the debate on this issue, it was responding to the growing awareness that school dropouts had become such an important concern that they commanded the attention and resources of the federal government. The interest in this issue grew to the point that the General Accounting Office's top seller in 1987 was "a report on innovative ways to reduce the number of school dropouts," which, remarkably, made it more popular than the government's publications on "Star Wars," defense spending, and health care issues.[68]

The dropout issue was moving to the congressional agenda at the same time that it was becoming a prominent issue among educators, public officials, and education association members in the states and at the grassroots level. Support for a federal dropout prevention program would continue to build in Congress as the issue began to receive more attention.

In 1986 at the National Governors' Association meeting which elected Governor Bill Clinton (D-Ark.) its chair, a linkage between declining U.S. economic competitiveness and school dropouts was made. The Agenda for the Nation's Governors in 1987, influenced by Governor Clinton, singled out dropouts as one of five areas of critical importance if the United States was to regain economic competitiveness in a changing world economy.[69] Clinton was selected as the keynote speaker at the first annual Dropout Prevention Network Conference in San Diego in 1989. Hence, the informal dropout network that had begun in 1985 with the meeting of a handful of educators and public officials was now an organization with annual meetings and a membership list of thousands.

In September 1989, President Bush and the nation's governors joined together in proclaiming six national educational goals to "boost achievement levels and improve the country's ability to compete economically in the next century." One goal was to increase "the high school graduation rate from 72 percent to at least 90 percent."[70]

Many Americans had already perceived the linkage between global competitiveness and education during the mid-1980s when educators and public officials began to talk about dropouts as a factor contributing to the United States' weakened economic competitiveness. As demonstrated in Table 2-2, Americans overwhelmingly felt that a good educational system

Table 2-2 Education and American Strength

QUESTION: "In determining America's strength in the future, say 25 years from now, how important do you feel each of the following factors will be—very important, fairly important, not too important, or not at all important."

	% responding "very important"		
	1988	1984	1982
Developing the best educational system in the world	88	82	84
Developing the most efficient industrial production system in the world	65	70	66
Building the strongest military force in the world	47	45	47

Source: Alec M. Gallup and Stanley M. Elam, "The 20th Annual Gallup Poll of the Public's Attitudes toward the Public Schools," *Phi Delta Kappan*, September 1988, pp. 44–45.

was the key to the nation's strength. The shift in emphasis to global economic competitiveness would fit in well with the attitudes of the American public. The remaining chapters will tell the legislative story of the first federal dropout prevention program and the efforts to keep it funded.

CHAPTER 3

Congress Creates a Dropout Program

In the mid-1980s the school dropout issue became embroiled with partisan and campaign politics. School dropout programs now became linked with a number of other policy issues, especially abortion, U.S. economic competitiveness, and trade policy. Temporal considerations also began to affect the issue. Since each Congress lasts only two years, both the House and Senate must both pass the same bill with identical language during this two-year period, and the president must then sign the bill (or the House and Senate must both have a two-thirds vote to override the veto). Looming at the end of each two-year cycle is a congressional election, with all 435 members of the House and one-third of the Senate up for reelection. And so it is that campaign politics can affect the fate of any legislative proposal.

MOVEMENT ON THE HILL

As the Ninety-ninth Congress got under way in January 1985, a coordinated effort to involve the U.S. Congress in the issue of dropouts began. By this time, the issue had been discussed in several hearings on the Hill, providing a wealth of information on the matter, and the nation's governors had begun to call attention to the issue. Moreover, educators interested in the dropout problem were beginning to coalesce in a national movement. Soon the reasons for federal involvement would clearly be articulated: "Federal leadership will give the problem a high national priority" and focus attention on appropriate strategies for dealing with the dropout problem."[1] In addition, "A federal program will find and foster the best strategies for dropout reduction and make this information available nationally. . . . [and] a Federal program will encourage standardized collection and reporting of dropout information."[2]

H.R. 3042, the Dropout Prevention and Reentry Act

Early in 1985 Representative Charles A. Hayes, a liberal Democrat from the south side of Chicago, and his legislative director, Howard Woodson, met with several Chicago constituents—Dr. Manford Byrd, the superintendent of the Chicago public schools, George Munoz, president of the Chicago Board of Education, and Jeff Simering, a lobbyist for the Chicago public schools.[3] The discussion focused on kids at risk, especially those dropping out of school.

While Hayes's district included the University of Chicago and the surrounding Hyde Park neighborhood, it also encompassed many housing projects with high crime rates on Chicago's south side.[4] It was these poor constituents that aroused Hayes's greatest concern, and he sought to help them through bills that would create job training programs and job guarantees and provide wages that would help break the cycle of poverty.[5] His efforts to help the dropouts in his Chicago district flowed naturally from his life-long battle for social justice.[6]

Several days after their meeting, Woodson told Simering that Hayes intended to introduce legislation that would tackle the dropout problem, and so began a collaborative effort between Simering and Representative Hayes and his staff.[7] This discussion expanded for a brief period of time to include representatives from the Children's Defense Fund, which had also been interested in dropout legislation. However, the Children's Defense Fund was pushing a bill that would be less programmatic and would focus more on the definition of dropout and data collection efforts rather than on concrete solutions.[8]

Shortly thereafter Michael Casserly, representing the Council of the Great City Schools, an organization dedicated to the interests of over forty of the largest public school systems in the country (including Chicago), was brought into the negotiations. Casserly was a good choice, for he had a good working relationship with the Children's Defense Fund and had known Simering for years. Therefore, he was in a good position to help mediate differences in the proposals offered by Simering and the Children's Defense Fund.

As a member of the House Education and Labor Committee and several of its subcommittees on education, Hayes was strategically placed to guide this legislation through the House in its most crucial phase—in committee. The work of Congress is done primarily in committee, especially by the committee chairs and subcommittee chairs and other leaders in both the House and Senate. Therefore, legislative proposals that are not shepherded through the process by a representative sitting on an appropriate committee have little chance of becoming law.

Hayes introduced the Dropout Prevention and Reentry Act (H.R. 3042) in the House of Representatives on July 18, 1985. The bill "would initiate a new Federal program of grants to school districts to mount demonstration programs. These programs would focus on identifying potential dropouts and preventing them from dropping out, encouraging youth who have already dropped out to reenter school, and developing model systems to collect information on the numbers of dropouts and their reasons for dropping out."[9] The bill authorized a four-year program costing "$50 million for fiscal year 1987 and such sums as necessary for three succeeding fiscal years."[10]

The proposed federal program in Hayes's bill would create demonstration projects, a popular means by which Congress can try out a program in a limited way. For example, several states, cities, or, in this case, schools and school districts are awarded funds to try out a program for several years. The programs are then evaluated and assessed to see if they are working in accordance with congressional intent and are meeting Congress's original objectives in passing the legislation. After evalutions are complete, Congress can then decide whether and to what extent the federal government should continue the programs. Demonstration projects may also provide a model of an effective program for states and local governments, or for the private sector to undertake, possibly with some federal support. Since 1985, with the passage of the Balanced Budget and Emergency Deficit Control Act of 1985, more commonly known as Gramm-Rudman-Hollings, the realities of deficit reduction pressures have also led Congress to think in terms of demonstration projects. Such projects allow the lawmakers to introduce new program areas but at lower levels of funding.[11]

S. 1525, The Dropout Prevention and Reentry Act

While the legislation was being hammered out on the House side, a sponsor on the Senate side was being sought. Casserly and Simering discussed the proposal with several Senate offices and found Senator Arlen Specter (R-Penn.) to be the most appropriate senator to sponsor a companion bill on the Senate side.

Specter (who would gain national notoriety with his aggressive questioning of Anita Hill during the Clarence Thomas confirmation hearings in 1991) was a moderate Republican, but he was not on the Senate Labor and Human Resources Committee, the committee with jurisdiction over education bills. Committee membership was not as essential in his case because power in the Senate is more fluid and open than in the House, owing to the Senate's smaller size. Therefore, senators find opportunities to bring bills before the full Senate for consideration which would not be allowed in the House. For example, the Senate allows consideration of nongermane floor amendments, permitting a legislative proposal to be brought directly to the floor and offered as an amendment to whatever bill is pending, and thus bypassing committee consideration.

In Specter's favor was his membership on the education subcommittee of the all-powerful Appropriations Committee which would have to provide the funding once authorization was approved. Moreover, Specter, a Republican, was a member of the majority party in the Senate in 1985 and therefore would be in a better position than any Democratic sponsor to gain the leadership's support in getting consideration of the bill. Another consideration adding to his choice was the fact that he was up for reelection in 1986, and one of the primary constituent groups he would have to woo for the moderate vote would be the education community. Pushing this legislation through would help him gain endorsements from the powerful teacher unions.[12]

As noted earlier, for any bill to become law, both the House and the Senate must pass it in exactly the same form in the same Congress. Within two weeks of the introduction of H.R. 3042 in the House, Senator Specter had introduced the same dropout bill (S. 1525) in the U.S. Senate. Therefore, this coordination of effort between Representative Hayes and Senator Specter was an important signal to colleagues that members of Congress were making a serious effort to involve the government in stemming the growing high school dropout rate. Representative Hayes even came over to the Dirksen Building on the Senate side of the Hill for a press conference held on July 30, 1985, by Senator Specter and his co-sponsors to introduce the bill.[13] Each Congress has two sessions, and 1985 was the first year of the Ninety-ninth Congress. Representative Hayes and Senator Specter coordinated their efforts to insure that the House and Senate would be considering identical bills early enough in the Congress to increase the chances of legislative success.[14]

Despite their efforts, the Dropout Prevention and Reentry Act met the fate of most legislation and failed to pass in both houses of Congress.

WHAT WENT RIGHT—THE HOUSE

H.R. 3042 had seventy-one co-sponsors, including seven from the Subcommittee on Elementary, Secondary, and Vocational Education of the House Committee on Education and Labor.[15] Ever since the congressional reforms pushed through the House of Representatives by the seventy-five "Watergate Democrats" elected in 1974, control over the substance of legislation has been relegated largely to subcommittees. Thus, gaining the support of nearly half of the membership of that subcommittee was important, and in shaping the legislative path of this bill, the support of the subcommittee chair, Augustus F. Hawkins (D-Calif.), would prove crucial.

Hawkins, chair of both the Subcommittee on Elementary, Secondary, and Vocational Education and the full Committee on Education and Labor, signed on as a co-sponsor.[16] Hawkins and Hayes were both liberal members of the Congressional Black Caucus, and Hawkins gave his support to this education initiative by his junior colleague from Illinois. Hawkins, who represented the Twenty-ninth Congressional District in Los Angeles, from 1962 until his retirement in 1991, came from a district that was not unlike Hayes's district; both districts were heavily Democratic, with large minority and poor populations.[17]

Hearings on H.R. 3042 were held before the Subcommittee on Elementary, Secondary, and Vocational Education in both Washington and Chicago. Field hearings like those held in Chicago have several purposes. They provide for a broader range of testimony from local public officials or people who work in program areas affected by the legislation under consideration. For these individuals, a trip to Washington to testify at a congressional hearing may be prohibitively expensive. As a result, hearings at the Capitol often draw on people who are readily available, such as individuals representing large interest groups and trade associations already collaborating on the drafting of legislation. A field hearing also lets members of Congress hear from those living beyond the Washington beltway; these people are often the ones who will have to implement federal programs or will be directly affected by the programs. These hearings provide an opportunity to hear how federal programs can best serve the needs of local and state governments. Local and state officials can provide information and insight into fiscal problems in states which may be alleviated through federal aid. These same officials can also explain what type of programs may be needed to best meet their needs and how federal funds can make a difference.

A hearing is, of course, a useful means for gathering information, and it can also serve as a dramatic set-piece, especially when witnesses are stacked in favor of one side or the other on an issue. In particular, field hearings can give local and state public officials increased visibility, and at the same time provide visibility for a member of Congress back in the district. The local media also benefit, for they are given access to a story through firsthand observation and will therefore get a better feel for how the business of Congress is done and what their own representative or senators are doing.

At the hearing in Representative Hayes's district, the witnesses included Harold Washington, then mayor of Chicago; the superintendent of the Chicago public schools; other local and state public officials; and several students, teachers, and a principal. Roberto Rivera, director of the Chicago Intervention Network of the Department of Human Services in the city of Chicago, spoke in support of federal funding for a demonstration dropout program and federal sponsorship of a national school dropout study. Such a study, as called for in the legislation, would "establish a standard definition of a school dropout," and gather consistent data and information on dropout rates and reasons for dropping out among different populations.[18] According to Rivera, this database would "allow us to truly gauge our efforts, to make corrections, to monitor educational decisions and reform; and finally, to make the school system an accountable system to communities, to students, and to the taxpayer."[19]

Movement in the House

With the support of the chair as well as many members of the committee, the House Committee on Education and Labor favorably reported the bill out of committee to the Committee of the Whole House on the State of the Union on July 23, 1986.

In order to expedite the consideration of legislation in the House, a procedure has been established whereby legislation is first considered and debated in the House of Representatives meeting as the Committee of the Whole House on the State of the Union. When the House is meeting as the Committee of the Whole, the most visible difference from a normal session is that the mace is moved from its prominent location on a pedestal near the Speaker's table to a lower pedestal. The mace, a symbol of the sergeant at arms's authority, is a 46-inch column of ebony rods bound together by silver and topped by a silver eagle.[20] The rules for the Committee of the Whole "are designed to speed up floor action."[21]

A quorum is only 100 members rather than the 218 needed in the full House, and amendments "are introduced and debated under the five-minute rule," which in theory gives each side five minutes to make its case.[22] General debate is usually one hour long, divided equally between both sides. Before a bill is brought to the floor, however, the chair of the committee that reports the bill out requests a rule from the Rules Committee. The Rules Committee works with the party leadership in helping to set the agenda for the House by deciding the order in which bills will be brought to the floor for debate. This committee also "governs the length of debate permitted once the bill reaches the floor and the extent to which a measure can be amended."[23]

In the case of the Dropout Prevention and Reentry Act, the Rules Committee set the time for debate at one hour, with thirty minutes under the control of Representative Hawkins, chair of the Committee on Education and Labor, and thirty minutes under the control of Representative Bill Goodling, the second most senior Republican on the Committee on Education and Labor and ranking member of the Subcommittee on Elementary, Secondary, and Vocational Education.

During debate, Representative Hawkins, a supporter of the bill, explained the provisions of the legislation and recounted the testimony given by witnesses during the hearings on the bill, emphasizing the extent of the dropout problem. Representative Goodling spoke in opposition to the bill. As a newly elected member in the 1970s, Goodling, a former teacher and principal, was considered "one of the most conservative members of the Pennsylvania delegation."[24] Nonetheless, he would usually join his Democratic colleagues in supporting education programs opposed by recent Republican presidents. In this instance, however, his conservative leanings dominated, largely because of the recent debate over the deficit. Goodling feared that if the deficit targets were not met, existing programs would have to be cut, and, under that scenario, a new education program could not be justified:

> My greatest concern for educational funding is that proven programs not be subjected to the sequestration process.[25] Programs of proven effectiveness such as Chapter 1 and Head Start would suffer serious cutbacks under this scenario.[26]
>
> As a member of the Budget Committee, I have worked hard to provide sufficient funding to maintain these existing programs. In my view, enacting new legislation such as H.R. 3042 not only would exacerbate the overall deficit situation making sequestration more likely, but could possibly damage those educational programs already in place.[27]

The bill did have bipartisan support, however. Representative James M. Jeffords, a Republican from Vermont, with a voting record that would make him one of the more liberal members of his party, and ranking member of the Committee on Education and Labor, spoke in favor of the bill. Jeffords recognized that a program that reduced the dropout rate would bring long-term benefits to society.

> It may seem unusual for me to be standing here in support of a bill which calls for new money. Now is a time when we are facing large budget

deficits, when we must face the task of reordering our priorities. However, the bill, H.R. 3042, can have an important effect on our economic competitiveness. Unless we can bring dropouts back into school in order to provide them with the basic and technical skills they need, they face the likelihood of an adult life of dependency and unemployment. We have to provide a means by which these youths can become productive adults.[28]

Jeffords also used his time on the floor to explain an amendment that committee member Pat Williams (D-Mont.) had added during the markup. (The markup is the committee session held after the hearings in which committee members and staff add, delete, and modify the language in the bill before the final bill is brought to the floor for consideration by the full House.) The Williams amendment helped ensure the support of members representing rural districts by adding language to the bill assuring that some grants would be awarded to school districts with fewer than 2000 students.[29]

During floor debate Hawkins offered a few "clarifying amendments," consisting of a few changes in words and phrases, to "simply focus the proposal more closely on education and instructional programs for school dropouts."[30] All were passed without any objection.

With only two members speaking against the bill, H.R. 3042 passed in the House without a recorded roll call vote.[31]

In spite of a large number of co-sponsors, favorable hearings, and the support of the committee and subcommittee chair in the House, the dropout prevention bill would fail to become law in the Ninety-ninth Congress for several reasons.

WHAT WENT WRONG—THE SENATE

When Senator Specter introduced S. 1525—the companion measure in the Senate to H.R. 3042, the Dropout Prevention and Reentry Act—in the Senate on July 30, 1985, he was joined by a number of other senators, including Robert T. Stafford (R-Vt.), chair of the Senate Subcommittee on Education, Arts and Humanities, Senator Pell (D-R.I.), ranking member of the subcommittee, and Senators Edward M. Kennedy (D-Mass.), Bill Bradley (D-N.J.), and John Chafee (D-R.I.). In the fall of 1985, hearings were held in Washington during which testimony was heard from several senators, a student, local and state educational officials, and representatives from education interest groups.[32] The bill gained another ten co-sponsors and seemed to be on track for approval in the Senate, but its journey came to a grinding halt one year later.

The Budget Deficit

One problem that had been identified during the consideration of the bill on the House side was the federal budget deficit. Representative Hayes himself identified the problem in May 1986: I realize that in this era of Gramm-Rudman, many of our colleagues have questioned [the funding authorization level of $50 million, but] I can tell you . . . it will be pennies compared to the value of the lives we can save.[33] (One summary of the action by Congress in the entire field of education policy during the first session of the Ninety-ninth Congress clearly revealed the difficulties in getting federal approval for any new education initiative: "States and localities continued to promote efforts to improve schools and colleges in 1985, but relatively little initiative came from federal officials. While proposals to boost education funding were weighed in legislatures around the country, Congress' appetite for expanding federal school aid was dulled by demands to curb the deficit."[34]) Representative Hawkins, chair of the committee, carefully explained the impediments to congressional approval of the program to local school officials during the field hearing in Chicago:

> The only question that seems to be at odds among the members of the committee—and this may reflect differences among the membership of the full House—is the $50 million to begin the program. It has been said that this program is not only valuable educationally, but that it is also cost-effective, socially desirable, and morally sound.
>
> However, we anticipate opposition from the administration, again based on the cost of the program itself. The implication of the administration is that if those of you at the local level think the program is so desirable, why is it not possible for you to raise the money at the state and local levels?[35]

The question was answered by Manford Byrd, superintendent of the Chicago public schools:

> One of our problems, unlike the Federal government, we cannot go into deficit funding.
> . . .
> It is always a matter of conflicting goods, and especially at the State level, where our dollars do tend to go more to human services than the Federal dollars go toward, and, in fact, if there was something I would say to address to your colleagues, it might be the idea that perhaps the greatest defense we could have of the Nation is in the strength and well-being of its individuals and not necessarily in missiles, but, of course, you hear that argument all the time.[36]

Dr. Byrd noted that most federal aid to education had been designed to equalize resources "not only among states, but within states."[37]

The budget deficit was clearly a great preoccupation for the Ninety-ninth Congress, since a deficit reduction plan, which began to be identified with the names of its sponsors—the Gramm-Rudman-Hollings bill—had passed in late 1985.[38] Gramm-Rudman-Hollings set a series of increasingly lower deficit targets to be met in each of six years, with a goal of a balanced federal budget by the year 1991. With deficit targets, Congress would now have to consider the overall costs of programs. As a result, the addition of a new federal program in education would receive more attention and scrutiny than it might have received in an earlier Congress. Clearly, for some legislators the cost of the program, even at the relatively low sum of $50 million, was too much in these times of deficit reduction.

Failure in the Ninety-Ninth Congress—Election-Year Politics

While the deficit may have helped build opposition to the bill in the Senate, two greater obstacles appeared to be partisan politics and the issue of abortion. As the November elections drew near, a series of sequential holds were alternately used by the Republican and Democratic leadership to block floor consideration of the bill. The Senate, with a smaller membership than the House, is more responsive to the individual needs of each of its members. As a result, a procedure known as a "hold" exists whereby any senator can ask his or her party leadership to consider delaying a matter. The identity of the senator requesting the hold is not revealed unless that senator so desires. It is often easy to make an educated guess as to who placed the hold, and efforts to accommodate a senator's objection may be attempted. When a unanimous consent agreement is raised to bring a matter to the floor, an objection by the party leader acting on a hold will prevent the legislation from being considered at that time.

On the Democratic side, by early October it had become clear that the Republicans' chances of holding on to control of the Senate in the November elections were dead even. According to analysts at the *Congressional Quarterly*, "it had been a close question all year . . . with a prediction of '50 or 51 Democratic seats.' "[39] If the Democrats were positioned to regain control of the Senate, then why should they help a Republican senator, Arlen Specter, who was up for reelection?

Specter sought the endorsement of the education groups in Pennsylvania as he forged an election coalition of the right—including the National Rifle Association and the Pennsylvania Pro-Life Federation—and more moderate camps.[40] Quick passage of this bill would help ensure the endorsement of education groups. And so it appears that partisan politics led some Democrats to request a hold on the bill. Therefore, when S. 1525 was brought to the floor of the Senate, Senator Robert Byrd (D-W.Va.), Senate minority leader at the time, objected to further consideration of the bill.[41] It was ironic, but typical of Congress, that four years later it would be Arlen Specter who would be a pivotal figure in the Democrats' efforts to continue funding for the program after it had finally been approved.

In 1986 the Democrats were also aware of the troubles Specter was having in holding on to the support of his fellow Republicans. Earlier that summer, Senator Robert Dole (R-Kans.), then Senate majority leader, acting on behalf of fellow Republicans who had put a hold on the bill, had objected to floor consideration of the bill.[42] The issue of the dropout program began to be linked to the abortion debate because of the provisions in the bill that required dropout projects funded under the program to "address the special needs of pregnant minors and school-age parents."[43] (The linkage was made because some female students had dropped out of school owing to pregnancy.) Senator Gordon J. Humphrey (R-N.H.) was among the senators who interpreted this provision to mean that school "counseling would include recommending abortion to teenage girls as a way of keeping them in school."[44] Humphrey, endorsed by conservative newspapers in his first bid for the Senate in 1978 on a pro-life platform, had vowed after the 1984 election to focus his attention on the issue of abortion.[45] Thus, these two forces—partisan considerations in an election year and the anti-abortion lobby—combined to kill the dropout measure; it never reached the floor of the Senate. In spite of overwhelming bipartisan support in the House of Representatives, it died in the Ninety-ninth Congress, as did so many other bills.

The November elections saw the Democrats maintain control of the House, a control held since 1955, and their return to majority party status in the Senate, with a 55–45 seat majority. While problems would still remain, including the size of the federal deficit and its impact on spending for any new domestic legislation, a Democratic majority in both the House and Senate would eliminate or at least mute the partisan tangling that had contributed to the Senate's failure to pass a dropout bill in the Ninety-ninth Congress. Especially encouraging for the bill's prospects was the election as chair of Senator Claiborne Pell, the ranking Democrat on the Senate Subcommittee on Education, Arts and Humanities and a strong champion of education issues.[46] Nonetheless, there would still be a need for cooperation: any legislation would still require the approval of Republican President Ronald Reagan, since neither the House nor the Senate had become veto proof.[47]

BACK ON TRACK—A NEW CONGRESS

As the One Hundredth Congress got under way in January 1987, it was clear to all knowing observers that the momentum needed to pass the school dropout program had finally been reached. With the Senate firmly in the hands of the Democrats, there was an eagerness to move on some of the education bills that had languished in the previous Congress. As Pell noted, "We're not going to go in waving the flag of confrontation, [but] I think we have the votes, if necessary, to prevail."[48]

S. 320: The School Dropout Demonstration Assistance Act

On January 16, 1987, Pell introduced the Dropout Prevention and Reentry Act. The new bill, S. 320, was renamed the School Dropout Demonstration Assistance Act. Eighteen other senators in bipartisan support joined Senator Pell in introducing this bill. This measure carried great significance for Pell, for it was the first education initiative he would introduce in the One Hundredth Congress. As chair of the subcommittee, his support would be critical in determining which education measures would receive the backing of the committee, since most of the work done in Congress is done in committee.

According to Pell, "the high number of school dropouts [was] . . . the most pressing problem facing our schools today."[49] Passage of the bill was to be "one of our highest priorities" in the One Hundredth Congress. Pell was optimistic and firm in his commitment to see this bill become law: "It is a bill that we will place on a fast track. Since hearings were held on this legislation in the last Congress, I hope to move it to the subcommittee and full committee markup without undue delay."[50]

Several modifications were made in the language of this bill from the bill introduced in the previous Congress. One change affected the allocation of funds. In order to gain the support of senators from rural states, school districts with fewer than 20,000 elementary and secondary school students would be allotted 30 percent of the available funds. (A set portion of those funds would be reserved for school districts with fewer than 2000 students.) This was increased from the 20 percent allocated to rural districts in the Ninety-ninth Congress. This strategy seemed to produce the desired effect: two Democratic senators from rural states who had not co-sponsored S. 1525, John Stennis of Mississippi and George Mitchell of Maine, joined Pell as co-sponsors when S. 320 was introduced.

A second modification was deletion of language referring to "pregnant minors." The original language used in S.1525 in the Ninety-ninth Congress called for the "development and implementation" of projects which would, in part, "address the special needs of pregnant minors and school-age parents." As we have seen, this language had contributed to conservative opposition to the bill in the Senate in the fall of 1986, derailing efforts to pass the legislation in the Senate before adjournment.

To avoid entangling the dropout program with the abortion issue, Pell eliminated all references to "pregnant minors." Instead, the new language was modified to read: applications for projects would "address the special needs of school-age parents."[51]

This bill appeared to be off to a fast start. With the chair of the Subcommittee on Education, Arts and Humanities as sponsor and the ranking member an initial co-sponsor, the bill was quickly cleared by the subcommittee in March. Indeed, passage of legislation to reduce the dropout rate had become a priority in the One Hundredth Congress. Several different strategies were followed to assure its passage. Initially, the Senate adopted a more cautious approach than the House with the introduction of a number of separate bills dealing with education. Instead of including a number of specific education programs in a massive education bill at the start of the session, S. 373, the major bill to reauthorize many of the programs providing federal support for elementary, secondary, and adult education through 1993 was kept simple and short. S. 373, only twenty-three pages long when it was introduced in January 1987, would eventually serve as the legislative vehicle for considering a number of education bills, including the dropout bill. For that reason, initially it was kept quite short.[52] In fact, by October 1987, when the education subcommittee voted on reporting the education package to the full committee, its length had grown to 253 pages, including the dropout legislation.[53]

Senator Pell and Senator Stafford, chair and ranking Republican of the education subcommittee, respectively, at first supported a "slow, piece-meal approach to reauthorizing education programs."[54] This was due to the fact that most of the education programs were authorized through 1988. A cautious approach would give the new Democratic leadership in the Senate "time to gauge the chamber's mood for new spending." However, in no time at all, it became clear that there was support for new spending, at least for education. Not only did the budget resolution (H Con Res 93) include additional funds, but "the Senate added more than $500 million a year in new budget authority for education to its version of an omnibus trade bill (HR 3)."[55] It did not take long for the Senate to act on this newfound support for education in the budget.

At the same time the dropout language was being included in this larger education package, the Dropout Assistance Act had become part of another legislative package, S. 406, the Education for a Competitive

America Act. This bill, reported out of the Committee on Labor and Human Resources on June 16, 1987, was "a freestanding legislative proposal . . . intended to be included as part of the omnibus trade legislation which include[d] initiatives of . . . other Senate Committees . . . designed to improve . . . economic competition in the global economy through a series of education initiatives in those areas which . . . directly improved the capabilities of our current and future workforce."[56] An omnibus bill serves as a catch-all bill, including a number of different measures, and may be forged through the work of committee chairs, party leaders, and staff. As more provisions are added, representing the different interests of members, the coalition supporting a bill will expand. In time, with enough votes won to gain support, the bill becomes a must-pass bill, providing a vehicle by which a wide range of measures may be added that would have less chance of support if brought to the floor individually.[57] In recent years omnibus bills have become a frequent tool of the leadership because they improve the chances of legislation passing and lessen the chance of a presidential veto for any one of the separate legislative proposals since the president is forced to vote "yes" or "no" on the entire package.

In the case of the omnibus trade bill, a number of committees drafted language for their own small niche of the final package. House Speaker Jim Wright (D-Tex.) worked with the Rules Committee to shape a coherent trade package in one bill for the full House to consider, and Majority Leader Robert Byrd took bills from eight committees to meld into one omnibus trade bill for the full Senate to consider.[58]

The School Dropout Demonstration Assistance Act was agreed to as an amendment to S.406 (the Committee on Labor and Human Resources' contribution to the omnibus trade bill) without objection.[59] Several other education bills were included in this package, including Senator Kennedy's Star Schools program which "would provide grants to telecommunications networks to provide instruction" in such areas as "math, science and foreign languages," as well as programs to increase literacy. These measures were overwhelmingly supported, with only three senators in opposition—Orrin Hatch (R-Utah), Dan Quayle (R-Ind.), and Strom Thurmond (R-S.C.). In fact, Quayle was the only senator to vote against reporting S.406 for consideration by the full Senate.[60]

With passage of the trade bill "a top priority for the new Democratic-controlled Congress,"[61] the education bills included in this package would insure their likelihood of passage. As a result, several programs favored by members of the education committee, including Pell's dropout legislation and Kennedy's Star Schools, were included.[62] By the end of July 1987, both the House and Senate had passed different versions of a trade bill. However, unforeseen economic and budget difficulties in the fall of 1987, including the October 19 Stock Market crash, pushed agreement on a trade bill with the House until the second session of the One Hundredth Congress, which began in January 1988.

The dropout issue had been redefined from an issue in education to one of economic competitiveness along with the other education programs. Through this redefinition, the coalition of support for these education programs, as well as for the massive trade bill, would expand. However, at the same time that the dropout program was being included in the conference discussion on the trade bill, it was also included as part of the omnibus education bill. By December 1987, when the education bill was finally approved by the full Senate, over twenty-six separate bills had been incorporated into S.373, the Senate omnibus education bill. Senator Pell clearly stated the purpose of including the School Dropout Demonstration Assistance Act in this omnibus bill: "A comprehensive elementary and secondary education bill must address the fact that 25 percent of our students drop out of school every year. We must make every effort to prevent these students from leaving school and to encourage those who have left to return and finish. I am therefore very pleased that this important legislation is part of our omnibus bill."[63] Given the problem in reaching a trade agreement that a majority of members in the House and Senate would agree to, Pell thought it was important to move on several fronts to insure passage of the dropout legislation. Thus, he pushed for its inclusion in the omnibus education bill as well as in the omnibus trade bill.[64]

In order to give program administrators in the executive branch some discretion, Congress often includes a statement of how legislation is to be implemented, thereby clarifying its intent for future program administrators and the courts. This is often done by including a statement of congressional intent in a committee or conference report released at the time a bill is being considered. Another approach that can be taken to clarify congressional intent without having to add to the language in legislation may be to hold a colloquy between two or more members of the House or Senate during floor debate. A colloquy is a brief discussion by two or more members which is often inserted in the *Congressional Record* and not actually spoken; its purpose is to clarify legislative intent, often through the use of examples. The colloquy will usually include the committee or subcommittee chair or ranking member who, working to gain support for the measure, will painstakingly outline what the legislative provisions of the bill will do.

In the case of the dropout legislation, Senator Pell had been careful to delete any reference to the counseling of pregnant teenagers in his original bill, and no language to that effect had been added during the committee markup. Still the report from the Committee on Labor and Human Resources which accompanied S.373 when it was reported to the full Senate included the statement that "It is not the intent of the Committee to use education funds authorized under this Act for health services. Such services are funded through various federal, state and local health programs, and it is not the intent of the Committee either to duplicate or to supplement such funding through this Act."[65]

This language had been inserted into the report accompanying the bill out of committee by concerned members on the Republican side of the aisle. Senator Orrin Hatch repeated these same words almost verbatim on the floor of the Senate during floor debate. Senator Hatch, the ranking member of the Labor and Human Resources Committee, undoubtedly was trying to ease passage of the bill through the Senate on his side of the aisle. Hatch, who is not as predictably conservative in matters that have come before the committee as his election campaigns would suggest, has often worked with Democrats to reach compromises acceptable to the majority of the Senate, although this approach has not always been successful.[66]

It was apparent that the concern was coming from the same source that had blocked floor consideration of the dropout bill in the Ninety-ninth Congress—those who feared the measure might promote abortion. Hatch's attempt to placate his Republican colleagues is most evident in his colloquy with Senator Jesse Helms (R-N.C.) inserted into the *Congressional Record* during the floor debate.

Mr. Helms. Mr. President, I would inquire of the distinguished managers regarding title VIII entitled, "Demonstration Projects Designed to Address School Dropout Problems and to Strengthen Basic Skills Instruction." On page 85 the report states, "It is not the intent of the committee to use education funds authorized under this act for health services."

My specific question is this: Does this means [sic] that Federal funds appropriated under title VIII of the pending bill shall not be used on or off the premises of any elementary or secondary school to provide the following:

First, contraceptive drugs or devices;
Second, prescriptions for such drugs or devices;
Third, transportation for such drugs or devices;
Fourth, referrals for such drugs or devices;
Fifth, counseling to encourage the child to use such drugs or devices;
Sixth, abortions;
Seventh, transportation for abortions;
Eighth, referrals for abortions; or
Ninth, counseling to encourage the child to obtain an abortion?

Mr. Hatch. The Senator is correct. Certainly that would be my intent.[67]

And so by December 1987, the Senate had passed both the omnibus trade bill and the omnibus education bill. However, given the complexity of each bill, and the large number of programs included in each, the bills were not identical to the bills passed in the House.

H.R. 5—The School Improvement Act of 1987

The approach taken in the House of Representatives was to push for a massive education package reauthorizing existing programs for five years in addition to the creation of new programs as soon as the One Hundredth Congress began in January 1987. Included in this omnibus education bill, H.R. 5, were provisions for a program of national demonstration grants for three years to be used for dropout prevention and reentry programs, in addition to a program of basic skills improvement for secondary school students. While the language of the bill called for an equal proportion of funds to go to dropout programs and basic skills programs, the secretary of education would still have discretion to make adjustments in the proportions based on applications received.[68] This caused a point of contention with the Senate, which was firmly on the path to approving funding specifically and solely for dropout programs.

The omnibus education bill had a relatively easy path through the House of Representatives, passing by a vote of 401–1 in May 1987.[69] At the same time, the House had also been considering an omnibus trade bill which passed in April 1987. An amendment to the original trade bill by the House Committee on Education and Labor included provisions to improve U.S. competitiveness through programs for literacy, vocational training, math, sciences, and foreign language training.[70] However, no provisions were made for the dropout program as was being done in the Senate. The trade bill was a massive and complicated piece of legislation—over 1000 pages long. The education provisions of the bill were but a small part of a bill designed to grapple with the rising trade deficit with "the most sweeping set of proposed changes in U.S. trade law since the enactment of the 1974 Trade Act . . . a comprehensive approach . . . , covering agriculture, education, intellectual property rights and other areas not traditionally included in trade legislation."[71]

By the time it had passed both the House and Senate, the trade bill had been considered by fourteen House and nine Senate committees.[72] The versions passed by the House and Senate were not identical; the House version, for example, omitted any provisions for the dropout program. Since legislation must be passed in identical form in the House and Senate in the same Congress, the differences in the House and Senate versions would need to be worked out in a conference committee. A conference committee exists solely for the purpose of developing legislative programs and language agreeable to both chambers. The conference committee members are appointed by the respective party leaders of the House and Senate, and usually reflect the interests of the committees that offered the bill. Because large omnibus bills often reflect the work and interest of a number of committees, the conference committee can grow quite large as happened in the case of the trade bill. In that case, subgroups or mini-conferences may be held, so that those interested in just one area—education, for example, will work through the language on that section of the bill. Throughout the fall of 1987, 44 senators and 155 House members divided into 17 subgroups met sporadically to iron out the differences between the two bills.[73]

A final trade bill did not emerge from conference until the spring of 1988. It was vetoed by President Reagan because of a provision in the bill which would have required a sixty-day notice of plant closings. In June, Representative Dan Rostenkowski introduced a new bill, H.R. 4848, which did not include the plant closing notification provisions, but reflected the conference agreement of the House and Senate. In this version, the School Demonstration Assistance Act of 1988 was included. By August the omnibus trade bill had won approval by both the House and the Senate.

In the end, the Omnibus Trade and Competitiveness Act of 1988 authorized the dropout program for fiscal year 1988. The Augustus F. Hawkins-Robert T. Stafford Elementary and Secondary School Improvement Amendments of 1988 authorized the dropout program for 1989, as the House went along with the Senate language creating a separate dropout program.

In fact, the program was passed a third time! In order for the program to be up and running in the fall of 1988, it had to be authorized early enough for the Appropriations Committee to approve funding since the committee does not normally approve spending unless a proper authorization has been obtained. However, since the program had the support of both the House and Senate and it was clear it would pass, with the only questions being when and through what legislative vehicle, in late December 1987 the Appropriations Committee had approved both an *authorization* and *appropriation* for fiscal year 1988 as part of a massive continuing resolution.[74] A continuing resolution is a joint resolution, which is used as a catch-all spending bill near the end of the fiscal year. "Whenever Congress cannot complete action on one or more of the thirteen regular appropriations bills by the start of the fiscal year, it provides temporary emergency funding for the affected federal agencies through a continuing resolution." Whereas in the past they "were employed to keep a few government agencies in operation for short periods," today they "are major policy-making instruments of massive size and scope."[75] The approval that was to come later in the normal authorization process, while technically not needed, would be needed to insure support for the program by the Appropriations Committee in the future.

In the end, a small separate demonstration program with funding targeted solely for dropout programs was agreed to, but only for a period of two years. In the first round of competition for demonstration project grants, the Department of Education selected eighty-nine sites. (See Appendix A.) The project grants were to be used by school districts, community-based organizations, and other institutions in partnership with schools to reduce the number of school dropouts by establishing and demonstrating

> 1.) effective programs to identify potential student dropouts and prevent them from dropping out;
> 2.) effective programs to identify and encourage children who have already dropped out to reenter school and complete their elementary and secondary education;
> 3.) effective early intervention programs designed to identify at-risk students in elementary and secondary schools; and
> 4.) model systems for collecting and reporting information to local school officials on the number, ages, and grade levels of the children not completing their elementary and secondary education and the reasons why such children have dropped out of school.[76]

A wide range of activities and services were allowed in projects designed to lower the dropout rate, including the use of work-study and apprenticeship opportunities to encourage students to stay in school, as well as remedial activities for those who were at risk of dropping out or who had dropped out, and staff training in schools for teachers and counselors to help meet the needs of those at risk of dropping out. In addition, the projects could experiment to make use of various broadcasting resources along with other technological aids to keep kids in schools or to encourage them to return.[77]

Some members of Congress expected that a larger program providing federal funds for "basic skills programs" for states to administer would be approved. This program would then enable states to decide best on the way to use these monies, including programs for dropouts. The states would be the best judge of which demonstration projects would provide a model for their own respective needs. Unfortunately for those involved with the dropout demonstration projects and interested in continuing a federal role in this program area, the increase in funding for "basic skills program needs," which was needed to continue these programs, failed to win congressional approval.

REAUTHORIZATION IN THE ONE HUNDRED AND FIRST CONGRESS

No one knew whether the appropriations needed for the large state-administered basic skills programs for secondary students would be approved in the One Hundred and First Congress. Yet by the end of the first year and a half of implementation, the dropout programs appeared to be succeeding in their objectives of increasing the high school graduation rate. As a precautionary strategy, Representative Charles A. Hayes introduced H.R. 2281 on May 9, 1989, to extend the authorization for school dropout demonstration programs for fiscal years 1990 and 1991. In June 1989, during floor debate, Representative Bill Goodling spoke to the funding requirements of the large state-administered basic skills program:

> As you know, the problem of students dropping out of school is a staggering problem in this country. Last Congress, we created two programs aimed at helping to combat this problem. The smaller program received funding; the larger did not. This bill extends authority to fund the smaller program. The larger program would need approximately 20 times the funding as the smaller program extended in H.R. 2281. At this time, I believe that such a large funding requirement is probably a budgetary impossibility. H.R. 2281 will allow us to continue our support of combating the problem of dropouts in a smaller and more targeted program. Through this bill, we can choose to fund either one or the other program, but not both.
>
> The larger program mirrors the chapter 1 program of the Elementary and Secondary Education Act of 1965, which targets Federal support for basic skills education. As a practical matter, money used in the chapter 1 program could be used for services in the high school; however, due to funding shortages, local educators almost without exception use all the chapter 1 money in the early grades. This program would direct money toward the higher grades. Even though I may prefer to have the larger program funded, the bill recognizes the practical reality of these fiscal times.[78]

The bill extending the authorization of the dropout programs (H.R. 2281) was approved by the House in June 1989 under suspension of the rules. However, the easy passage in the House did not reflect the growing obstacles the program would soon face in its legislative journey. Again the path would not be simple.

CHAPTER 4

Who the Program Serves

A small federal program, such as the school dropout demonstration assistance program, can seem removed and distant from the lives of most citizens. But for those who had dropped out, this small program made the difference between a life on welfare and a world of possibilities never before envisioned. No longer beyond their reach were a high school diploma, a good job, a college degree, newfound self-esteem, and even an optimistic outlook on life. Nonetheless, few people knew anything about this program, which is typical of much of the legislation passed by Congress.

The program was designed to help increase the high school graduation rate not only in urban areas, but also in rural communities. In order to provide a better understanding of what this program was all about, this chapter will present the two sides of the programs through a brief portrait of one of the beneficiaries of the program who lived in Milwaukee's inner city, and a sketch of West Valley Academy's program for at-risk students in rural Oregon.

THE PORTRAIT OF A DROPOUT

June Moore was a high school dropout.[1] In 1990 she was a participant in one of the demonstration dropout prevention projects, the Milwaukee Area Technical College's (MATC) Project Hold program. Her life would be profoundly affected if lack of funding brought the program to a halt.

Moore dropped out of high school in her sophomore year at the age of fifteen. At the time she was a B student, but she was a single parent and felt compelled to choose between staying in school or taking care of her newborn son. June tried to work toward a high school degree by taking GED classes but found the pace too slow. The only alternative at the time was enrollment as a regular student in the public high school system. June was enrolled in a high school plagued with some of the most serious problems found in inner city schools, and after sitting in the classroom for one day she realized this would not work.

June next tried the Milwaukee Area Technical College's high school program and found the approach more suitable for her needs than that offered by an alternative high school. MATC is known throughout Milwaukee for providing alternative paths to getting a high school degree. As June puts it: "I fit in a lot better around here [MATC], and people treated me like I was a person, rather than a kid. It was hard trying to go to high school when you had kids. You feel real out of place and I wanted to be somewhere where I didn't feel so out of place." Even the initial step of beginning this high school program took a great deal of effort. As Ron Fancher, an outreach specialist for Project Hold who has worked with many high school dropouts, has observed, "We get so many calls, with people just calling to inquire about returning to school; 'What would I have to do. . . . How can I do it.' " But a lot of people don't follow up that call with enrollment in a high school program. "Oftentimes individuals make that call two or three times, and it's on the third, fourth, or even fifth time that they actually take advantage of walking through the door," Fancher states.

June was like many of those who call, but unlike many, she did eventually join the program. June would call for information and then say, "Okay, I'll call back." A month would pass and she would make another call, and again ask for information on the program, this time responding, "Okay, I'll see you down there," and still she would not follow through. After repeating this pattern over several months she finally said to herself, "Forget it, I'm not going to call. I'm going to get dressed and I'm going to go down there."

This decision was not easy. According to June, "You're scared at first because you don't know what to do and you don't know what they are going to think about me. Am I going to be smart enough to fit in? All of these things run through your mind before you even begin to make that first phone call. And then once you begin the program you wonder if you can make it in this class."

One of her instructors, Sue Martell, was instrumental in steering June to Project Hold. June developed a friendship with Martell as she helped her work through several personal problems. As June recounts, "I wanted to come to school, but I didn't have any money to get to school, or any books or supplies."

June was one of the first participants in the state of Wisconsin's controversial Learnfare program, which began in 1988. Learnfare requires school attendance for all children between the ages of thirteen and nineteen who are on welfare (i.e., including sons and daughters "of a mother receiving payments under the Aid to Families with Dependent Children [AFDC] program, or a mother herself"[2]). The program is punitive in that "[I]f a student accumulates 10 absences in a semester, the state is informed and begins monitoring attendance records. If the child has three additional, unexcused absences in a month, that child's share of a welfare grant is cut. The sanctions continue until monthly attendance improves."

The Learnfare program has been criticized for a number of reasons. One problem that has often been cited is that support services and systems, such as child care for student mothers, were not worked through in the original program.[3] One observer has noted that "you have to drop out and get sanctioned before you get the support that you need."[4] Willie T. Little, the community affairs director for the Milwaukee public schools, noted two years after the program was under way that "There are families out there that need help. The question is who is going to provide that assistance. . . . That's the problem with Learnfare: It does not go into problem-solving."[5] June knew of some mothers who had waited two years to get into a state-funded day care program.

Through her instructor, June was put in touch with Ron Fancher at Project Hold. The support services provided by Project Hold gave June the extra support and guidance she needed to complete the requirements for her high school degree. But even when she was already on campus and encouraged to talk with the staff at Project Hold, it took a while for her to take that first step. According to June, "I felt that they were going to look down on me because I am young, have kids, and am a high school drop-out. I looked down on myself during those times and I felt that everybody else had their eye on me, and it made me feel real uncomfortable. I thought I was the only person in this situation at the time. When you are young, you don't know anything about life, you don't know anything about people . . . so you think all kinds of things."

At MATC students can follow one of three tracks—a GED, an adult high school, or a high school equivalency diploma (requiring extra courses in civic literacy, health literacy, and career planning). As Maureen Coffey, program administrator for Project Hold, explains, "we don't provide the instruction. We provide the support for students after we help them get in the instruction."

Ron Fancher and other outreach specialists in Project Hold work closely with each student to provide ongoing support and encouragement to keep them going. More importantly, most outreach specialists are so well attuned to the students' needs that they can, as Maureen Coffey puts it, identify "the barrier the student is experiencing right now that may threaten her to drop out again." Each individual case is examined on an individual basis to determine whether the specific need is child care, or drug treatment, or a dollar for bus transportation, or even a textbook. "There are all sorts of reasons why people drop out, and most of the time it isn't because they're not smart enough to finish school, it's because of personal obstacles," Coffey states. Outreach specialists not only help students learn about drug and alcohol counseling services, and job opportunities, but they may help get a student into a program that is already oversubscribed and with a waiting list.

With a textbook costing between $25 and $50 and with four or five classes taken per semester, the costs associated with staying in school or returning to school may be prohibitive, especially when daily transportation costs and even child care expenses are also involved. Project Hold helps keep the material costs down by enabling a student to borrow textbooks for a semester.

Assistance is sometimes needed in identifying child care providers. Some mothers wishing to gain access to state-funded child care services may be on a waiting list for as long as two years. While Project Hold does not provide or fund child care, the outreach specialist may be aware of the services and support mechanisms available to students and furnish referrals and contacts to get a student on the waiting list or even placed higher on that list. Fancher describes his job as an outreach specialist as follows:

> I help develop a track, paint a picture, create a path, and continue to motivate and inspire students to continue to push on. Sometimes students get so bogged down with the day to day duties and things that they have to do just to cope with family situations, life, and then you add education to that also. It's conducive to just have someone to tie all that together for you and just turn it into motivation. A lot of our students are being successful every day with what they have to deal with but they're so bogged down that they don't even realize sometimes the effort that it took to make it through each day.
>
> We continue to keep students in touch with what they are actually doing, the strides that they are making, and the dividends that it is paying.

Fancher described the relationship that developed between June and himself:

> The majority of our students, because of the at-risk nature or the disadvantages they come from, have to choose alternative methods to be successful and to achieve, so that calls for alternative strategies. June and I have become friends. I know a lot about her and her home life and she knows the same thing about me: how many kids I have and what has happened with my kids, because those kinds of situations are real. So she's in touch with me and my emotions and feelings when we meet. I know when she has had a bad day with the kids. . . .
>
> We both like carrot-nut-raisin muffins and coffee, so we've had numerous conversations over those bran muffins and coffee. We talk about all kinds of things—from physical condition, healthy lifestyles, raising children. . . .
>
> She has given me a lot of just old home remedies to deal with differ-

ent medical child care stuff . . . so when you begin to discuss all of these traditional, non-traditional, ordinary, unordinary things that happen in life, a bonding takes place, and it's all built upon a trust factor. A trust factor so that when June tells me that she needs something, because I'm so in tune with what she has to deal with, what she copes with, I know how important it is to her.

June adds:

You only get so much money from the state, and it only goes so far. I use the money that I get from the state to pay my bills and to buy my kids shoes and clothes, or whatever they may need, and sometimes the money that I have left over I use for transportation, but that money only goes so far. . . . So sometimes I wouldn't even be able to get to school because I just ran out of money and there was nothing I could do about it. . . . And I would say, "Well, Ron, I really need to get home. Give me a bus ticket. . . ." And Ron would give me a bus ticket and I would be able to get home.

Based on the relationship they had built, Fancher would know that this was a genuine need. As Fancher noted:

We help students to continue to focus on their future. Sometimes, the individuals that are closest to us and the individuals that we have the most contact with are not as supportive to our endeavors and to what we are going through. I recall numerous conversations that June and I had about her mom thinking that she should be doing other things than going to school, or pursuing a certain career at a particular time.

June observes:

My mother was never a really big help to me at all. When I first had my son, she put me out while I was in labor [at the age of 15]. I really had no support from anybody in the family because she had everybody shun me like they do in other countries. So I had no help. I always heard, "Well, you know you're never going to be anything . . . you're going to be another statistic. . . . So I didn't have any friends, and I didn't have anybody to turn to during those times for me. And then when I met Ron it was hard for me to trust people, really hard. Ron knew this because I told him, "Well, you know I don't trust people very easily. I always think there's something behind the reason they're doing things."

Fancher:

It was real important for me to help June to understand that though your mom may be saying certain things or doing certain things, this doesn't mean she doesn't love you. She's going through and coping with her own things. She's drawing from her past and her background, where many women were not as assertive, and were not pursuing non-traditional fields. So she was saying these things to June to say: "you stick to this." When June walks across that stage [at graduation], her mom is going to jump for joy more than anyone else and say "That's my baby, all right," and mean it, and be for real, so I felt it was real important not to take the things her mom was saying for how they sound. There is love, there is support, there is caring . . . but her mom is going through things also.

As Fancher sees his job, he needs to keep the students focused, so that they can learn to view a crisis or hardship that develops as "just another storm of life you're going to have to weather." Fancher was able to help June see that she could do her own thing, in her own way. As June observes, "I can be my own person without having to worry about what everybody else is thinking about, so it made it a lot easier because then I stopped worrying about what everybody else thought about me and went on to do what I thought was right for me. So it made it easier for me to cope with school and everything else."

Of her two brothers and one sister, June is the only one who has a high school degree. Although June is not sure if her parents ever completed high school, her mother always stressed the importance of graduating from high school. According to June, "I rebelled . . . I got tired of always being the one to stay home and read. Now I see that my mother was right about a lot of things."

The demonstration dropout program has given June a different outlook. Before coming into this program, June didn't trust anybody.

> After hearing how bad you are for a long time you begin to think you are that way. Ron used to tell me, "You know what, you can do it. You're too smart not to." When I would show him my report card, even if I got all C's, Ron would say, "This is a great report card. You did really well for being in the situation you are in." So I would feel good about myself.

Fancher noted that the counselors in the program have to be careful about putting labels on people. "We don't put labels on students. . . . It is so important for us to tune into the most minute successful event or activity or endeavor that a student has achieved and make them aware of that."

The program has had a spillover effect in that its graduates often become role models for family and friends in similar situations. For example, June has served as a role model for her older sister who returned to finish school after having dropped out of the seventh grade. When her sister told June she had failed a test, June responded: "You haven't failed. . . . Even if you didn't pass the test that you wanted to pass, you did pass the test to see whether or not you could stick with it."

After June completed her high school studies, she stayed in touch with the Project Hold staff, and in particular Ron Fancher, who had become a special friend to her over the years. She had kept in contact even when she had moved into a new program for welfare recipients seeking training beyond a high school degree who needed help with child care, transportation, textbooks, and tuition. She found her experiences in this program to be "dehumanizing" because everyone was "treated as a number, and not as a person." Rather than finding encouragement, the program administrators put "her down for being on AFDC." As a result, she remained in contact with the Project Hold staff as she worked through a two-year associate degree program in applied science in welding technology and graduated from that program on May 20, 1992. As Coffey has noted, "our obligation as far as funding is just to get them through the high school and then try to transition them over . . . but automatically there is so much bonding that goes on in this part that we often have people who continue with us at a personal level." Even as June was completing her associate degree, she was recruiting others to join the program, and follow in her footsteps.

June is just one of hundreds of students who benefited from this demonstration dropout prevention program in Milwaukee. As is true of most of the successful demonstration projects, the support services it provides have been a key to its success in graduating students who dropped out of school.

A DEMONSTRATION PROJECT IN A RURAL SETTING

As was mentioned earlier, nearly eveyone tends to associate the problem of high school dropouts with the nation's inner cities, but rural communities, too, face this problem. One of the eighty-nine project grants was awarded to West Valley Academy in Sheridan, Oregon, an alternative school serving at-risk students in the rural Willamette Valley in Oregon in grades K–12. West Valley is a community-based, private nonprofit educational institution that works with a number of public school systems and Native American tribes.[6] Instructional methods are tailored to meet the needs of each individual student, with the staff "organized into three flexible teaching teams, each consisting of credentialed teachers and teaching assistants with degrees in specialized areas . . . supported by a counselor and a full service student testing and evaluation center."[7] Academic progress is measured in ways other than standardized tests, and not all students are taught in the same way.

Again, support services are critical to the success of the program. Some of these services include maintaining frequent contact with parents; representing children or parents in meetings with various social service agencies and "acting as an advocate [of the student] who understands and is not intimidated by 'the system' " in those meetings; and counseling students in a number of different areas.[8] To give an idea of the level of support, all absences from school are investigated. "The van drivers, who are usually also teachers, know all of the children and even go into homes after them if they are not at the pickup point. The children, and their parents, soon learn that we are serious about attendance."[9] Students who are pregnant or who are mothers also receive "training in child development, home economics, and practical skills of survival."[10] In addition, mothers can bring their children with them to school, and the children can participate in a preschool program while their mother is in class.[11]

THE ROLE OF DEMONSTRATION PROGRAMS

Maureen Coffey has observed that "there are so many variables in peoples' lives that inhibit them from going back to school. . . . You can send out a million letters [requiring students to stay in school] but it is not going to solve the problem. You have got to have a support system that goes with it." Many high school dropouts do not have access to the network of support many others have. Some have no family or even a spouse to provide assistance in child care, or pick up assignments and books if a student is sick. By way of example, one student in MATC's program was the victim of gunshot wounds to the scalp, with a bullet lodged in the stomach. An outreach specialist consulted with each of the student's course instructors and reviewed a plan for the student either to get an incomplete or to do out-of-class work assignments to make up the missed course work. For one assignment the student had to do a book report. So the outreach specialist went to the library and picked up the book and then dropped it off at the student's home.

These are the types of programs funded under the demonstration dropout program, and they have served as models for other schools. Based on site visits conducted by the Department of Education, a number of successes were recorded at program sites across the country in the first year and a half of the program's implementation.[12] Despite all these positive signs, by December 1990 it looked like the program might come to an end.

CHAPTER 5

A Legislative Impasse

While the nation's first federal program devoted exclusively to the school dropout problem was under way, the nation's political leaders were establishing an increase in the high school graduation rate as a new national goal. In the summer of 1989 President Bush called for a meeting of the nation's governors for an education summit conference.[1] Only twice before in the nation's history had a president convened the nation's governors—President Theodore Roosevelt on the issue of conservation in 1908, and President Franklin D. Roosevelt on the Great Depression in 1933.[2]

At the summit conference, held on the campus of the University of Virginia in September, the president and the governors agreed to work on setting national education goals and establishing a means by which to report on the nation's progress in achieving those goals. The authors of this new agreement described it as "a Jeffersonian compact to enlighten our children and the children of generations to come."[3] Governor Bill Clinton of Arkansas, a leading proponent of a stronger commitment to education, noted that "This is the first time in the history of this country that we have ever thought enough of education to commit ourselves to national performance goals."[4]

President Bush followed up on this commitment in his State of the Union Address in January 1990. He stated as one of America's education goals that "the United States must increase the high school graduation rate to no less than 90 percent."[5] However, in spite of apparent success and the growing national rhetoric on the need to do something about the dropout problem, the dropout program's very existence was in jeopardy. Ironically, at the same time that the nation's governors and the president had declared "the time for rhetoric is past; the time for performance is now,"[6] the administration rejected an opportunity to move beyond the rhetoric by continuing the only federal dropout program in existence.

Although the goal of a higher graduation rate was clearly articulated, the role of the national government in this campaign was ambiguous. Historically, the federal government has only had a small role in education policy. "Education has always been primarily the responsibility of the states, a product of historical development, public preference, and the reserve powers clause of the Constitution."[7] In fact, the federal share of the nation's spending on education is less than 10 percent.[8] Following in the footsteps of Reagan and other Republican presidents beginning with Richard Nixon, Bush advocated a New Federalism that reflected not only an ideological predisposition to return the power to states (power that had been accumulating in the hands of Washington policymakers since Roosevelt's New Deal in the 1930s and Johnson's War on Poverty programs in the 1960s), but also a growing awareness that the deficit limited the federal government's capacity to fund programs.[9] Thus it was that the administration passed up its opportunity to lead Congress in funding the dropout program.

CATCH-22: WHY WE ARE WHERE WE ARE

Several approaches had been taken to authorize spending for a national school dropout prevention program. In creating programs, Congress could follow several different strategies, one of which was to establish a narrowly focused *categorical program* targeted at a certain segment of the population, with Congress setting parameters as to how the money could be spent and administered. Another option was to establish a *broad-based block grant program administered by the states,* with state agencies deciding how funds should be allocated and spent within the states.

In 1988, in the original authorization for the demonstration dropout prevention program, the House of Representatives had sought to include funds for dropout programs under a broad-based basic skills program for secondary school students. With a growing interest in finding tangible measures of educational success (e.g., a higher high school completion rate), some thought the popular support for funding dropout programs would enable support to coalesce around a more costly basic skills program by linking the two programs together.[10] Representative Pat Williams (D-Mont.) favored the broad-based basic skills program, while Representative Hayes embraced the narrowly focused program that solely addressed the dropouts' educational needs. In the end, a compromise was forged as the two programs became linked together.[11]

In the House bill, the combined secondary school basic skills/dropout prevention program was seen as "a new, two-pronged approach for addressing the special problems of disadvantaged, secondary-school-age youth," with programs "aimed at (1) effective dropout prevention and reentry strategies; and (2) effective secondary school basic skills improvement programs."[12] According to the report of the House Committee on Education and Labor:

> The bill includes both components because the problems of dropouts and low achievement among secondary students are intertwined. A General Accounting Office study of the dropout problem cited poor grades and other school-related problems as a major reasons [sic] why students drop out. Students who are two or more years behind grade level are one of the highest risk groups of potential dropouts.[13]

By way of clarification, activities designed to improve basic skills at the secondary school level include programs fashioned to "meet the special needs of secondary students"; remedial and peer tutoring programs; training programs for staff; as well as various counseling and support services.[14]

The Senate had kept the narrowly focused dropout program separate and distinct from the basic skills program. When a difference arises in the content and wording of legislation passed by the House and Senate, a conference committee consisting of members of both houses is formed to try to reach an agreement acceptable to both chambers. In the final compromise agreement, the House went along with the Senate's approach. However, as part of the agreement, the narrowly focused program would be authorized for only two years. After two years, the broad-based basic skills improvement program would allow states to use funds for a variety of purposes, including dropout prevention programs.[15]

Although this broad-based program scheduled to begin in 1990 was authorized by Congress to begin in that same fiscal year, no funds were ever appropriated for the program. The $400 million price tag for the larger state-administered program was too high given the budget deficit. While efforts were still made to establish a program of large discretionary grants to the states for basic skills instruction and dropout prevention activities, it became clear that *appropriations* to fund the program would not be forthcoming.

A TEMPORARY SOLUTION—EXTEND THE PROGRAM

Realizing that the funds needed for the large discretionary grant program would not be approved in May 1989, Representative Hayes introduced H.R. 2281—a bill to extend the reauthorization of the demonstration dropout program.[16] Hayes was joined by Representative Augustus Hawkins (D-Calif.), the chair of the House Education and Labor Committee, and Representative Bill Goodling (R-Penn.), the ranking member of the House Education and Labor Committee. Since the Democratic and

Republican leaders of the House Education and Labor Committee fully backed this effort, there was no question that this legislation would quickly pass in the House.

Speaking to his colleagues in the House, Representative Hayes warned that unless the current demonstration dropout program was extended, "it is virtually certain that the Federal Government will abandon any effort to help public schools come to grips with their dropout problems. In short, the Federal focus on school dropouts will drop off the national agenda."[17] And so in June 1989, the House of Representatives easily passed legislation extending the demonstration dropout program for two additional years, through fiscal year 1991, under a procedure used to expedite consideration of noncontroversial legislation—suspension of the rules.[18] The situation in the Senate proved more difficult, however.

The Senate did not pass legislation reauthorizing the dropout program until the last days of the 1989 session, and when it finally did, it complicated the issue by passing the dropout provision as a rider to another piece of legislation, the reauthorization for the Taft Institute. Unlike the House, which because of the size of its membership adheres to a set of rules and procedures to expedite the flow of legislation, the Senate works to accommodate the interests of all its members. Thus, one strategy allowed in the Senate, but not in the House, is the use of riders (i.e., amendments that usually are not germane to legislation pending on the floor). Such amendments are often added to popular legislation near the end of a session. Legislation added as a rider would probably not be brought to the floor as a standalone bill for any number of reasons, including the lack of time in the schedule for full floor debate and consideration of the bill, especially as time runs short near the end of a session. The legislation may also be bottled up in committee, and the rider then becomes a mechanism to bring the legislation to the floor for consideration by the full Senate.

The Taft Institute, an educational organization highly regarded by members of Congress, was founded in 1961 in memory of Senator Robert A. Taft, a former majority leader and Republican presidential candidate who died in 1953. Senator Daniel Moynihan (D-N.Y.) described the institute, which had received federal funding for its programs since 1980, to his colleagues:

> The institute is a non-profit, nonpartisan organization dedicated to the . . . task of improving civic education. The Taft Institute provides elementary and secondary school teachers direct access to government leaders. Lecturers have included President George Bush, former Vice Presidents Walter Mondale and Hubert Humphrey, and Supreme Court Justice Sandra Day O'Connor . . . public servants and professors of government.

Over the years, the Institute has taught thousands of teachers, and in turn, it has reached several million students. In the past year, it conducted 30 seminars in 27 States. Teachers are taught how to educate young people in civic responsibility.[19]

The dropout program language was added to the Taft Institute language because with the session quickly drawing to a close, the Senate felt a sense of urgency in reauthorizing the dropout program. This appeared to be the only way to get the legislation passed. The authorization would have to pass in this session in order to get the approval of appropriations that would keep the program running. For the most part, the House Appropriations Committee does not act to fund a program until it has an authorization for appropriations as recommended by the appropriate standing committee and passed by both the House and Senate. The House had already passed the reauthorization for the dropout program earlier in the year, in June, and the Appropriations Committee would soon begin its work on funding programs for fiscal year 1991. However, without Senate approval, the Appropriations Committee would not consider the program for funding.

A SECOND APPROACH—THE PRESIDENT'S EDUCATION PACKAGE

At the same time, the House and Senate were considering President Bush's education proposal, the Excellence in Education Act (S. 695). The Senate Labor and Human Resources Committee reported out S. 695 and included legislation to reauthorize the popular dropout program for an additional two years as a part of this education package. With the Republicans rallying behind the president's package, which included the dropout language, program supporters argued that, given the sense of urgency in getting the dropout authorization passed, there was a compelling case for its passage. Thus, an amendment extending the dropout legislation for two years was easily passed as a rider to the Taft Institute reauthorization. And so the reauthorization for the dropout program had now passed both the House and Senate.

LEGISLATIVE IMPASSE

As noted earlier, legislation must pass the House and Senate in identical form in order for it to be sent to the president for signature or veto. By the end of the first session:

The Senate had passed the dropout reauthorization but had attached it to the reauthorization for the Taft Institute.

The House had passed a separate bill reauthorizing the dropout program.

The House had reported out from subcommittee a separate bill reauthorizing the Taft Institute.[20]

In essence, two popular programs had won the approval of members of both houses of Congress, yet had not passed the respective chambers in the same form. The Senate had combined the dropout reauthorization and Taft Institute reauthorization in one bill, whereas the House had a separate dropout bill and a separate Taft Institute bill.

From my perspective as a new arrival on the Hill, it seemed that this problem would be an easy one to resolve, but to my dismay, I learned that was not to be the case. A call to a staff member on the House Committee on Education and Labor revealed that the House would not budge from its position. The House would not pass a reauthorization of the Taft Institute with the dropout language attached. Two reasons were given:

1. The House had already passed a separate bill reauthorizing the dropout program, so why should it have to pass another bill with the dropout program? As I listened to this explanation, I had my first lesson on the kind of complexity created when a two-chamber legislative body was set up. It was clear—the beginnings of a battle for turf between the House and Senate was taking shape. But as the staff member I had called went on, I realized that the dropout program was caught up in a battle between the House and Senate that had been played out the year before and had more to do with a longstanding hostility resulting from differences in how the House and Senate handle legislation.
2. In the previous year, the House had passed a "modest measure to reauthorize the Taft Institute at a cost of $750,000 a year for fiscal 1989–91"[21] However, as the 1988 elections neared, the Senate added a number of projects to the bill, and when the bill came back to the house for a final vote after conference, it had grown with a price tag of $59.1 million.[22] Representative Newt Gingrich (R-Ga.) compared the bill to "a little herd of pigs rushing through Congress."[23] While it was never said, the inference was clear: The House would teach the Senate a lesson in fiscal responsibility.

The Taft reauthorization, with that price tag of $59 million, was rejected that year, but it did leave a bad taste with the members of the House who remembered how the Senate had cost them approval of the Taft Institute the year before. This time the House would play hardball politics. If the dropout program was to be reauthorized, it would have to be done as a clean bill, or at least not as an add-on to the infamous Taft Institute reauthorization.

By the end of the first session of the One Hundred and First Congress in December 1989, the school dropout program had not been reauthorized. While it had easily passed the House, it had yet to pass the Senate in identical form. Without a reauthorization, neither the House Appropriations Committee nor the Senate Appropriations Committee would approve any money for FY90. Some considered making an attempt to amend the Labor-Health and Human Services-Education appropriations bill when it came to the floor of the Senate in the fall of 1989, but such an amendment was given little chance of success, since the program authorization had yet to be approved. And so by December 1989 it appeared that the program would not continue. The stage was set for a legislative impasse.

CHAPTER 6

Senator Kohl and His Staff
Join the Coalition

My life as a congressional staff member began in December 1989, in the middle of the One Hundredth Congress, just as the first session had come to a close. The policy area assigned to me was education. Of special interest to me was access to educational opportunities, which had affected my life directly. When I was in college, I worked to pay my way, unaware of the range of financial aid programs, aside from scholarships, that were available. This experience taught me that not only must educational programs be available, but information about them must be aggressively disseminated. (While working in Kohl's office, I was able to work on a bill involving access to such information.)

Unlike almost all legislative assistants on the Hill, as a congressional fellow and therefore a temporary staffer, I had only one policy area to handle for the senator. Most legislative assistants must divide their attention between a number of different policy areas. For example, one legislative assistant might handle agriculture, transportation, and communications issues; another might be responsible for health, labor, and social issues. For this reason, some senators and representatives have learned to take advantage of the free help of a midcareer professional and seek out fellows for their offices. This is especially true for those members who need an expert in such areas as health care; and so they use physicians and other health care professionals who come to Washington as congressional fellows for a year.

As a result of my narrow assignment, I was able to devote a great deal of attention to one area of education policy, the continued funding for the school dropout demonstration projects. In addition, this was one of the first issues brought to my attention, and without a backlog of work (my desk was quite clean, except for the aforementioned popcorn!), I was able to immerse myself in this issue. It was too soon for me to begin developing education initiatives for Senator Kohl himself to sponsor, because I had much to learn. For now I had enough to do in simply responding to policy questions from constituents.

Sherry Hayes, Senator Kohl's legislative assistant who handled education, along with labor, health care, and other social issues, proved to be a great teacher. Not only did she have the energy and enthusiasm for Congress which is expected of most senior staff, but she also cared deeply about these issues. As I have said earlier, she also believed in the total immersion technique, which is how she herself had learned the system in her first job on the Hill working for Senator Paul Simon. Her philosophy is that you learn best by doing, which for a newcomer to the Hill can be quite daunting. Early on she sent me to the floor of the Senate to accompany Senator Kohl when he was giving a floor speech in the area of education. She drew me a diagram of the Senate floor, including the "well" where only the senators are allowed to congregate, as well as the aisles, entrances, and staff benches in the back, with a careful map of where I as a staff member would be allowed to walk and sit. When I received my first call from a constituent asking for help, Sherry gave me the name and phone number of the appropriate Senate committee staff member to call, along with a script of what to say and how to say it, and I was on my way—I was being introduced to the Washington game of "phone tag." Until a staffer has established an identity and a certain credibility on the Hill, it may take days, or even a week or two, to get phone calls returned. (Some of my calls were never returned.) What seemed to prompt the fastest return of a call was if you had been able to get through the first and second rounds of "phone tag"—that is, I call Staff person A; Staff person A returns phone call to me, but I'm away from my desk; I then return the call, and say "I'm returning Staff person A's call"; I may then finally establish contact with the person I've been trying to reach over a period of days.

EDUCATING THE STAFF

One of the first calls I received in December 1989 was from Maureen Coffey, a member of the Milwaukee Area Technical College's Project Hold, one of the federally funded school dropout prevention programs.

Constituent Concerns

The Milwaukee Area Technical College (MATC) received federal funding to run dropout programs in the Milwaukee area under two federal programs—vocational education and the national school demonstration dropout program. Funding for the Milwaukee programs under both federal programs appeared to be in jeopardy in December when I began work. The original call to Ann Young, a staff member on Senator Pell's education subcommittee, concerned the vocational education funding. But the two programs were related in terms of the purpose and populations being served, and both programs in Milwaukee had received national acclaim.

Maureen Coffey and Joe Pellegrin, director of high school relations for MATC, patiently helped me understand that two programs were in danger of losing federal funding. Pellegrin began his career as a teacher in the Milwaukee Public Schools, but, dismayed by the overwhelming problems facing teachers and administrators in the inner city schools in the 1960s, he soon left teaching for a series of administrative posts elsewhere in Wisconsin. He returned to Milwaukee in the early 1980s to head the High School Relations Division for MATC, with a personal commitment to "do something about the problems that I had seen back in the 1960s that I couldn't do anything about."[1] And so he developed a series of programs to deal with the school dropout problem, creating opportunities by drawing on available state and federal resources. For her part, Coffey's tenacity, coupled with her dedication and caring for those served in the dropout programs, makes her one of the strongest advocates for dropouts. In spite of limited resources and slow progress, both Pellegrin and Coffey have retained their optimism, along with a determination that should be the model for any constituents seeking help in Washington. Pellegrin has observed that, if needed, they "would march on Washington."[2]

As noted earlier, MATC's Project Hold had received one of the eighty-nine original demonstration dropout prevention project grants. This was the middle of the second and last year of funding of the project, and there was a concern as to whether the funding would be continued. And if it was continued, would existing projects be eligible for an extension of funding or subject to a new round of competition?[3] Given the academic year calendar, program participants felt a real sense of urgency. In academia hirings for fall programs are made in the spring; with funding uncertainty, program staff would begin to seek other job opportunities, and projects would begin to be pared back.

In order to effectively judge the merits of a legislative proposal, congressional staff make use of a number of resource tools, including the professional staff members of relevant subcommittees and committees with jurisdiction over the legislation (who may even be of the opposite party); transcripts of committee hearings and committee reports; personal staff of sponsoring members; online databases that can provide detailed searches of legislative histories; reports and materials from constituents, interest groups, and lobbyists; executive branch personnel—from the Office of Management and Budget to actual program administrators in departments and agencies; as well as a network of individuals with specialized knowledge whose names and phone numbers have accumulated in rolodexes throughout the Hill. That staff member must not only become convinced of the value of a program, but also will most likely have to sell the idea to a legislative director or chief of staff before it is presented to the senator or representative for consideration. In addition, in the era of Gramm-Rudman-Hollings and massive deficits, on the Senate side many offices have added a staff member with expertise in the complicated budgetary rules affecting most legislative proposals requiring funding. And so requests involving money (in effect, any substantive legislation) must also be subjected to the scrutiny of the designated "budget enforcer" or, put more positively, the designated "reality checker."

Committee Staff

The education committee staff members who would prove essential as the dropout story unfolded were Ann Young, David Evans, Amanda Broun, and Terry Hartle. Broun and Hartle both worked for Senator Edward M. Kennedy (D-Mass.), chair of the Senate Committee on Labor and Human Resources. Each committee in Congress has staff hired to do the work of the committee, with the majority staff working for the chair and the minority staff working under the direction of the ranking minority member. The professional staff serving on committees often bring longtime expertise to the substantive policy matters of the committee.[4]

Broun, chief education counsel on the committee in 1990, was formerly an attorney with the New York City Board of Education and legislative counsel in New York City's Office of Management and Budget.[5] Throughout her career Broun has shown an abiding concern for meeting the education needs of our nation's young people. Hartle, education staff director for the committee, formerly worked with the Educational Testing Service and was director of Social Policy Studies at the American Enterprise Institute (AEI), a conservative think tank.[6] Some on the Hill speculate that Hartle, co-author of *Excellence in Education: The States Take Charge,* published in 1986 by AEI, is a conservative counter to Senator Kennedy's liberal leanings.

The subcommittee of the Senate Labor and Human Resources Committee with jurisdiction over the dropout program was Senator Claiborne Pell's Subcommittee on Education, Arts and Humanities. The members of Pell's staff most involved in the school dropout issue were David Evans and Ann Young. Evans, staff director on the subcommittee, draws from a wide range of experience, with service on the subcommittee going back to 1981. This experience, coupled with his long-time interest in education policy, has earned him the respect of many educators. Ann Young, a professional staff member on the committee working with Evans on the majority side, has detailed knowledge of educational policies and programs from her years on the subcommittee, which would prove invaluable for the dropout coalition.

Committee staff benefit immeasurably from their interactions with the personal staff of other members of Congress. Specifically, the office staffs of the United States' 100 senators can provide insight into the breadth of programs throughout the fifty states. Under our federal system, each state has powers in certain areas; as a result, we have a governmental system that allows for flexibility and adaptation to the differing needs of citizens in each state. As admirable as this system is, its allowance for fifty different state governments, laws, and governmental structures does present complications when Congress is trying to write federal legislation that can accommodate the interests of all fifty. A program that may work in one state may not work in another.

The ties that the committee staff can build to members' staff can help facilitate the drafting of legislation that will be in accordance with congressional intent, yet still accommodate the needs of the various states. Without this interaction with the personal staff, legislation passed by Congress would result in unanticipated consequences. For instance, with a change in legislative language a program receiving federal money might lose eligibility because of the administrative structure of the state. Congress might subsequently have to pass legislation to correct this problem. I learned that constituents have needs, but they are also needed to provide detailed knowledge of the effects of federal programs. Lawmakers also have to know the possible impact of making slight changes in the wording authorizing a program that may cut out a particular state, city, or program from continued participation. This information can be beneficial to committee staff who are the ones who painstakingly craft the language of a bill. Committee staff may also act as entrepreneurs, seeking out " 'new ideas' for hearings, bills, or amendments" to sell to their bosses, as well as troubleshooters, working through problems and negotiating agreements to gain support for the committee's legislation.[7]

Coffey and Pellegrin were able to provide a careful, succinct explanation of the funding problem to Ann Young and David Evans. This would help efforts to keep the demonstration dropout program running, and, later in the year, to craft language for a vocational education program able to accommodate Wisconsin's educational administrative structure.

"Issue networks" have an important role in the policy process. Whether one is in the executive branch or Congress, or an outside interest, "the policy technocracy has established a common language for discussing the issues, a shared grammar for identifying the major points of contention, a mutually familiar rhetoric of argumentation."[8] Part of the reason why Senator Kohl and his staff were ultimately able to help is that Coffey and Pellegrin did a very effective job in explaining both the nature of the problem and the impact of federal action on the programs to Senator Kohl's staff as well as the committee staff. These constituents and the committee staff had a common language, shared with the program administrators in the Department of Education and others in the education community, which helped facilitate discussion. They all knew the program thoroughly, either through the role of practitioner and implementer, or as creator of the original legislation. They were familiar with the same studies, data, models, and other specialists in this policy area. But I had a lot to learn in a very short time if I was to be of any assistance.

Program Administrators in the Executive Branch

Once I had familiarized myself with some of the details of the dropout program, in January 1990 I made a call to John Fiegel in the Department of Education, who administered the dropout program. Knowing that Congress had set up this program as a demonstration project, I assumed the program must have had an evaluation component that would permit members of Congress to assess the effectiveness of the program in reducing the nation's dropout rates. Congress usually builds an evaluation component into the legislation that creates a demonstration program because one objective of demonstration projects is to provide field experiments to see which approaches work best.

Fiegel told me that each of the project sites had its own evaluation mechanisms and that the Department of Education had awarded a contract to the American Institutes for Research in August 1989 to conduct an outside evaluation of the program. However, forms for the evaluation would probably not be approved until the spring of 1990, with the result that the evaluation would not be available until January 1991. One reason for the delay is that Congress initially required that an evaluation be undertaken for the demonstration projects, but no funds were provided. In addition, OMB needed to review the evaluation forms before they could be sent out, which further delayed the evaluation process before it could get under way. (I was to learn later that a draft of the evaluation study was not ready until February 1992.[9]) For Congress, the evaluation component as to the "impact of the policies on society" is usually the weakest stage of the policy process. As Randall Ripley has noted, with few incentives for members of Congress, "congressional 'evaluation' tends to consist of judgments based on political considerations, anecdotes about the benefits conferred by programs or individuals . . ., and gut feelings and intuitions."[10]

Fiegel did note that several of the projects that had completed self-evaluations were having very good results and that site visits by the Department of Education indicated the program was working. He indicated that all funding would come to an end by September 1990 unless new appropriations were made. But first the reauthorization was needed. And, yes, it did make sense to reauthorize the program as a demonstration program, until the evaluations were completed. A decision could then be made as to any further federal involvement, based on the results of the evaluation which would indicate which approaches were working both in increasing graduation rates and reducing dropout rates.

Based on this information, as well as specific data on the success of the projects in Wisconsin which had been forwarded by constituents, I concluded that it made sense for the senator to go to bat for this program. (In addition to the Milwaukee Area Technical College, the Milwaukee Public Schools and the Lac du Flambeau Band of Lake Superior Chippewa Indians also had demonstration dropout programs.) At that time I did not realize the authorization would still prove problematic and that Senator Kohl, in seeking program funds, would eventually take on a role usually reserved for committee chairs.

In order to get a better sense of the issues at hand, I took advantage of one of the online databases many members of the House and Senate can subscribe to, Legi-Slate, and quickly ran a legislative history of the dropout legislation to determine its status. Legi-Slate can quickly produce a detailed legislative history of a bill—that is, when it was introduced, by whom, co-sponsors, committee status, passage in the House or Senate, and when it was signed into law.

REAUTHORIZATION ATTEMPTS

I soon discovered that the original two-year authorization would come to an end in September 1990. I also learned the status of the reauthorization. That is, the House had reauthorized the program for one more year, as had the Senate, but the Senate had tacked its reauthorization to the Taft Institute reauthorization. In addition, language to reauthorize the dropout program had been included in the president's massive education bill, introduced by Senator Nancy Kassebaum (R-Kans.).

The matter seemed simple to me. I could reassure Coffey that the program appeared to have ample support, which would therefore easily assure its reauthorization. It had passed the House and the Senate and was included in the president's education package, so why wouldn't it pass? As the weeks went by, I became acutely aware that this relatively simple and straightforward program had already suffered a long and complicated birthing process, and that the reauthorization would be just as complicated.

The reauthorization of the dropout demonstration program was not among the Hill's top priorities, but it was at the top of *my* agenda. After a number of phone calls, I learned that the "simple" reauthorization would not be so simple.

Senator Kohl and his staff were serving a role of intermediary in the authorization process. They kept constituents informed as to when the authorization would come to the floor for a vote by relaying information from the Senate Subcommittee on Education, Arts and Humanities to constituents affected by the program. When it came time to do battle for appropriations, however, Senator Kohl and his staff emerged as key players. In fact, during January and February 1990, at the same time the reauthorization process was proceeding in the Senate, guided by Senators Pell and Kennedy and the education committee staff, Senator Kohl's staff was laying the groundwork for the leading role the senator would take in March after the authorization had been passed.

Since the Senate had passed the dropout reauthorization attached to the Taft Institute, I called an education committee staff member on the House side to find out when the Taft reauthorization would be passed. It was a popular program in both the House and Senate, and would facilitate passage of the dropout program. I heard a brief chuckle on the other end of the line, and then the reply, the gist of which was: The House has already passed the dropout reauthorization as a stand-alone bill and would not link the dropout bill, or for that matter any other bill, to the Taft Institute reauthorization. Hadn't the Senate learned its lesson about passing a clean Taft Institute bill—that is, with no extraneous amendments? No, the House would not help the Senate by passing the dropout measure a second time (i.e., this time attached to the Taft Institute bill). If the Senate wanted the dropout program reauthorized, it would have to pass it in the same form as the House—as a stand-alone bill.

Again, that did not seem to present too large an obstacle to this neophyte staff member. It had already passed the Senate in November, and the nation's leaders had strongly voiced their support of efforts to increase the high school graduation rate. In fact, the president had just called for an increase in the high school graduation rate to no less than 90 percent in his annual State of the Union Message delivered to Congress on January 31, 1990. In addition, the president's FY91 budget included $45 million for a school dropout program in FY91. Surely this popular program would have strong bipartisan support.

I soon discovered the political problems.

The President's Education Agenda

During the 1988 presidential election contest, candidate George Bush had pledged to be "the education president." In April 1989 President Bush "sent Congress a proposed 'Educational Excellence Act' . . . , asking law makers to authorize $423 million for cash awards to excellent schools and teachers, math and science scholarships, and alternative methods for certifying teachers."[11] By the time this bill was reported out of committee in the summer of 1989, several provisions were added, including the reauthorization of the school dropout demonstration assistance program.[12]

On February 7, 1990, the bill was passed by the Senate.[13]

The Republicans backed the president's *entire* education package—S. 695—and saw no necessity to vote on a separate authorization for the dropout program. Even so, both Democratic and Republican leaders tried to bring the stand-alone bill (H.R. 2281) to the floor, but they were unable to do so because a "hold" had been placed on the bill.

In this case, Jesse Helms was the prime suspect in requesting the hold. In earlier years, concern had been raised in Congress over the type of "counseling" to be given students participating in the federally funded dropout programs, especially in the case of pregnant teens. As noted in Chapter 3, the dropout program legislation had been derailed once before when it had become linked to the abortion debate. Some legislators had been concerned about whether counselors might encourage pregnant teens to get an abortion simply to get them to stay in school. Helms was also suspect because of his fundamental philosophical objection to the federal government's role in education policy; in his view, education was an issue for state and local governments. In this case, however, no senator ever came forward to publicly announce his or her objection to consideration of this legislation, and so the identity of the senator remained unknown.

The logjam on the dropout measure was finally broken when a series of education issues were brought to the floor of the Senate on February 6,

1990. Among these issues was a measure near and dear to First Lady Barbara Bush, a literacy bill designed to "launch a comprehensive and coordinated campaign to erase adult illiteracy,"[14] as well as the president's education package, which passed on February 7, 1990. Perhaps prodding from the White House to get the literacy bill out helped release the logjam blocking the education bills. Just as the party responsible for requesting the hold remained unknown, so the reason for the release of the hold remained a mystery. Regardless of the reason, the hold was soon off the dropout bill, and it was brought to the floor of the Senate on February 20, 1990, under a unanimous consent agreement. After one hour of debate, it was approved unanimously, 94–0. At long last, the dropout reauthorization language had been passed in identical form in both the House and Senate as a separate bill, not linked with any other legislation.

Senator Kohl joined a number of other senators, including Senators Pell, Kassebaum, and Kennedy, in speaking in favor of the bill. As is often the case in floor speeches, given the Senate norms of courtesy, Senator Kohl thanked his colleague Senator Pell for bringing the bill to the floor for consideration and then focused attention on the relationship between this legislation and his constituents back in Wisconsin. Kohl described Project Hold, a "nationally acclaimed program at the Milwaukee Area Technical College [MATC], working with young people, to help reduce the dropout rate in the Milwaukee area."[15] This program had received funding since August 1988 under the original dropout demonstration assistance program. Kohl cited the success of the program: "60 students have received high school diplomas, and 16 have received their GED. Over 50 percent of these students have gone on for advanced training in a postsecondary institution."[16]

Kohl then described how the MATC program works at the middle school level to keep kids in school, at the high school level to "put [dropouts] . . . back into a situation where they can learn and succeed," and with adults to the age of 25 in programs designed to provide basic skills and eventually a high school degree.[17]

After leaving the chamber, Senator Kohl ran into Mike Casserly and Jeff Simering, an encounter that was to prove fortuitous in the life of the dropout program. At the time Casserly was associate director for legislation and research at the Council of the Great City Schools, and Simering was a lobbyist representing the Chicago public schools. Both had supported the dropout program legislation from its earliest days back in 1985. They thanked Senator Kohl for his support, and the senator in turn observed how effective the program was and that it made sense to continue.

Because of time constraints and personal reticence, many members, including Senator Kohl, will insert a speech into the *Congressional Record* rather than deliver it in person. (A "bullet" symbol located before a passage in the *Congressional Record* indicates a speech or insertion not spoken by the senator on the floor.) Casserly and Simering noted that the junior senator from Wisconsin, who was not on the education subcommittee or even on the Senate Committee on Labor and Human Resources, had indicated his strong support of this legislation through a floor speech delivered in person to his colleagues. They tucked this piece of information into their minds, not realizing at the time how important a role Senator Kohl would play in the survival of this program.

With the bill now having passed in the House and Senate in identical form, it was sent to the president who signed it on March 6, 1990.

FUNDING?!

The phone calls from Maureen Coffey kept coming to my desk. "What about the funding?" In the euphoria of the moment at seeing the dropout program finally reauthorized by the House and Senate and signed into law by the president, I seemed to have forgotten the other half of the equation—the appropriations needed to fund the program.

Coffey gave me a refresher course on Congress and patiently explained that, while it was fine that the program had been reauthorized without objection in both the House and Senate, it meant nothing if appropriations were not forthcoming. I recalled the lectures I had given students in my Congress course where I had explained that for some legislative proposals members of Congress may jump on the bandwagon and unanimously authorize a program, knowing full well it won't get appropriations. In this way they can claim credit with constituents for helping pass the legislation, while blaming others—the members of the Appropriations Committee, the "guardians of the Treasury"—for a program's demise.

Would this be the fate of the dropout program? Though popular, successful, and politically timely, would it be allowed to die for lack of appropriations? I naively thought this was not possible. I still assumed that if a program was good and had member support, the legislative system would keep it going. Only many months later, on the day funding was finally approved, did I realize that perhaps my naivete had contributed to its successful journey through a maze of obstacles: I had a blind faith that Congress would come through, and I continued to work toward that end. By then I would also discover that that same conviction produces many little triumphs on the Hill.

I checked with the Democratic staff on the Senate Appropriations

Subcommittee on Labor-Health and Human Services-Education, and the Senate Committee on Labor and Human Resources and its education subcommittee to find out if funding for the program was likely. Then I would make a recommendation to Senator Kohl's staff and, eventually, the senator himself.

Conversations with the committee staffs helped clarify the problems. The budget cycle and the appropriations process within that cycle, I was told, would present nearly insurmountable odds against funding for this program.

AUTHORIZATIONS, APPROPRIATIONS, AND BUDGETS

While an authorization creates a program or may continue a program either indefinitely or for a set period of time, only an appropriations bill will give Congress "legal authority to spend or obligate money from the Treasury. The Constitution disallows money to be drawn from the Treasury 'but in consequence of Appropriations made by law.' "[18] At times this two-stage process blurs when authorizing language extending a program or even creating a program may be added to an appropriations bill. Many members of Congress frown on this practice because it enhances the power of party leaders and those committee leaders who fashion the continuing resolution package at the expense of the authorizing committee.[19] The power of the individual members, especially the chairs of the Appropriations Committee and its subcommittees, is often enhanced, increasing the overall power and prestige of the appropriations committees in both houses.

The dropout program had been originally authorized through an appropriations bill—that is, a Continuing Resolution. However, in order to gain support for the program in subsequent years, a separate authorization was also obtained in the trade bill for fiscal year 1988 and in the education bill for fiscal year 1989. This would help "legitimize" the program in the eyes of the other members of Congress.

Beginning in the mid-1970s, a new layer was added to this process. Congress began to be concerned with an overall budget that would coherently address the issues of revenues coming into the federal Treasury (primarily through taxes and user fees), with expenditures made from the U.S. Treasury. Now the standing committees, which work on authorizing language for programs, as well as the Appropriations Committees, would have to consider how program needs fit into a broader budget. The budget committees would make recommendations to the House and Senate for spending targets for different program areas (e.g., defense, education), as well as for revenues needed to pay for those programs. (Another set of committees is responsible for raising revenue: the powerful House Ways and Means Committee and Senate Finance Committee.)

The "Era of the Budget"

During the 1980s the budget deficit grew to $200 billion and became a source of growing consternation among both policy leaders in Washington and observers outside the beltway.[20] The deficit "tripled the national debt . . . in the 1980's."[21] In addition, a growing portion of the federal budget pays for entitlements, which "now account for about half of federal spending. With interest charges added in, mandatory costs constitute almost two-thirds of total spending. These expenditures rise automatically each year, regardless of the condition of the budget or the needs of other government programs," making reduction in the deficit a difficult political issue.[22]

In 1985, with the deficit over $200 billion, Congress responded with the Balanced Budget and Emergency Deficit Control Act of 1985 (Gramm-Rudman-Hollings).[23] This act did not seek to create a new structural mechanism to enhance congressional power and control over the budget as was the case with reforms in 1974 (which created House and Senate budget committees, as well as a timetable and series of procedures for congressional consideration of the budget). Rather, it was designed to limit congressional decisions over the budget if targets set to reduce the deficit each year could not be met. A sequestration process was put in place, which would allow automatic across-the-board cuts in the budget if the deficit reduction targets were not met.[24]

Even after the Gramm-Rudman-Hollings reforms were launched, however, the deficit continued to rise. White and Wildavsky clearly explain the problems facing Congress in resolving the deficit in this "era of the budget":

> Budgeting involves meeting obligations, keeping promises. It involves choices about values, about which purposes are of highest priority. It involves questions of power: How are we to be governed, and by whom? Most of all, tax and spending decisions involve real people with real pain and real benefits. What happens to any of us—the fate of farmers, the poor, or General Dynamics—may have meaning to others. In the rhetoric of deficit reduction, these other matters are either disparaged as "special interests" or, worse, ignored. Persistent deficits are blamed on a lack of courage or good will. Wrong. Deficits persist because all choices are bad. Choices are hard because important values are helped or hurt by all alternatives.[25]

Some observers maintain that divided party government has exacerbated the problems faced by political leaders in Washington. Divided government was the case for twelve consecutive years until 1993, with the Republicans in control of the White House and the Democrats in control of at least the House of Representatives. "President Ronald Reagan said cut taxes and spend more on the military. Democrats argued that the outcome of such a policy would be cuts in social security and other benefits. Each side won its round. What was left was a political system that could neither raise taxes nor cut programs."[26]

The themes dominating much of the debate over the budget in the late 1980s and 1990s show that the needs of competing interests were answered through compromise and accommodation. The tension between a decentralized, fragmented budget process and a need for centralized control remains a problem in the 1990s. In the summer of 1990, the Democratic leadership of the House and Senate worked out an agreement with the Republican White House, the Budget Enforcement Act of 1990, which reflected the compromise struck between Congress and the president. Briefly, this act continued Gramm-Rudman-Hollings, but it made the probability of sequestration unlikely until 1994. Limits were put on discretionary spending (nonentitlement programs) by category—defense, foreign aid, and domestic. If the spending limit is breached within any of these categories, then across-the-board cuts within that program area are put in place. (There are exceptions for emergencies and unforseen costs— e.g., inflation; if the president declares an emergency; or if the Savings and Loan bailout costs increase.) Under this agreement deficit reduction is not the goal; rather, limits have been placed on spending. "The proposal recognize[d] that Congress has little power over the economy and that economists' forecasts do not have the accuracy to predict what a likely deficit will be 18 months or more in the future."[27]

The introduction of a comprehensive budgetary mechanism in the 1970s for Congress and the adoption of new procedures to confront the growing deficit have added some complexity in the ability of Congress both to create and to expand programs. At the same time the public continues to expect the federal government, especially Congress and the president, to solve the nation's problems.

While it is difficult and challenging, it is not impossible for programs to receive funding even in an era of fiscal austerity. As this case study will demonstrate, the president's annual budget message to Congress, the congressional budget resolution, and the Appropriations Committee all played important roles both in the regular appropriations cycle and the supplemental appropriations bill. They were all part of the legislative odyssey to continue funding for one small domestic program that consumed only $20 million out of a total budget of over $1 trillion.[28]

Budget Cycle

An extension of the dropout program for FY90 and FY91 was authorized by the Senate at the end of February 1990 and signed into law by the president in early March. The 1991 fiscal year would begin on October 1, 1990. However, most programs in the Department of Education are forward funded, in part to accommodate the needs of an academic calendar which begins in August or September. Therefore, if funds are appropriated for FY91, schools will use them in the 1991–92 academic calendar year. Even if the appropriations were obtained for FY91 through the regular appropriations cycle, the funds would not be available until October 1, 1990. With the FY91 appropriations just beginning their way through committee and not likely to be approved by the full House and Senate until the fall of 1990, it would be too late for new programs to be up and running and serving students in an academic year that had already begun. It would also be too late for existing programs to benefit from a one-year extension. In order to retain staff, the dropout program would need to know in the spring of 1990 if it was to continue in the fall. Teachers and counselors funded through the dropout program would have to know if their position would continue or if they would have to seek a new position in the spring when most vacancies are announced and filled. Otherwise, the program would have to scale back operations or close owing to the uncertain status of federal funds.

The President's Budget

The president's budget with specific programs and funding levels detailed (now submitted to Congress on the first Monday in February) is several years in the making.[29] As a result, it is difficult to respond immediately to world changes. Although the president and governors had agreed in 1989 and early 1990 to reduce the school dropout rate, it would take at least a year for this goal to show up in the annual budget request the president sent to Congress.

This timetable would be reflected in the action taken by the appropriations committees since the committees use the president's budget as a guideline for spending decisions.[30] But the national interest in "dropouts" came too late to be included in the president's FY90 budget. This budget, which came to the Hill in early 1989, had requested no funds to continue the dropout projects. By the spring of 1990, the administration had already released its FY91 budget. As a result, in spite of the rhetoric on school dropouts, the administration would not make any recommendation to Congress to amend or supplement its FY90 budget since the FY90 budget decision had already been made in the previous year. The administration's budget process was forward looking and could not go back and reassess previous budgets. Whereas in subsequent years the president's budget would include requests for funding of the dropout program, the standard procedure whereby the president made a request and the appropriations committees responded would not work if the programs were to continue in the fall of 1990. Whether there were to be appropriations in FY90 was up to Congress.

Appropriations in an Era of Fiscal Austerity

Under Gramm-Rudman-Hollings, spending restrictions are set by policy areas, with each subcommittee of appropriations working under a spending cap imposed by the full Appropriations Committee. In order to add spending to the FY90 budget, funds would have to be tranferred from one program to another within the same policy area(s). It would not be easy, for example, to transfer money from Defense spending to a domestic spending program without being subject to a point of order. Before long, I would become acquainted with other aspects of the congressional budgetary process—for example, "unobligated balances," "outlays," and "spend out rates"—that would prove to be vital pieces of information in the quest for funds.

In learning about the problems encountered in securing funding for the dropout program for the 1990–91 academic year, I became acutely sensitized to the tradeoffs facing both members and their staffs in their day-to-day decision making. The fiscal realities of the 1990s were so grave that there was little, if any, flexibility in a budget that was already in place.[31]

Supplemental Appropriations

To add appropriations for this program for FY90 would require the use of a supplemental appropriation. In addition to the thirteen annual appropriations bills, Congress usually passes one or more "supplemental" appropriations bills once the fiscal year has begun—either to respond to an emergency or to make up for a planned or unanticipated shortfall in the regular bills. These bills have been referred to as "midcourse corrections."

Typically, they will include emergency funding for relief to victims of natural disasters. These appropriations bills are still subject to the guidelines set by the budget committees. And, in the post–Gramm-Rudman-Hollings era, they are more difficult to fashion and pass due to the required offsets.

While it is difficult to add spending once the fiscal year is under way, especially given the restraints imposed on the budgetary process by Gramm-Rudman-Hollings, one of the few options available was to have the funding added as a "dire emergency" to the supplemental appropriations bill likely to be considered by the House and the Senate sometime in the spring focusing on aid to the " 'emerging' democracies in Eastern Europe, Panama, and Nicaragua."[32]

In the spring of 1990, the Appropriations Committee was asked to add funding in a number of areas. The staff of the Subcommittee on Labor-Health and Human Services-Education could do little for a junior senator from Wisconsin who was not on the Appropriations Committee or on the Committee on Labor and Human Resources, given the competing demands of more senior members and the spending caps on domestic programs. In fact, their response seemed typical: they called on the budget resolution and funding allocations to say their hands were tied and that they could be of no help, even if the project appeared worthwhile. While the budget resolutions do put limits on the Appropriations Committee, it is clear that the Appropriations Committee is also making choices. One staff member on Appropriations explains:

> subcommittee clerks and members added the Budget Act to the armament of reasons for stiffing a request that they don't want to fund. One of the clerks explained how this works: "the budget resolution has given the subcommittee and the full committee a tool to resist increases over and above what the committee would otherwise recommend. We've used it this year saying, "Gee whiz, we'd like to put that in but we've got the budget ceiling and it would take us over." It has given the committee a crutch to resist what they might want to resist anyway.[33]

Thus, support would have to come from elsewhere.

Senators Kennedy and Pell, though strong supporters of the school dropout program, had to seek funds for other programs as well. Any request for funds from Appropriations would have to be limited. Neither senator could add the dropout legislation to his list, even though the price tag, about $20 million, was relatively small.

On the House side, the delay in reauthorization by the Senate (from June 1989, when the bill passed the House, to late February 1990, when the bill passed the Senate) had prevented a request for appropriations for

FY90 in the normal appropriations cycle. In addition, the House and Senate seemed to have different philosophies on the use of the "dire emergency" supplemental appropriations mechanism. Whereas senators tended to view this mechanism as an *opportunity* for a midyear course correction to accommodate shifting needs, the House regarded the supplemental bill as a means to deal with true "dire emergencies."

I soon came to realize that no matter how appealing it might seem, we would not be able simply to take the money from a B-2 bomber and move it over to fund the education program. Instead, it would take a more creative approach, one that was in accordance with the new budget rules and that would require resources beyond just the staff of one senator.[34] To produce this small legislative triumph, which ensured continuation of a small but successful program, would require the combined efforts of

Senator Kohl's staff

The staffs of the Senate Committee on Labor and Human Resources and its Subcommittee on Education, Arts and Humanities

The House Committee on Education and Labor and its Subcommittee on Elementary, Secondary, and Vocational Education

Both the Democratic and Republican staff on the Appropriations Committees and Subcommittees on Labor-Health and Human Services-Education

Interest groups

Constituents

Program directors

Members of Congress

CHAPTER 7

The Forces Come Together

The 100 senators and 435 representatives who make up the Congress obviously have different agendas; therefore, forming the majority needed for passage of legislation in either House can prove challenging. Coalition building in Congress may be facilitated, however, as members help each other out. Certain issues can become legislatively linked together, even if they involve different substantive policy areas. For instance, several bills can be added together into one package, creating an omnibus bill. The parts of such a bill might have a better chance of passing if the supporters of each separate bill are united in a coalition that will then favor passage of the entire package. Such a coalition may also be strong enough to override a presidential veto. In addition, the informal rules of Congress—the norms and folkways, such as reciprocity whereby "I'll scratch your back if you scratch mine"—can also work to link bills and issues that appear to be totally unrelated. In an institution where alliances shift from day to day, if not hour to hour, given the issue at hand and the constant vigil as to the potential impact on constituents, the work of Congress demands that a set of informal rules also guide the members' behavior and actions.

THE INFORMAL RULES

Over thirty years ago, political scientist Donald R. Matthews identified six norms and folkways of the Senate: apprenticeship, legislative work, specialization, courtesy, institutional patriotism, and reciprocity.[1] Although some of these informal rules are less applicable to the Senate of the 1990s, they are still important in understanding how things are done, especially for those who have been long-time members of the chamber. As Matthews writes, "new members are expected to serve a proper apprenticeship."[2] They should "show respect for their elders . . . and . . . seek their advice."[3] They also must do their legislative work, and each member is to "specialize, to focus his energy and attention on the relatively few matters that come before his committees or that directly and immediately affect his state."[4]

Members mute conflicts by extending courtesy to one another: "A cardinal rule of Senate behavior is that political disagreements should not influence personal feelings."[5] In addition, "Senators are expected to believe that they belong to the greatest legislative and deliberative body in the world. They are expected to be a bit suspicious of the President and the bureaucrats and just a little disdainful of the House. They are expected to revere the Senate's personnel, organization, and folkways and to champion them to the outside world."[6] Matthews notes that this attitude is no more "an emotional investment from their members" than is the case with members of other institutions, including large corporations or law firms.

The final norm, and the one most important for this discussion, is that of reciprocity. "Every senator, at one time or another, is in a position to help out a colleague. The folkways of the Senate hold that a senator should provide this assistance and that he be repaid in kind."[7] In an institution that is by design destined to produce disorder and chaos, with few of the formal rules and procedures that are used in the House, these norms and folkways help to bring some order to the Senate and allow its work to be done.

For example, reciprocity goes beyond the mere trading of votes. Rather, it defines the working relationship among members and provides a means by which the work of the Senate can be accomplished.

> . . . this implicit bargaining . . . explains much of the behavior of senators. Each of them has vast power under the chamber's rules. A single senator, for example, can slow the Senate almost to a halt by systematically objecting to all unanimous consent requests. A few, by exercising their right to filibuster, can block the passage of all bills. Or a single senator could sneak almost any piece of legislation through the chamber by acting when floor attendance is sparse and by taking advantage of the looseness of the chamber rules. While these and other similar powers always exist as a potential threat, the amazing thing is that they are rarely utilized. The spirit of reciprocity results in much, if not most, of the senators' actual power not being exercised. If a senator *does* push his formal powers to the limit, he has broken the implicit bargain and can expect, not cooperation from his colleagues, but only retaliation in kind.[8]

As a result, members and their staff always look beyond the narrow scope of any one bill to see what the broader picture looks like. For example, they anticipate what legislation is coming up for a vote, what coalitions are forming, whether there is legislation they should be aware of that can help their constituents, or whether they are in a position to help a colleague get their bill passed. For any bill coming to the floor for debate and a vote, each member of the House and Senate must be aware of the implications of a vote, in terms not only of its impact on constituents, or good policy, but also of how colleagues in the chamber view that vote.

Throughout the second session of the One Hundred and First Congress, several matters commanded the attention of members and staff, including the Clean Air bill. This landmark piece of legislation came after a ten-year legislative impasse, and wrote into law tough new federal standards "on urban smog, automobile exhaust, toxic air pollution and acid rain."[9] Many disparate policy matters coming before Congress can be linked, and debate over the Clear Air bill began to affect strategic planning for the dropout legislation.

THE CLEAN AIR BILL

Passage of the Clean Air bill would be one of the major legislative accomplishments of the One Hundred and First Congress. This bill was of particular importance to Majority Leader George Mitchell (D-Me.). Mitchell, a proponent of tough environmental laws, had begun his career on the Hill as a legislative assistant to Senator Edmund Muskie (D-Me.), who had made his mark in the area of environmental policy.[10] This bill was also important to former Majority Leader Robert Byrd, who as leader had blocked any clean air legislation that would add environmental regulations detrimental to his West Virginia coal miner constituency.

In observing the movement of the Clear Air bill through the Senate, I realized that one amendment offered by Senator Byrd, the chair of the Appropriations Committee and President Pro Tem of the Senate, was of particular importance to Byrd. Elected to the Senate in 1958, Senator Byrd became President Pro Tempore of the Senate by virtue of having served in the Senate longer than any other member of the majority party. This seniority gave him the opportunity to chair the Appropriations Committee in 1989. He stepped down from the post of majority leader in order to take on that powerful position, pledging to help the people of West Virginia by ensuring that they received a fair share of federal pork.[11] For Byrd, the citizens of West Virginia came before the interests of the nation, since it was the people of West Virginia who elected him. This kind of "pork barrel politics" has wreaked havoc on the ability of Congress to come to terms with the budget deficit and make national policy. A clear example in the post–Cold War era is that many members favor cuts in defense spending, until it leads to the closing of bases in their districts or the scaling back of a defense industry in their state, with resulting job loss.

Byrd, a master of parliamentary procedure and the rules of the Senate, remains one of the most respected members of that body in spite of any objections his "West Virginia first" policy might provoke. He has earned that respect by virtue of hard work. His move up the leadership ladder to the position of majority leader was the result of this hard work and attention to the needs of individual members. "He was never too busy to attend to the petty details that can make the lives of Senators easier: keeping them informed of the pace of floor debate and the scheduling of upcoming votes, helping them to get amendments before the Senate, arranging paired votes, and even getting taxis. . . . understanding the political situations of each Senator, their strengths and weaknesses, and . . . mastering the details of substantive legislation and parliamentary procedure."[12] As one former aide has said, Byrd " 'has a special way of making people feel endeared, sympathetic, respecting of his integrity, indebted to him.' "[13]

Senator Wyche Fowler (D-Ga.) has observed: " 'He puts the institution and its traditions above any personal agenda. . . . He has used his power on behalf of protecting the Senate as a constitutional institution rather than using it to further the politics or policies of Robert Byrd.' "[14] But his pledge to the people of West Virginia was not an empty pledge.

One section of the Clear Air bill was aimed at reducing the acid rain produced in burning high-sulfur coal. The provisions in this section would make it both more difficult and costly for utility companies to use high-sulfur coal, which was mined primarily in West Virginia, other Appalachian states, and several states in the Midwest. As a result of these new restrictions which would force utilities to switch to other fuels, it was estimated that 3,000 to 5,000 coal miners would lose their jobs. The Byrd amendment would "provide financial support and job-training benefits" for these workers.[15] Their benefits would be far more generous than those earmarked for other displaced workers who were losing their jobs as a result of other provisions in the Clean Air bill.[16] The cost of the proposal was initially expected to run to $1.4 billion. Over a period of weeks, the size and scope of the benefit package was reduced to $500 million, but this would still be too costly for the Bush White House. For Senator Mitchell, Byrd's successor as the majority leader, the environment was just as passionate a cause, and he wanted to see a Clean Air bill passed. According to Byrd, " 'Senator Mitchell is fighting for what he believes in. . . . And I'm fighting for what I believe in.' "[17]

The importance of this provision in the bill to Senator Byrd became clear to me when he paid a personal visit to Senator Kohl. The sight of the highly respected and most senior Democrat calling on one of the two most junior senators made a lasting impression in my mind.[18]

Byrd was investing a level of personal energy and involvement that is rarely seen in the Senate. "Byrd, a man with 32 years' worth of IOU's in one vest pocket and countless future chits to hand out in the other, had gone door to door" in the weeks leading up to the vote "to meet with Republicans and Democrats alike and had penned and typed them many notes."[19]

On March 29, 1990, when the vote on Byrd's amendment was taken, it was defeated by the narrowest of margins, 50–49. The only senator not voting, Senator Bennett Johnston (D-La.) who was delayed in returning from a funeral by the weather,[20] announced he would have voted with Byrd.

Byrd lost several votes he had been counting on, apparently including Senator Joseph Biden (D-Del.). Biden withheld his vote until the end of the roll call and left the floor during the vote with Assistant Minority Leader Alan Simpson (R-Wyo.) to take a call from John Sununu, chief of staff for President Bush.[21] Feeling a need to explain his vote immediately following this defeat for Byrd, Biden took to the floor of the Senate and stated that Sununu had "guaranteed me the President was going to veto the bill"[22] if the amendment passed. Biden went on to explain, "I had indicated to Senator Byrd that my sympathies were with his position—I like him, would like to help the coal miners—and if this were not a deal buster, if this would not kill this bill, I would vote with him. But if it would, I would not."[23]

Senator Kohl voted with Senator Byrd.

In the midst of the passionate discussion on the Hill in the aftermath of the vote, I considered the ramifications of Senator Kohl's vote for the dropout bill. Perhaps reciprocity could come into play, and Byrd's support could be marshalled in the battle for funding the dropout program.

The next day I went through the Department of Education's list of program grantees and organized them into several categories:

Projects in states with senators who voted with Byrd

Projects in states with senators who voted against Byrd

A breakdown of the above lists by party and membership on the Appropriations Committee

The lists were organized with two questions in mind: (1) to what extent would there be potential support on the Appropriations Committee coming from those members who had projects in their states? (2) With reciprocity in mind, had a sizable number of senators with projects in their states voted with Senator Byrd on the crucial coal miner vote?

Looking at the composition of the lists, I thought it might be possible to get the senators on the Appropriations Committee to add funding for this program if it was perceived as an issue of some importance to the senators who had projects in their states. A review of the lists also showed that thirty-two of the sixty-one senators with projects in their states had voted with Senator Byrd. A thirty-third senator, Bennett Johnston, who was not present for the vote, indicated he would have voted with Byrd. Thus, among this group of senators there was a greater percentage of support for Byrd than he had received overall from the Senate on his amendment.

At this point, it appeared that a supplemental appropriations bill—a "midcourse correction"—might be passed to allow for additional funding for programs that had not successfully received funding in the regular appropriations cycle. But many of these projects would be subjected to intense scrutiny to determine whether they could meet the test of a "dire emergency." This would be especially true of those requests for funding coming from senators who were not on the Appropriations Committee, since members of this committee were concerned about the interests of their own constituents.

Earlier in the session the parameters of a supplemental bill had been uncertain. For example, would it only allow funding for foreign aid programs? Now it appeared that the bill would be open to domestic, foreign, and defense requests alike. But the task remained rather daunting. How, and by whom, would the funding be added to the massive supplemental appropriations bill being considered in the Appropriations Committee?

THE FORCES IN MOTION:
BEYOND THE BELTWAY AND INSIDE THE BELTWAY

A key to including the dropout program in the supplemental appropriations bill was to find a member on the Appropriations Committee who would usher it through. This task would prove difficult given the competing requests for funds made of members.

When we look at Congress and the policy process, most of the focus seems to be on activities in Washington, D.C. However, forces at work beyond the Beltway often trigger, if not parallel, activity on the Hill. In fact, a strategy to keep the program funded had developed in a setting far from Washington, back in 1989 before the reauthorization was ever approved. In time, the forces on the Hill, elsewhere in Washington, and beyond the Beltway, all working to keep the dropout program running, would be joined in a common effort.

Beyond the Beltway

A number of the dropout demonstration project directors belonged to the National Dropout Prevention Network (NDPN). Initially, this network of teachers, educational administrators, government officials, and interest group representatives met informally. It soon grew to an organization of over 3000 members committed to improving educational opportunities for some of the most hard-pressed segments of society, focusing on at-risk youth and dropouts. The NDPN's first annual conference was held in the spring of 1989 in San Diego, with over 1500 participants sharing information on effective strategies in dropout prevention.[24]

At that meeting, John Fiegel, the Department of Education coordinator for the demonstration dropout program, spoke to the project directors. The strategy of this group was stimulated by a warning from Fiegel, who noted that this was the second and last year of funding for the program. The program had not yet been reauthorized and had no further appropriations. He emphasized that the Department of Education could do nothing on its own and that no one in Congress would be able to help them at this point.

Maureen Coffey went up to Fiegel and promised that she would not permit the program to die, a sentiment shared by many other conference participants. Fiegel, while unable to do anything officially, was instrumental in encouraging the program's advocates to continue their lobbying activities. By telling the conference participants that "You people have to make it happen—I can't do it," he was, in his own way, giving encouragement to try.[25] (A year later, in January 1990, Fiegel would also give me enough information about the projects and the work being done on them to persuade me that this program was worth fighting for.)

A career civil servant, Fiegel would prove to be one of the most important voices in the Department of Education supporting the effort to keep the program going. As Mike Casserly has noted, "He's always been very, very helpful and supportive and kind of our secret agent. He always loved all this stuff we did, and helped it along."[26] Based on conversations with people who know Fiegel, he genuinely cares about the program he administers, as well as the education needs of young people. He also wants the educational system in the United States to work, even if it requires change in long-standing practices.

The conference activated the dropout network and helped generate an intensive grass-roots lobbying effort. Throughout the remaining months of 1989 and in 1990, this grass-roots network pushed for reauthorization of the dropout program. Once the Senate finally approved the reauthorization in February 1990, the network's attention shifted to the push for funding. Maureen Coffey was not only calling Senator Kohl's office for assistance in securing continued funding for the program, but was also in touch with others in the network who were sending letters and calling their senators and representatives. In Iowa, the project directors in the Des Moines public schools approached the staff of Senator Tom Harkin (D-Iowa), and in Oregon, the project directors at the West Valley Academy approached the staff in Senator Hatfield's (R-Ore.) office.

The members of the Appropriations Committee became critical targets. From a strategic standpoint, Senators Hatfield and Harkin were central individuals, for both were on the Senate Appropriations Committee. Senator Hatfield was the ranking member (the most senior Republican) on the committee, whereas Senator Harkin was the chair of the Subcommittee on Labor-Health and Human Services-Education.

Since both Oregon and Iowa had dropout projects, it was assumed that these two senators would support continued funding of the projects. Surprisingly, that support failed to materialize. The Des Moines public schools actually became discouraged by the apparent lack of support from Senator Harkin's office, which was attributed to a top staff assistant's lack of enthusiasm for the program.[27]

Senator Bob Kasten (R-Wis.), who was also a member of the Appropriations Committee and could have helped, refused to give any support until weeks later when it was certain the amendment would pass. Thus, it appeared that no member of the Appropriations Committee would request the funding from fellow members on the committee.

While Coffey was calling Senators Kohl and Kasten, projects in Tennessee, Delaware, and Texas generated a great deal of activity to get constituents to contact their respective senators.[28] In addition, another set of forces had been set in motion—interest groups and their lobbyists.

Inside the Beltway: Interest Groups

The two chief lobbyists for continued funding were Michael Casserly, of the Council of the Great City Schools, and Jeff Simering, representing the Chicago public schools. Casserly is highly respected within the education community. His encyclopedic memory has proved invaluable in providing information on programs, participants in the policy process, and the legislative histories of the major education bills passed in the last decade. It has also served his organization well in planning strategies to gain support for programs, for it is important to know where your allies may lie, where support has been obtained in the past, and where favors may be owed.

Jeff Simering, a government relations consultant with several clients, including the Chicago public schools, has had a long-time interest in education policy and wrote a book in the 1970s, *The Federal Funding Guide for Education,* to assist the education community in its search for federal support. Simering is also a respected member of the education community, and because of his work on most of the major education bills in the last ten years he has accumulated detailed knowledge of the policies, programs, and participants in this area. Simering and Casserly became such a fixture on the Hill that during one education hearing Representative Bill Goodling (R-Penn.) good-naturedly referred to them as the "Pork Brothers." This is not a bad sobriquet considering that most perceive the cause—education—to be a good one.[29]

In spring of 1990, after the authorization had passed and it had become clear that a supplemental bill that could serve as the legislative vehicle for funding the dropout program would be forthcoming, Casserly and Simering met to go over the list of senators who had projects in their states and might be interested in taking the lead on this issue. Through the dropout network they learned that two of the most logical choices—Senators Hatfield and Harkin—could not be counted on to help.

Another approach would be to persuade the leadership of the committee that controlled the authorization for education programs (Senator Kennedy, chair of the Senate Labor and Human Resources Committee, or Senator Pell, chair of the Subcommittee on Education, Arts and Humanities) to request the funds from members of the Appropriations Committee. Both senators and their staffs supported the program, but, given their other priorities, they could not afford to have this program be the one for which they asked a favor from Senator Byrd and his committee. However, the Kennedy and Pell staffs pledged their support if another way could be found to request the funding. There would have to be another way.

Casserly began to make calls to the offices of the sixty-two senators who had projects in their states. One call was placed to Senator Kohl's staff.

THE FORCES COME TOGETHER

That brief conversation showed that the battle for funding was being waged on several different fronts. Casserly was impressed and amused that a political strategy similar to his own was being mapped out in Senator Kohl's office. The crucial question that still remained was how best to approach the Senate Appropriations Committee. After the conversation had ended and Mike and Jeff were plotting their own strategy, they realized that, although Senator Kohl would not have been their first, second, or even tenth choice to lead the fight for appropriations, he could be their only choice!

Elected in 1988, Senator Kohl ranked last in seniority in the Senate. He was not on the Appropriations Committee, and he was not even on the Senate Labor and Human Resources Committee. Few in Washington, including Jeff and Mike, even knew of the senator's personal commitment to education, as demonstrated by his generous scholarship and teacher awards program in Wisconsin. The junior senator from Wisconsin, who seemed to follow the norm of apprenticeship, was not a very outspoken or visible member, and so seemed an unlikely choice to do battle with the Appropriations Committee.

As Simering and Casserly would later recall, however, upon their first meeting in February, just after the reauthorization of the dropout program had been unanimously approved by the Senate, Senator Kohl had appeared to be genuinely supportive of the program. He had been one of the few senators not on the Senate Labor and Human Resources Committee to take the time to come to the floor of the Senate and speak in favor of the program.

Within a few days, a coalition of forces formed on the Hill to attempt what few thought possible at the time: secure funding via the supplemental appropriations bill, now in committee. The coalition included Simering and Casserly, Ann Young and David Evans from Senator Pell's staff, Amanda Broun from Senator Kennedy's staff, and Sherry Hayes, Mike McCarthy, and myself from Senator Kohl's staff. (McCarthy, the legislative correspondent who primarily responded to constituent mail in the area of education and labor policy, was typical of many young Hill staffers. A recent college graduate, he possessed the energy and endurance needed to balance the demand of answering volumes of constituent mail with the requests of legislative assistants who needed help on a particular bill.) At times this group would expand to over 100 people on the Hill. The coalition in Washington was supported by the work of the dropout network throughout the United States, with the major players including Maureen Coffey, of Wisconsin's "Project Hold," and Jan Davidson, of Oregon's West Valley Academy.

This coalition, though unique to the issue of school dropouts, was typical of many coalitions that form around a given policy area. Committee staff, interest group lobbyists, and constituents benefiting from the program united to fight for the dropout program. As is typical in such coalitions, program administrators in the executive branch are consulted, information is shared, data are gathered, supporters and opponents identified, strategies plotted, statements prepared, legislative language to be used in amendments or bills is drafted, opposition is anticipated, and votes are lined up.[30]

Although the task seemed nearly impossible, enough people thought that the effort was justified. A few, including this author, maintained a sense of optimism that yes, even in an era of fiscal austerity, the congressional system would work and be responsive to an educational policy that was a "dire emergency."

A Number of Different Senate Strategies

With the coalition in place, the difficult work of finding a way to add the funds for the dropout program began. The task would not be easy. It was not just a simple matter of requesting funds from the Appropriations Committee, for the committee was working under the limits set by the budget resolutions agreed to by both chambers. In order to fund the dropout program at this stage of the process in the supplemental appropriations bill, a tradeoff would be necessary. Funds would have to come from another program area that had already been funded; that is, an offset would need to be identified which would allow the addition of funds for the dropout program to be deemed "deficit neutral." Time was of the essence. It was already mid-April, and the Appropriations Committee would soon be marking up the supplemental, that is, going over requests line by line in committee, adding language, and modifying and deleting provisions, until a bill could be readied for consideration by the full Senate.

AN APPEAL TO THE CHAIR

The first step was to approach the leadership of the Appropriations Committee. Senator Pell sent a letter to Senator Byrd, chair of the Appropriations Committee, asking that an appropriation of $21 million be approved to continue the program. Pell, the author of the original authorization passed in the Senate, wrote that the funding was "of very considerable importance to me, my state and the nation's educational well-being." He included arguments that others would use to gain support for the program: the program was the only federal program whose sole focus was on reducing the nation's school dropout rate; the projects were succeeding in increasing the high school graduation rate; and the Bush administration had requested $45 million for the program for fiscal year 1991. In his letter to Byrd, Pell also referred to a successful project in Providence, Rhode Island, that would have to close if continued funding were denied. In addition, Pell personally added a handwritten note that reminded Byrd of his vote with the senator on the Clean Air amendment which would have helped West Virginia coal miners.[1] Senator Pell followed up his note with a personal request for support. Senator Kennedy sent a similar note to Senator Byrd. In an institution where staff has to handle much of the communication between offices owing to the volume of legislative business, the personal request of one member to another carries considerable weight, demonstrating to fellow members the special importance of the particular matter involved. Time was running out, however, and there was no indication that Byrd would respond favorably to either Pell or Kennedy. Another approach was needed.

Given his junior status in the Senate, Senator Kohl decided against the personal strategy Pell and Kennedy had used in attempting to persuade Senator Byrd and other members on the Appropriations Committee of the importance of this legislation. Instead, Kohl settled on an approach that was more suited to a member out of the leadership circles: He would seek the support of other senators in approaching the Appropriations Committee. If a number of senators voiced their support along with his, perhaps the committee members might be persuaded to add the funding needed in the supplemental.

On Friday, April 20, 1990, two of Senator Kohl's staff members would be doing the legwork needed to get other senators and staff the information needed in order to gain their support. For his part, the senator would have to tackle a number of different responsibilities that day. To gain a sense of the typical day of a senator and the many demands placed on every member, Senator Kohl's agenda that day included a meeting with other Democratic senators to discuss strategies on campaign finance reform legislation; a hearing held by the Governmental Affairs Committee's Subcommittee on Federal Services on federal employee health benefits; a Judiciary Committee hearing on immigration; a half hour call-in show on a Wisconsin public radio station; meetings with staff to go over pending legislation; meetings and photo ops with two high school groups from Wisconsin; interviews of several job applicants for a legislative assistant position; and meetings with more constituents from Wisconsin.

Senators Kohl, Pell, and Kennedy were all torn in several different directions and could not focus solely on the dropout issue. Therefore, they had to depend on staff to coordinate the lobbying efforts. Yet the informal approach—discussing the issue of funding for school dropout programs or answering a senator's questions in a few brief minutes of conversation while waiting for the reserved elevators for members of Congress, or in the Cloakroom after a floor vote—would be instrumental in winning over the support of colleagues once their staffs had done the groundwork.

And so, on that Friday, shortly after Senators Pell and Kennedy had sent out their letters to Byrd, Kohl's staff got to work. A memo was hand delivered to the education legislative assistant in each of the Senate offices of states that had a demonstration dropout project that was receiving federal funds. Attached to the memo was a draft of a letter to Senator Robert Byrd urging that funding for the school dropout demonstration assistance program be continued (see Box 8-1).

The memo to the education legislative assistants (LAs) explained that the Appropriations Committee would be marking up the legislation on late Monday afternoon, April 23. Since thirty-one states had projects that would be affected if the funding were not continued, there seemed to be a reasonable chance that a quick and strong response might convince the Appropriations Committee of the value of this program. Given that it was already Friday afternoon by the time the memo was in the hands of the LAs, signatures would have to be collected on Monday morning. LAs were urged to call for more information as soon as possible, or to indicate the willingness of their boss to sign Senator Kohl's letter.

Earlier in the week, Senator Kohl's staff had placed a call to Mike Casserly at the Council of the Great City Schools, inquiring whether the Council had the staff capacity to call the sixty-two Senate offices with demonstration projects to explain the letter and urge the senators to sign it. The Council reported that it did have the capacity. (Later, I learned that, remarkably, it consisted of just two people, Isabel Salinas Almendarez and Mike Casserly.)

A copy of the draft letter was faxed to the Council.[2] By the end of the week, Isabel was making calls to the federal relations coordinator in each of the public school systems represented by the Council to explain the situation and to ask them to call their senators to urge them to sign the letter being sent to Senator Byrd.[3] She also called each of the projects receiving federal funds, even if they weren't at the public school systems represented by the Council of the Great City Schools, and told them "it was imperative" also to get two or three other people to call and ask that the letter to Byrd be signed. Information was faxed to everyone who requested it.

A chain reaction began whereby calls were being generated from the Council of the Great City Schools, certain project coordinators, the school systems, and other participants in the "dropout network." According to Isabel, this activity was "typical of most grass-roots motivating-type efforts." The nature of the issue is communicated to the organization's membership, the key members of Congress are identified for contact, and

Box 8-1   Draft of a Letter to Senator Robert Byrd

April 23, 1990

The Honorable Robert Byrd
Chairman
Appropriations Committee
United States Senate

Dear Robert,

We are writing to ask for your support for Fiscal 1990 funding for the National School Dropout Demonstration Assistance Program. As you know, on February 20, 1990, the Senate unanimously passed HR 2281, reauthorizing the Dropout Program for FY 90 and FY 91, and the President signed this bill on March 6.

This is the only federal program devoted solely to reducing the rate of dropouts. It would be ironic if this program were to lapse in funding in the very year the Nation's Governors have set as a national goal, that "by the year 2000, the high school graduation rate will increase to at least 90%," and in a year in which the President has called for an increase in the high school graduation rate to "no less than 90 percent" in his State of the Union message.

The Department of Education is in the middle of a multi-stage evaluation process of these projects, and early reports suggest the projects are working, and accomplishing a great deal. However, the evaluation process will not even be completed by the time the program loses funding August 31, when programs will be forced to close their doors.

It really makes a great deal of sense to continue the support of a program that is working, and is helping to reduce a disturbingly high dropout rate. The President's Budget includes a request for a $45 million appropriation for FY 91 that, if enacted, would begin a new cycle of programs for FY 91. However, money would not be available for those programs until August, 1991.

We urge the Appropriations Committee to include a supplemental appropriation of at least $21 million for Fiscal Year 1990 for the School Dropout Demonstration Assistance Program. This will enable current programs to continue until the Fiscal 1991 appropriation is considered.

Sincerely,

suggestions are given as to what to say when contacting the congressional delegation.[4]

In no more than two days, thirteen senators made a commitment to sign the letter. The physical challenge of obtaining the thirteen signatures was given to Mike McCarthy, a legislative correspondent (LC) in Senator Kohl's office.

In terms of legislative strategy, bipartisan support for any measure is an important asset. If possible, the first two signatures on a letter like the one to Byrd should be one Democrat and one Republican. In the case of the Byrd letter, the first and only Republican to sign on was Pete Wilson of California. Wilson, with a moderate voting record on social issues, was beginning his campaign for governor of California.[5] With six demonstration projects in California, including projects in the Los Angeles and San Francisco school systems, Wilson would be able to claim credit for helping these programs if funding were continued, thus adding to his record as a public servant in his campaign for governor. And so, the first two names on the letter were those of Senators Kohl and Wilson.

As soon as Senator Wilson's signature was obtained, Mike McCarthy began his travels through the corridors of the Hart, Dirksen, and Russell Senate office buildings to get the signatures of the senators who had agreed to sign. Even though the actual signature is usually obtained from an office auto-pen, Mike still had to visit each office, talk with the education LAs or LCs, let them read the final letter, and then have the letter signed. Given the limited amount of time he had to obtain signatures and the fifteen-minute walk from the seventh floor of the Hart Senate Office Building to an office in the Russell Building, McCarthy developed a phone relay system. After obtaining a signature, he would call back to Senator Kohl's office to see if any more senators had agreed to sign on, in order to get as many signatures as possible in the Russell or Dirksen buildings before returning to the Hart Building. After several hours, McCarthy had obtained the signatures of thirteen senators: in addition to Senators Kohl and Wilson, the signers included Edward M. Kennedy (D-Mass.); Paul Sarbanes (D-Md.); Richard C. Shelby (D-Ala.); Paul Simon (D-Ill.); Joseph R. Biden, Jr. (D-Del.); Christopher J. Dodd (D-Conn.); Donald W. Riegle, Jr. (D-Mich.); Carl Levin (D-Mich.); Joseph I. Lieberman (D-Conn.); Claiborne Pell (D-R.I.); and Howell Heflin (D-Ala.).

One strategy used as a way to increase support, as well as a courtesy to other offices, was to let a senator's office know as soon as the other senator from the state had signed on. This often worked in reverse: We would call asking for support, and one of the first questions asked would be, "Has Senator X [i.e., the other senator from the state] signed on?"

There appeared to be a sense of safety in numbers, and, in addition, a fellow senator was used as a cue-giver for what to support.[6]

Some offices were grateful for the "heads up" phone call alerting them to the opportunity to help constituents in their state. Other offices had already received numerous calls from constituents in support of the funding.

Senators have many different and often competing responsibilities: to serve constituents, to make good policy, to help support the party leadership, to support the president, and, in an institution that does its work in committees, to serve the best interests of that committee. Members of the Appropriations Committee, as I soon learned, are particularly serious about the last-named responsibility. Senators serving on the Appropriations Committee, though supportive of the cause, would not sign on to a letter asking for the support of the chair, Robert Byrd, in a single request for appropriations. Many senators felt that such an approach was inappropriate, perhaps jeopardizing any power and influence they would have within the committee. Most, if not all, members of the committee had their own list of programs for which they were seeking funding. From a strategic standpoint, singling out support for one program before the committee markup began by signing a letter in support of that program, thus prioritizing requests, might endanger the funding of other programs that were equally espoused.

Despite this well-organized effort, the supplemental appropriations bill that emerged from the Appropriations Committee failed to include funding for continuing the dropout projects. Several factors had worked against the success of this effort.

First, although constituents from the Des Moines and Oregon schools had approached their respective senators for support, they were never able to get the firm commitment of Senator Hatfield or Senator Harkin, two of the most powerful members of the Appropriations Committee, to back the continued funding efforts. The support of Senator Harkin, as chair of the Subcommittee on Labor-Health and Human Services-Education, was particularly important. In the past, Harkin had received support from education groups. Thus, one would have expected his support, but it never materialized. This failure proved frustrating to the Des Moines public schools that had received federal funding for their dropout project. In Oregon, strong Republican supporters of Senator Hatfield at one point thought they had a commitment of Hatfield's support from a member of the senator's staff. But even that commitment, coupled with a call from the governor of Oregon to Hatfield, did not bring his support.[7] In addition, in looking at the list of senators who had signed on to the letter, six of the thirteen had voted against Senator Byrd on the crucial coal miner vote, including Senator

Biden. Thus, Senator Byrd might not feel inclined to help these senators when they needed his support, just as they had not voted to help his West Virginia constituents when he had asked for their support.

Second, although a request for funds was being made, the letter to Senator Byrd made no suggestion as to how this additional funding could be offset. Given the budget requirements, the work of the members of the Appropriations Committee was more difficult than that of a previous generation in that the bill would have to be deficit neutral. If new funds were to be spent, offsetting revenues or cuts elsewhere in the budget would be needed.

While the first approach had failed, the fact that thirteen senators had been successfully importuned to support the request within only a matter of days spurred the coalition to try again.

Throughout this period, the sole emphasis was on the Senate taking favorable action. The Senate has a long history of adding spending requests to supplemental appropriation bills. With senators representing whole states and thus a diverse constituency, they have to accommodate more interests than their counterparts in the House. In addition, given the smaller number of senators than representatives, the members of the Senate Appropriations Committee have more committee responsibilities than do the members of the House Appropriations Committee. Therefore, the Senate Appropriations Committee may not view "guarding the Treasury" as its primary role.

Finally, with appropriations bills generally originating in the House, the Senate has become the "court of last resort" for interest groups and agency personnel seeking increases in funds.[8] Members of the House Appropriations Committee tended to frown on this Senate behavior, especially Representative William H. Natcher (D-Ky.), a member of the House since 1953 and chair of the House Appropriations Subcommittee on Labor-Health and Human Services-Education, "who didn't like earmarks for specific projects."[9] As we will see, this difference in perspective would lead to a confrontation between the House and Senate.

With prospects for success so slim in the Senate, it was not worth risking political capital even to begin an attempt in the House unless the Senate first approved it, since gaining the support of House members, such as Natcher, would prove extremely difficult. In addition, 1990 was an election year, and there was a sense that the Senate might be more responsive to constituent concerns.

The Senate Appropriations Committee would be quickly moving the supplemental bill to the floor for full consideration by the Senate. Only a brief period of time—a matter of days—would be available in which to map out a new strategy.

AMENDING ON THE FLOOR

With the failure of the committee approach, the next option was to attempt to amend the supplemental bill on the floor. While the work of Congress is done in its committees, the amendment process is a means of broadening and modifying the work of the committee. Interests ignored in committee may have a second chance to be heard on the floor, a broader coalition of support may be formed, and an amendment may even change the substantive focus of the bill.

Clearly, continued funding of the dropout program had strong support. Most, if not all, who heard the case for funding agreed that the program was effective in demonstrating approaches to lower the school dropout rate and increase the high school graduation rate. The question remained—was there enough support in the Senate to add this as an amendment on the floor? If so, who would offer the amendment?

The next strategy session took place in the Senate Chef—a very small snack bar located in the underground corridor connecting the Hart and Dirksen Senate Office buildings. Those present were Simering, Casserly, Amanda Broun, Ann Young, Sherry Hayes, and myself. We quickly agreed that a floor amendment might be possible and that Senator Kohl should be the one to offer it since he had led the fight thus far.

The discussion quickly turned to the more difficult task at hand—that is, determining a way to propose an amendment asking for additional appropriations without being subject to a point of order that would be raised if the amendment was not deficit neutral. If we asked for additional spending, we would have to suggest a means to pay for the program, either through a tax increase or other revenue enhancement measure, or through a spending cut in a program already receiving funds. Since there would be no means of increasing revenues through a tax or user fee, we would have to find a way to offset the funding.

Three different approaches were considered. First, we could take funds from a program that might have little support and therefore arouse little objection from constituents with a strong attachment to the program. Second, we could tap a pool of funds—unobligated balances that were lapsing—that were not being spent by departments or agencies (e.g., funds that may be available in a number of departments, which when added up together would provide the offset we needed). Or third, the start of the funding date could be delayed until October 1, the first day of the new fiscal year. The last approach would prevent the dropout funding from being counted against FY90 spending limits, and would defer the accounting until the FY91 budget. This approach, while the simplest and most appealing as a short-term strategy, would draw fire from the Appropriations Committee because it would limit the pool of funds available to the committee to work with in FY91 and might generally foreclose future options. If Senators Kohl, Pell, or Kennedy, the principal forces behind the amendment in the Senate, requested appropriations in the next fiscal year cycle for other programs, they might find themselves being reminded that they had, in effect, already received funds for FY91 in terms of the accounting procedures in place. This option was given serious consideration by the ad hoc group, until a Democratic staff member of the appropriations subcommittee said it would not work. Later we learned this information was misleading.

At this stage of the process, I discovered the importance of the Congressional Budget Office (CBO). CBO, created to give Congress the budgetary and staff expertise to match the expertise which the president receives from the Office of Management and Budget (OMB), would determine whether an amendment was deficit neutral. CBO would need to score any request for spending in order to determine its impact on the federal budget. If we proposed an amendment requesting $20 million for school dropout programs, CBO would certify that the means we had come up with to provide funds to offset that request would be equal to $20 million. Therefore, the amendment could be offered as deficit neutral.

In addition, I learned that programs have different spend-out rates, that is, the rate at which authorized money is spent. "In a given year some appropriated funds may remain unspent."[10] Therefore, a program or department's actual spending, or outlays, is important. Because different programs spend appropriated money at different rates, depending on when the bills come due, those rates affect the way in which CBO scores a budget proposal. The school dropout program was scored with a low spend-out rate. As a result, in order to offset the $19.945 million needed to fund the dropout program, an offset of only about 2.8 million would be needed. This figure then became the target sum needed to transfer from existing spending, either by identifying unobligated balances that were lapsing or by transferring money from another program to the dropout program. One alternative (never given serious consideration, however) was that the offset be taken from defense spending, given that some defense systems had been canceled during the past year. In theory, this would open up a pool of available funds. However, we assumed that the Appropriations Committee had already used any available funds for disaster relief and other program needs. The transfer of monies appropriated for the strategic defense initiative (SDI) program to fund the dropout program was also tempting, but such a move would probably generate a storm of controversy over what we hoped would be a rather simple and noncontroversial floor amendment.

Because of the difficulties involved in taking an offset from another program area, we focused on potential offsets that could be identified in the Department of Education budget. At the end of each year, the budget reveals that funds remain unspent in some accounts. Therefore, if one of those accounts with a surplus of funds could be identified, it would be possible to use some of those funds as the offset in a floor amendment. We realized that the only way to get the information on which accounts would have a surplus of funds would be through the Department of Education. That appeared an unlikely option since the Bush administration had made it clear that, although it supported the goal of achieving a 90 percent high school graduation rate, it had not supported continued funding for existing dropout programs in the FY90 budget. It is important to recall that the president's budget involves a multiyear process. When the dropout program was first authorized, Congress had planned to set up a larger basic skills program that would give states discretion in funding programs that best met their particular needs, including using funds for dropout programs. However, given the nationwide attention to dropouts in 1989 and 1990, funds had been requested in the FY91 budget for dropout programs.

As a way of forcing the Department of Education into assisting the coalition that was working to identify surplus funds, Senator Kohl, joined by Senators Pell, Kennedy, McConnell, and Levin, submitted an amendment to H.R. 4404, the supplemental appropriations bill, on Thursday, April 26, 1990. The amendment simply stated the following:

> The Secretary shall transfer—
> $2.867 million of amounts made available in fiscal year 1990 from the Department of Education, Departmental Management, to carry out the provisions of the School Dropout Demonstration Assistance Act of 1988, for expenses necessary to extend current grants authorized under title VI, part A of Public Law 100–297 for one additional year, $19,945,000, to remain available through September 30, 1991.[11]

While the Kennedy and Pell staffs had helped coauthor the amendment, Senators McConnell and Levin would allow their names to be used as supporters of the amendment even though they did not assist in the actual crafting of the amendment. Thus, all would appear as co-sponsors with Kohl.

In a statement inserted into the *Congressional Record* when the amendment was introduced, Senator Kohl explained the amendment to his colleagues and indicated that he was ready to play hardball. His amendment proposed that the funding be offset by taking funds from the Department of Education's management budget, which included spending for travel and other expenses. In that statement, which is included below, he refers to a phone call he had received the night before from the under secretary of education, Ted Sanders. Sanders, who had learned of the impending amendment and proposed offset, stated that the Department of Education would face considerable difficulties if it was forced to cut $2.8 million from salaries and expenses in order to offset outlays for the dropout demonstration program. Sanders then proposed several alternatives, including the cutting of funds for Howard University, an historically black college. In no uncertain terms Senator Kohl informed Sanders that would not be done.[12]

With no other acceptable alternative, Senator Kohl went ahead and submitted the amendment. He included a list of the thirty-one states currently receiving dropout prevention funds, along with the amount of the awards each state received in 1988, to be published in the *Congressional Record*. He went on to explain why this funding request should be added to the Dire Emergency Supplemental Appropriations bill and why this approach was justified:

> What this amendment seeks to do is to provide emergency funding for a program that supports school dropout assistance in 31 States throughout this Nation. Last year, when we considered the Labor, Health and Human Services Appropriations bill for fiscal year 1990, we did not have an authorization for this program. Since that time, the Senate has voted unanimously to reauthorize the program and the President has signed that legislation. But unfortunately, the funds needed to continue this needed program will cease to be available this summer. $19,945,000 is needed to carry the program through the next academic year.
>
> Without a Federal commitment to continue the funding, without a strong signal from us, these programs will not be in operation when the academic year begins in September. It is that simple, and I believe it is critical that we respond now.
>
> The problem, of course, is not a lack of support for the School Dropout Assistance Program. This, in fact, is the year of the dropout. The dilemma is finding an appropriate way to pay for it. So I have been searching for an offset. Now I would like in a perfect world, to have the luxury of financing this program through some other subcommittee's allocation—no offense to my distinguished colleagues who appropriate for defense, or foreign operations. In this Senator's mind, the Labor, HHS and Education funds are pretty lean, picked to the bone if you will, in contrast to spending in other areas.
>
> But I anticipate those types of offsets won't be tolerated for the purpose of floor debate, and I'm trying to play by the rules.
>
> So I have searched high and low within these accounts to find an offset, perhaps to the amusement of those members who serve on the Labor, HHS and Education subcommittee, who have already scratched through what little was there to begin with. The choices aren't pretty.

After exhaustive efforts, we have decided to file the amendment with the least of the evils as an offset.

The offset, which has been cleared by CBO as sufficient, would cut 0.8 percent—eight-tenths of one percent, or $2.8 million—from the Department of Education departmental management budget of $331 million. Last year the account received a 10-percent increase after $1 million had lapsed, unobligated. Approximately 60 percent of the program administration money is used for salary, consultants and benefits. I do not seek to displace workers. But somewhere in that 40 percent, I think there must be some room to find $2.8 million without causing excessing [sic] havoc.

But I am not locked into this particular offset. I have spoken with the Under Secretary of Education and I believe there is a mutual interest in getting funds to these dropout prevention programs this year—it is a matter of how to do it.

I want to alert my colleagues to my deep commitment to getting this job done, as well as my willingness to work within the confines of the rules to do it in the least detrimental manner.[13]

Senator Kohl's apparent determination to push ahead with this amendment prompted a flurry of activity in the Department of Education, resulting in a series of conversations and faxes between the two offices. Included in the material was a detailed budget for the department, indicating that, while the salaries and expenses budget in fiscal 1989 had lapsed funds available, the fiscal 1990 budget would not have any surplus funds available.

The following morning, the Office of the Secretary sent out a statement detailing the points the under secretary had made to Senator Kohl: If the salaries and expense budget was cut by $2.8 million to provide the offset for the dropout program, a four-day furlough would result for all employees in the Department of Education. The department argued that since it was already in the seventh month of the 1990 fiscal year, the only way to cut the $2.8 million budget was through a furlough that would "severely disrupt Department operations." According to the department:

Most Education programs award funds in July, August, and September. A four day furlough could disrupt all awards under such forward funded state grant programs as Chapter 1, Education for the Handicapped, Vocational Education, and Pell Grants. It is unlikely that the Department could obligate many of these awards in time for the 1990–91 school year.

A 4 day furlough would also delay the Department's default initiative which has extensive work scheduled in working with schools on their default management plans to reduce the $2 billion cost of defaults.

The under secretary wanted to go after the most popular programs and threaten their viability in order to challenge Senator Kohl to back down from taking funds from the salaries and expenses budget. This was the administration's standard ploy whenever a disagreement arose with Congress over funding. (For example, in 1986, when the appropriations bills had not been passed on time, the United States Park Service closed down the Washington Monument and the Statue of Liberty to tourists, complying with a federal directive ordering "nonessential personnel" home. Within hours Congress had passed an appropriations bill to keep the government running.[14] This is referred to as the Washington Monument syndrome.) But Senator Kohl refused to back down. Since he had identified a strategy for funding a program which did not violate any of the budget rules and procedures, the under secretary was aware of the implications if others were to follow suit and use the same approach. It would be better to present an alternative solution. Soon a compromise was achieved: the under secretary asked several individuals in the Department of Education to go through the budget and find an offset that would be agreeable to both sides.

After careful scrutiny by several people, including Bettilou Taylor on Senator Specter's staff, it was revealed that the actual offset needed was only $2.4 million. The compromise finally offered by the Department of Education was an offset of $2.4 million obtained from surplus funds available for teacher cancellation payments under the Perkins Loan Cancellation program.[15] Taylor, a professional staff member on the minority side of the aisle who had come to work for the subcommittee in December 1989, proved to be the Appropriations Committee's most valuable member throughout this entire process of amendment crafting. While new to the Senate committee, she had brought with her a wealth of experience from fifteen years of work on the House Appropriations Committee, serving in every position—from secretary, to office manager, to administrative assistant—"everything but professional staff member." This experience would prove particularly helpful when the Senate went to conference with the House.

Throughout the spring of 1990, the education community had united to fight for, at minimum, maintaining current levels of federal funding. The different groups representing the postsecondary and primary and secondary education communities agreed that transferring funds from primary and secondary programs to postsecondary programs, and vice versa, would not be acceptable and would meet strong resistance from the education community. As a result, a careful statement was crafted to explain that the use of the Perkins Loan Cancellation funds did not violate this principle. In fact, since the Reagan-Bush administrations had not requested any funds for this program throughout the 1980s, stating that the program created "heavy and unnecessary Federal interest subsidi[zation]" and that "collection from prior loans . . . [was] expected to be sufficient to provide new loans to students without additional Federal capital contributions,"[16] Pell's and Kennedy's staff were concerned that this approach would decimate another program the administration opposed. Ann Young and Amanda Broun, after careful review of the implications of using these funds as an offset, concluded that this approach would work and would not jeopardize the program in any way.

An explanatory statement was distributed to those concerned about the transfer of these funds:

> Of the $19,945,000 that would be made available for Dropout Prevention Projects, it is estimated that $2,400,000 would outlay in the current fiscal year. Under the proposed language, the offset for this $2,400,000 would be obtained from surplus funds that are available for Teacher Cancellation payments under the Perkins Loan Program. These payments are made each year to reimburse postsecondary education institutions for Perkins loans that have been forgiven for students who enter certain fields of public interest, such as teaching or the Peace Corps. Requirements for these payments have been declining each year, and only $15,000,000 will be used in 1990. Since almost $44,000,000 is currently available, there remains a surplus of about $29,000,000. *Using $2,400,000 of these surplus funds for an offset will not curtail or eliminate any activities or have any effect whatsoever on any program or recipients.*

When the amendment was brought to the floor, Senator Kohl carefully explained that

> The offset for this amendment is acceptable to the administration. Indeed it was developed with their cooperation, appropriately scored by CBO, and cleared by the Budget Committee. The offset would be obtained from surplus funds that are available for cancellation payments under the Perkins loan program for certain public service careers.
>
> As I indicated to my colleagues last week, I would have preferred to not have to transfer money from one education account to another. But my understanding from the Department of Education is that requirements for these payments have been declining each year. Using $2.4 million of these surplus funds for an offset will not curtail or eliminate any activities or have any effect whatsoever on any programs or recipients.[17]

These remarks seemed to satisfy any worries about the offset. Kohl's office received only one call voicing concern over the precedent of transferring funding from a postsecondary to a secondary school program.

As is often true on the Hill, members of both parties frequently find support and assistance from others, regardless of party affiliation. In part, this is because most legislative proposals benefit a number of senators' constituents, regardless of the party affiliation of the bill's sponsor. As stated in Chapter 3, Senator Specter played a major role in the early history of the dropout program with his introduction of the dropout legislation in 1985. While it failed to pass the Senate in that Congress, his support came full circle through the work of his staff member, Bettilou Taylor. For those of us working in an area new to us—that is, the drafting of language needed to secure an appropriation—her help proved invaluable. Not only did she help craft the language needed to ensure the proper communication of our intent, but also later, when the Senate went to conference with the House, she realized an additional phrase would be needed to insure that funding would be available in time for the start of the 1990–91 academic year, and she added the appropriate language. We were most fortunate that she had moved over to the Senate side in December 1989. Without her attention to detail, the projects might not have received the intended funding.

The amendment was now ready to go to the floor.

CHAPTER 9

The Broader Picture

Members of the House and Senate are pulled in a number of different directions. Representatives average nearly seven total committee and subcommittee assignments per member, and senators, being fewer in number yet needing to cover the same policy areas as the House, average over eleven committee and subcommittee assignments per member.[1] Members must assess the needs of their constituents, the president, their own party leadership, the committees on which they serve, and their own individual preferences in a wide range of policy areas, including foreign, domestic, and economic policies. Not all matters are as simply focused as was the case with the dropout legislation. This chapter will put the dropout program in the context of the broader picture—the overview of Congress that is most familiar to outside observers—by examining the major policy items on the agenda of the One Hundred and First Congress from January until May 1990. It is in this context that the work of Congress is done, unobserved by most.

One of the major legislative actions before the Congress was the Clean Air bill; this legislation would dominate the agenda of Congress for weeks. The passions aroused by the members' deep concerns for both the environment and the needs of constituents and industries in each respective state led to an emotional involvement that is not often seen in the Congress. In addition, two policy areas on the agenda early in the second session of the One Hundred and First Congress—the budget and foreign aid—became intertwined in the debate over the Dire Emergency Supplemental Appropriations bill. The dropout funding, as was the case with many other such items considered in the dire emergency supplemental, was only a minor issue in the months of debate over that bill.

BUDGET DEFICITS

With a Gramm-Rudman deficit target set at $64 billion for fiscal year 1991 and OMB budget forecasts of a $100 billion deficit as of January

1990, about $36 billion in cuts would be needed in the FY91 budget.[2] Now that the transformation of Eastern Europe and the Soviet Union was under way, many Democrats were pushing for "deep cuts in defense spending, a 'peace dividend.' "[3] However, if the president and Congress could not agree on cuts to meet the $36 billion needed to meet the deficit target, a process of sequestration (i.e., automatic cuts to meet the existing deficit targets), half from defense and half from domestic programs, would then take place. For the president and his budget director, Richard Darman, sequestration perhaps appeared to be a preferable option, since defense would not take as bad a hit as many members of Congress were pushing for and domestic programs would also be slashed. Yet not everyone in the administration would favor this approach, especially Defense Department officials, who would find that "the Gramm-Rudman ax slices arbitrarily without distinguishing between programs of higher and lesser priority."[4]

The impact of the deficit and the consequences facing members if the deficit target was not met forced all members, but especially those on the appropriations committees, to deal with the reality of limited spending in a tough manner. As a result, when the dire emergency supplemental called for increased appropriations to meet specific and urgent needs, committee members would also have to come up with the funds to pay for those programs in a manner acceptable to their colleagues.

Meeting the deficit target became a particularly acute situation as the 1990 session progressed. "Congress failed in its first attempt to pass a budget resolution, settling temporarily for an ad hoc arrangement that allowed the House to begin working on appropriations bills."[5] For the Democratic leadership, the problem tended to focus on two areas: (1) the use of the "peace dividend," that is, given the end of the Cold War, how much money could be transferred from defense to domestic programs, and (2) hesitation in raising taxes at the same time Bush was reiterating his 1988 campaign pledge of "no new taxes."[6] Throughout the winter and early spring, as the economy worsened, budget projections began to be revised, indicating a need for greater cuts to meet the deficit target. Eventually, early in May, President Bush brought the congressional leaders of both parties to the White House to begin discussions of budget talks. Throughout the summer and early fall, high-level budget talks were held with top officials in the Bush administration and congressional leaders of both parties. At one point when talks became stalled in the middle of the summer, President Bush, as a way of moving them along, agreed to consider tax increases as a part of any deficit reduction agreement. This retreat from his 1988 campaign pledge of "Read my lips, no new taxes," brought a negative reaction from members of his own party, including Pat Buchanan, who would remind voters of the broken promise two years later in his campaign against Bush for the Republican party's presidential nomination.[7]

As the session wound down and the start of a new fiscal year approached, the threat of sequestration spurred the executive branch and congressional negotiators to reach an agreement, which they finally did in October 1990. This agreement modified deficit targets and the budget process.

The impact of the deficit on the Dire Emergency Supplemental Appropriations bill was clearly revealed in Senator Hatfield's opening remarks to his colleagues as debate began on the supplemental:

> I might comment that the original dire emergency supplemental bill was primarily concerned with aid to Nicaragua and to Panama. And as you see in this bill print now, that issue is no longer the sole or main issue within the supplemental, because it has been joined by a number of other very important matters and policies of pressing concern, all of which deserve the careful, though I would say expeditious, hearing, and consideration here today.
>
> I remind my colleagues on this side of the aisle, especially, that deficit neutrality will characterize all successful attempts to amend this supplemental appropriation bill. If an amendment is urgent enough to be considered at this time on the floor, it certainly then has to be important enough to merit the appropriate offset from another part of the measure.
>
> We urge this not because of any policy of the committee, but by the Budget Act itself, which we are functioning under to give this bill an opportunity to move to conference at the soonest date possible. We must move this bill. To that end, I hope that our debate today will be not only purposeful, but I hope it will be very brief.[8]

FOREIGN AID

While budget deficits did much to structure debate, the dire emergency supplemental was driven, in part, by the issue of foreign aid, as Senator Hatfield mentioned in his remarks above when the bill finally reached the floor. In fact, "President Bush got the supplemental bill started on January 25 when he requested $570 million—$500 million of it for the new government of Panama, which had taken office following a U.S. military invasion in December 1989, and $70 million for assistance to cover the larger-than-budgeted cost of arriving refugees, most of them Jews from the Soviet Union."[9]

Unlike other years, the United States was not facing a major domestic emergency requiring immediate relief, and so the foreign aid packages became the only legislative vehicle "politically powerful enough to drive the rest of the train."[10] The Nicaraguan elections (which "accomplished in one day what more than eight years of bitterly contested U.S. policy had been trying to do" with the election of opposition leader Violeta Chamorro on February 25), led the president and Congress to consider an economic aid package to Nicaragua.[11] In March, President Bush added a $300 million request for aid for Nicaragua to the fiscal 1990 supplemental appropriations bill.[12]

The foreign aid package of $870 million received some criticism from members of Congress who saw equally compelling needs on the domestic front. Senator Patrick J. Leahy (D-Vt.) observed that "the Administration is asking for more money for Panama and Nicaragua than the 'state of Vermont will use in two years.' "[13] In addition, the foreign aid package was subject to the provisions of Gramm-Rudman-Hollings in that an offset would be needed to be identified in order to keep the bill deficit neutral. Without a proper offset, the bill "would be subject to a point of order on the Senate floor" and would then require sixty votes for approval.[14]

Although the offset was targeted to come from defense cuts, the president and Congress could not agree on precisely what part of the defense budget would be cut.[15] Another complication arose from the changing political scene in Eastern Europe and the disagreement over "how much to spend to promote free-market economic development, as well as political reform" in these former communist states.[16] Some lawmakers proposed that some of the funds requested for Panama and Nicaragua be shifted to help assist Eastern European countries.[17]

By the time the bill reached the floor of the House for consideration in April, an additional $1.5 billion was added for domestic programs, including disaster relief for the damage caused by Hurricane Hugo and the 1989 San Francisco earthquake, and $510 million for the food stamp program that was soon going to run out of funds.[18] Along with a number of other programs, the supplemental now cost $2.4 billion.

By the time the supplemental reached the floor of the Senate, it had grown to include requests of $3.4 billion in appropriations, with a good chunk of the money for domestic programs. Additions included "$110 million for the Bureau of the Census to complete the decennial head count" since a large percentage of households had not responded to mail questionnaires and the Bureau of the Census had to "hire additional workers to conduct door-to-door interviews."[19] Another addition was the $20 million for high school dropout prevention programs.

One of the more controversial add-ons was $185 million for a new facility for the FBI that would house an automated fingerprint file system. The only site being considered for the new operation was in West Virginia, the home state of Robert Byrd, chair of the Appropriations Committee.

However, William S. Sessions, director of the FBI, also endorsed this measure.[20]

Before the bill would finally pass, it would also became entangled in U.S. foreign policy on El Salvador. Congressional leaders pushed to cut military aid to El Salvador as part of a "carrots and sticks" approach to get the Salvadoran government and leftist guerrillas to negotiate to end a war begun eleven years before.[21] Congressional action was speeded up by the release of a report on April 30, at the height of the Senate debate on the supplemental, by a task force of Democrats in the House, headed by Representative Joe Moakley (D-Mass.). "The group—including supporters and critics of official policy toward El Salvador—found that an investigation there into the brutal murders . . . of six Jesuit priests and two women ha[d] come to a 'virtual standstill.' "[22] In addition, the report noted that the United States had given millions of dollars in aid to subsidize the Salvadoran judicial and military systems. Yet the report concluded:

> Despite a decade of promises, . . . and repeated statements that progress is just around the corner, the Salvadoran justice system remains essentially an oxymoron—neither systematic nor just. . . .
>
> The murder of the Jesuits was a symptom of a too-frequent failure within the military to accept civilian authority and to pattern its own actions on the requirements of law.[23]

RULES AND NORMS OF THE SENATE

Once the bill moved to the Senate, the role of the individual rights of senators was clearly tested: first, in the issue of legislation being written on an appropriations bill; and second, in the right of members to engage in a filibuster.

When the supplemental moved to the Senate, the debate expanded to include abortion and the death penalty. Unlike the House, the Senate does not observe a strict test of germaneness for amendments added to bills. Thus, the Senate allows for a revisitation of issues that have come before the chamber in earlier debates, as well as new issues, which may have no direct relevance to the matter at hand.

While the bill was in committee, Senator Brock Adams (D-Wash.) pushed through an amendment that would allow the District of Columbia to use local funds to finance abortion. This was the continuation of a debate begun the year before. In 1989 President Bush had twice vetoed the appropriations bill for the District of Columbia, permitting it to use its own funds to pay for abortions.[24] When procedural efforts on the floor of the Senate and veto threats from the White House failed to remove this provision, Senator Phil Gramm (R-Tex.) moved to amend the abortion package by adding language that would allow the death penalty for drug-related crimes committed in Washington, D.C., which resulted in murder.[25] And so two of the most divisive issues that have ever come before Congress—abortion and capital punishment—became entangled with the dire emergency supplemental. As we will see in the next chapter, Senator Hatfield, ranking member of the Appropriations Committee and a strong opponent of the death penalty, helped move the debate through the use of a filibuster, threatening to delay any action until an agreement could be reached to move forward. The abortion and death penalty issues were left for the House and Senate conferees to resolve; both provisions were eventually dropped.[26]

A Tribute to Byrd

Respect for the individual rights of senators and courtesy and respect for the members themselves were also clearly illustrated in the heat of the partisan debate over the supplemental and the question of the germaneness of the abortion language in the supplemental. In the middle of debate on April 27, 1990, Senator Byrd cast his 12,134th vote, a new Senate record for total Senate votes ever cast, breaking the prior record of retired Senator William Proxmire (D-Wis.). Byrd was congratulated by Majority Leader Mitchell and Minority Leader Dole, as well as his junior colleague from West Virginia, Senator Jay Rockefeller, and by Strom Thurmond, the only senator more senior to Byrd. Thurmond, in his brief remarks, observed that Senator Byrd "is a remarkable man. He has made a remarkable record in the Senate. He is one of the ablest parliamentarians who ever served in this Senate throughout the history of the Senate. I think we all owe him a great debt of gratitude. I would like to express my personal appreciation to him for the fine service he has rendered to the United States of America."[27]

After Byrd spoke for a few minutes, all the senators present stood and gave him a round of applause. Following this brief interlude demonstrating respect for the achievement of a colleague, the Senate resumed debate. Although this exchange further delayed action, it reinforced the idea of civility and common courtesy that allows members to put aside the most strongly held partisan positions to come together when needed.

The norms and folkways of the Senate can make things a challenge for members, however, especially the leadership. April 27, 1990—the day the abortion and death penalty issues became linked on the floor of the

Senate—was a particularly trying one for all concerned. Senator Mitchell, the majority leader of an institution that respects the individual rights of all 100 senators, reflected on the problems of the Senate in the closing minutes of the day's session. He and Senator Hatfield had just cleared a number of nominations on the executive calendar, including the nomination of D. Brock Hornby of Maine to be U.S. district judge for the District of Maine.[28] That was the same district court judgeship that Senator Mitchell had held before his appointment to the Senate to fill the vacancy created by Senator Muskie's departure to take the job of secretary of state for President Jimmy Carter. Senator Mitchell shared some thoughts on his days on the bench and the difficulties of moving the Senate's agenda forward with Senator Hatfield, ranking member of Appropriations and the acting Republican leader in Senator Dole's absence.

> And I might say to my distinguished colleague here, the acting Republican leader, there are many days and nights when I as majority leader think wistfully of my days as a U.S. district judge for the District of Maine, and today was one of them; nothing to do with the manager of the bill that we are considering, but rather to do with the subject matter, the difficulty, that we are considering.
>
> When I was a judge, it took only one vote to do anything. Nowadays it takes 51 and sometimes they are hard to come by.[29]

No member, not even the leadership, has absolute control over the agenda. Members find that they have responsibilities in several different policy areas and to a number of different constituencies (including constituents, party leaders, the president, and committees). In an institution that respects the individual rights of all members, gridlock and paralysis may temporarily stop action, but only until a consensus is reached to move forward.

CHAPTER 10

Action on the Senate Floor

On Wednesday, April 25, 1990, the Dire Emergency Supplemental Appropriations bill was brought to the floor by Majority Leader George Mitchell for consideration by the Senate.[1] It got off to a slow start, having been delayed in its consideration by the full Senate because of a last minute addition of language that would allow the District of Columbia to pay for abortions with funds raised within the District. The rules of the Senate are usually bypassed through a unanimous consent agreement to proceed with business. In the case of the dire emergency supplemental, the report from the Appropriations Committee accompanying the bill was not available until Wednesday morning. With a two-day rule in place of not considering legislation "until 2 days have elapsed following receipt of the report,"[2] unanimous consent would be needed to bypass that rule. And it would not be forthcoming.

Senator Gordon Humphrey (R-N.H.) took to the floor of the Senate to explain that a unanimous consent agreement could not be reached because of the abortion provision. Humphrey also raised the issue of a presidential veto of the entire supplemental appropriations bill if the language remained. Humphrey read several passages from a letter by Richard Darman, the director of OMB:

> We understand that an effort may be made in the Senate to use H.R. 4404 as a vehicle for modifying the abortion provisions in the fiscal year 1990 District of Columbia Appropriations Act. The President vetoed H.R. 3610, the second D.C. appropriations bill, because of language identical to that which the Senate would consider.
> . . .
> We strongly believe that the appropriations legislation should not be used to reconsider nonemergency issues that were resolved in the regular 1990 appropriations process. If Congress presents the President with the bill that contains the abortion language that was included on H.R. 3610, the senior advisors will recommend that he veto the bill, and I am virtually certain that he would do so.[3]

After several more hours of consultation among the leadership from both sides of the aisle, a unanimous consent agreement was finally reached which would allow consideration of the bill.

Even though the bill was brought to the floor on April 25, there would be no other debate on the bill, other than a statement by Robert Byrd, chair of the Appropriations Committee, until the following day. The delay would also accommodate the nine senators who were in Nicaragua for the inauguration of Mrs. Chamorro.[4]

On Thursday, April 26, Senator Kohl submitted his amendment. Senators Pell, Kennedy, McConnell, and Levin joined Senator Kohl as co-sponsors of the amendment to the supplemental appropriations bill, H.R. 4404:

> The Secretary shall transfer—$2.867 million of amounts made available in fiscal year 1990 from the Department of Education, Departmental Management, to carry out the provisions of the School Dropout Demonstration Assistance Act of 1988, for expenses necessary to extend current grants authorized under title VI, part A of Public Law 100–297 for one additional year, $19,945,000, to remain available through September 30, 1991.[5]

As described in Chapter 8, that evening Senator Kohl talked with Under Secretary Sanders about the source of the offset, and on Friday morning a new amendment was drafted. The new amendment was mutually acceptable to both the Department of Education and Senator Kohl and his coalition of supporters on the Hill. The new amendment read as follows:

> For an additional amount for "School Improvement Programs," $19,945, 000, to remain available until September 30, 1991, for continued funding of existing dropout prevention demonstration projects funded in 1989, as authorized by title VI-A of the Elementary and Secondary Education Act of 1965, as amended: *Provided,* That $2,400,000 of the amount provided herein shall be derived by transfer from funds appropriated in Public Law 100–436 for part E, section 465, of the Higher Education Act, as amended.[6]

Meanwhile, one matter had to be resolved: what was Senator Pete Wilson (R-Calif.) up to? On Thursday night, the leadership of both parties had asked senators to indicate what amendments they planned to offer. Senator Mitchell offered a unanimous consent request that the amendments to the dire emergency, H.R. 4404, be limited to the list the leadership had compiled.[7] The list had over sixty amendments offered by a third of the members of the Senate. Not all these amendments would be brought to the floor for consideration, and some were offered as part of the members' strategic maneuvering to insure their voice would be heard, if not on this bill, then at a later point in time. Therefore, some were amendments in name only, with no known substantive content, and were offered as part of the parliamentary maneuvering for strategic advantage. Surprisingly, the list included an amendment to be offered by Senator Wilson on dropouts and a Wilson second-degree amendment to a Kohl amendment on dropouts.[8] As Senator Mitchell continued to read the list of amendments, including the Kohl amendment on dropouts, Senator Kohl's chief of staff, on hearing the Wilson strategy, immediately phoned the Democratic Cloakroom to add a Kohl second-degree amendment to the Wilson dropout amendment.[9] The second-degree amendment would thus give Senator Kohl the opportunity to shape the debate on dropouts, since his amendment to the Wilson amendment would be considered first.

This parliamentary maneuvering was a means of "filling the amendment tree," blocking other amendments and allowing one's position to be considered first by using parliamentary rules that govern the types of amendments which are in order and the order in which the amendments will be considered.[10] Senator Kohl didn't know what Wilson was up to, but at least he would have a strategic position secured in order to respond to whatever Wilson had planned. Kohl did so to insure that any effort Senator Wilson and his staff might make to derail the Kohl dropout amendment could potentially be blocked if Wilson had plans to offer a substantive amendment on dropouts.

The question became—What were Senator Wilson and his staff trying to do? The suspicion was that the Wilson office was trying to take over the momentum that was building on Kohl's amendment and then claim credit for continuing the funding if the amendment passed. This scenario was plausible given that Senator Wilson was in the midst of a campaign for the governorship of California, and California had six projects that had received nearly $2 million from the federal dropout program. Senator Wilson was no stranger to this ploy.

In 1989, for example, Senator Kohl had organized a hearing for the Governmental Affairs Committee on coordinating federal drug policy programs for substance-abusing women and their children as part of the fact-finding, data-gathering stage of the legislative process. Kohl then planned to introduce comprehensive legislation later in the year for families affected by substance abuse. As is standard, Kohl's staff had briefed the staff of other members on the committee in advance of the hearing, and shared advance copies of the testimony of witnesses. "Crack babies" were just beginning to capture the attention of the media by the time the hearing took place. To the surprise of all at the hearing, Senator Wilson announced *he* was going to introduce a bill *that very day* on programs dealing with substance abuse during pregnancy! In response, Kohl asked if he might see a draft of Wilson's bill. However, the bill was not yet ready. Wilson introduced his bill in the Senate later that day, but it took another day until the text of the bill appeared in the *Congressional Record,* along with a statement from Wilson explaining the bill. In that statement he drew from the testimony of witnesses appearing at the Governmental Affairs Committee hearing the day before. Thus it appeared as if Wilson was trying to steal the thunder from his colleague who had done much of the background work in moving this issue onto the Senate's agenda.[11]

Although Senator Kohl's office was concerned about sharing information on our offset, it was important to learn what Wilson was planning to do. Phone conversations with Wilson's LA revealed that the Wilson amendment proposed an offset that was unacceptable to the rest of the Senate. His proposal was to take the money from the food stamp program for an offset. Given that the food stamp program was receiving additional funding in the supplemental, it was unlikely that senators would vote to curb the program. It was clear that they were interested in learning our proposed offset.

As Richard Fenno has observed, although members and their staffs are not shy about claiming credit for legislative initiatives, the desire for recognition isn't always a driving force, at least not in terms of legislative action. This may be due to a junior member's inexperience, staff oversight, or the member's involvement in many and varied legislative activities at any one point in time. Or it may simply be that the "proposition that senators are perpetually preoccupied with credit-taking publicity" is wrong.[12] In the case of Herb Kohl, here is a senator who does not care to take center stage or to look for ways to take credit for legislative activity on the Hill. His staff, however, after months of work on securing funding for the dropout program rightly felt a proprietary interest in the issue and had no intention of yielding the credit for this amendment to Senator Wilson. A fear was also expressed that the under secretary of education, who was helping to identify an offset, would be more interested in helping a fellow Republican in the Senate than Democratic Senator Herb Kohl, and so circumspection was needed.

At a Friday morning meeting between Kohl's chief of staff, Bob Seltzer, and legislative assistant, Sherry Hayes, and Wilson's legislative assistant, Karen Strickland, it was suggested that the two senators work together on this issue since they had a common objective—continued funding of the dropout program. Senator Wilson agreed to join Senator Kohl as a co-sponsor on his amendment.

Later that morning, a call came from the Department of Education suggesting the alternative offset—one that would not affect the Department of Education or its clientele in an adverse way. As stated in Chapter 8, the Department of Education proposed that the offset be derived from funds that were available but not being used by the Perkins Loan Cancellation program.

Once the offset was identified, the amendment was sent to legislative counsel for crafting as well as to Bettilou Taylor, who had offered to review the language to insure that our intent was reflected in the actual language. As noted earlier, her years of experience on the House Appropriations Committee were of immeasurable help. In addition, Amanda Broun on Senator Kennedy's staff took the amendment to the Congressional Budget Office for "scoring" to be sure that the offset we had identified would keep the amendment deficit neutral. The amendment was also taken to the Senate Parliamentarian to insure that it did not violate any budget rules.

CO-SPONSORS

Meanwhile, the task of finding co-sponsors began in earnest. In an effort similar to the one that had been made several weeks earlier to get the Appropriations Committee's approval, both the staff in Senator Kohl's office and the staff of the Council of the Great City Schools made phone calls to every Senate office with a demonstration project in their state—sixty-two offices in all—alerting them to the revised amendment. Copies of the amendment, along with explanatory language reassuring the senators that the offset would not cause any adverse effects to anyone participating in the Perkins Loan Cancellation program, were quickly faxed or hand delivered to every Senate office with a demonstration project in its state. In addition, each office was informed of the Department of Education's assistance in identifying an offset they could now live with. The support of the Republican administration helped convince a few Republican senators that they could now support this amendment.

As a courtesy, the co-sponsors of the initial Kohl dropout amendment, which had been introduced the day before, were approached first and asked to co-sponsor the new amendment. Senators Pell, Kennedy, McConnell, and Levin all readily signed on to the new amendment and were soon joined by Senator Wilson. Members may sign on as a co-sponsor for many different reasons, including their genuine support of the measure; the benefits the bill can give to constituents; as a favor to another member or an interest group; or for use in publicizing their record back home. Although the number of co-sponsors is important, it is often more crucial to see who has signed on—for example, the leadership, both Democrats as well as Republicans, both liberals and conservatives from each party, and relevant committee members. As the day progressed, the number of co-sponsors continued to grow as senators and their staff became informed of the issue.

ACCOMMODATING THE INTERESTS OF 100 SENATORS

Each party in the House and Senate has its own policy committee, under control of the party leadership. While "the policy committees provide advice on scheduling, encourage party unity, study substantive and political issues, and discuss broad questions of party policy," they "do not make policy."[13] The policy committees alert members of pending floor activity. Legislative bulletins often include a summary of legislation coming to the floor, including committee action, possible amendments and their sponsors, the pros and cons of each amendment, and the administration's position. The Cloakroom staff, working for the party leadership, assists in the scheduling of bills and amendments, and members and their staffs use the Cloakroom both to alert the leadership of pending amendments and to learn of the day's legislative schedule.

We kept the Democratic Cloakroom and Democratic Policy Committee alerted to our amendment, and an explanation of the amendment (along with a number of other amendments) had been distributed to all Democratic offices over the course of that week. The Democratic Policy Committee's legislative bulletin also listed a contact to reach in Senator Kohl's office for further information.

The party leadership thus provides a useful service for members by keeping them informed about upcoming votes, possible amendments, and the pros and cons of particular legislative proposals. In return, members keep the leadership informed about any amendment they plan to offer, whether the amendment will be noncontroversial and able to be dispensed with through a voice vote or will require a roll call vote, and even travel plans to assist in scheduling votes that may be particularly close.

The leadership also crafts the unanimous consent agreements that will let senators know which bills will be debated, at what point in time, and for how long a period of time. Unanimous consent agreements can be rather detailed, listing amendments that will be considered, as well as the length of time allotted for debate on a particular amendment. The leadership works to accommodate the interests of all members, which is essential for the Senate in order to bypass its rules and expedite the consideration of legislation.

As the day progressed, more and more senators began to leave for their home states. Following the schedule worked out by the party leadership, the expectation was that the entire dire emergency would be over by Thursday, or early Friday. However, as noted in Chapter 9, the floor debate on it would move from abortion funding in the District of Columbia to the death penalty. Senator Phil Gramm wanted the Senate to consider an amendment that would "set out concrete penalties and minimum mandatory sentences for murder related to a drug felony in the District of Columbia [and] . . . put into place the availability of the death penalty where the court determines that that penalty is warranted."[14]

Senator Hatfield was a strong opponent of the death penalty.[15] In addition, as ranking member on the Appropriations Committee, he was the Republican floor manager for the supplemental appropriations bill and was determined to do his part in getting the bill through the Senate. Thus, in a strategic move that was not expected but nonetheless acceptable, given the respect for the rights of individual members in the Senate, Senator Hatfield signaled to members that he was about to begin a filibuster—and had a huge notebook before him

> put out by the National Coalition to Abolish the Death Penalty, and it deals with substantive issues like arbitrariness, cost of execution, crime rate statistics, death qualification, deterrence, extraditions, general death penalty, innocence in death row, juveniles, and many other chapters.
>
> I will read quickly, but I do want the Senate to be fully aware that we are dealing with a very serious issue here, and I am going to make every effort to be certain the Senate does not adopt this amendment in the second degree.[16]

With this introduction, Senator Hatfield was about to embark on a filibuster as a means of forcing the senators to choose between passing a supplemental appropriations bill with the aid to Nicaragua and Panama which most supported, or prolonging and expanding debate to include some of the most divisive and emotional issues to come before the Senate—that is, abortion and the death penalty. An exchange developed between Senator Alan J. Dixon (D-Ill.) and Senator Hatfield:

Mr. Dixon.   Mr. President, will the Senator from Oregon yield for a question without yielding his right to the floor?[17]

Mr. Hatfield.   I am happy to yield.

Mr. Dixon.   This Senator and others had obligations tonight of some importance, but we are prepared to stay to do what is necessary. Is my friend from Oregon telling me that if I stay tonight, I am going to have the distinct pleasure of hearing the Senator from Oregon enlighten us about every line, every comma, every period in that particular looseleaf binder he has just referenced in his earlier remarks?

Mr. Hatfield. Mr. President, does the Senator suggest I should put this to a vote as to whether I should read this?

Mr. Dixon. Mr. President, I request my colleague only answer this Senator's question.

Mr. Hatfield. I am very happy to respond. I merely want to say I am prepared to debate this issue on its merits and at length. I am not in any way trying to set this amendment aside, or the committee amendment aside, or the death penalty issue aside for other business of the Senate. But, until whatever the leadership wishes to do is announced, I shall proceed to read.

Mr. President, chapter 1. And I will yield to the leadership at any moment the leadership wishes me to yield.

Mr. Dole. How about Monday?

Mr. Hatfield. "The arbitrariness."

Mr. Mitchell. Will the Senator yield?

Mr. Hatfield. Without losing my right to the floor.

Mr. Mitchell. We hope to be in a position to interject in just a few moments. In the meantime, I know we all look forward to hearing the Senator's dissertation.

The Presiding Officer. The Senator from Oregon.

Mr. Hatfield. Mr. President, in this whole matter of the death penalty, the argument is being used that it is a deterrent, and that is the main argument we constantly hear from the Judiciary Committee and all these other enthusiasts for the death penalty; that it is a deterrent. We impose the death penalty and that discourages crime. . . .[18]

With that the filibuster continued, only to be interrupted by pleas from the presiding officer that "the Senate . . . come to order. Those Members in the aisles will please take seats. Members conversing will please cease audible conversation or go to the cloakrooms."[19] The Senate as a collectivity was not happy. Plans were thrown into chaos as the uncertainty of the schedule of the remainder of the day continued.

During that afternoon, as the Hatfield filibuster proceeded, the leadership on both sides of the aisle struggled to come up with a unanimous consent agreement that would reduce the number of amendments from over sixty to fewer than ten. By the time Senator Mitchell came to the floor, the list had been pared to only eight amendments. Senators Dole and Mitchell were able to reach agreement among their respective members that the controversial matters of abortion and the death penalty be left to another debate.

Included in the eight amendments was Senator Kohl's dropout amendment and a possible second degree amendment to Kohl's amendment by Senator Wilson.[20] A look of surprise flashed across the staff faces watching the proceedings on C-SPAN in Senator Kohl's office. What was Senator Wilson up to now? A quick phone call to Wilson's staff revealed that this was an error; there would be no second degree amendment, and Wilson would indeed join in as a co-sponsor of the Kohl amendment. We were all reassured when shortly thereafter, on the floor of the Senate, Majority Leader Mitchell stated: "I have just been advised that my previous statement of a possible second-degree to the Kohl amendment will not occur. We were advised that was a possibility. Evidently, it will not now occur."[21]

With a unanimous consent agreement reached outlining the schedule of debate on amendments and votes for Monday, April 30, the rest of the session that Friday afternoon would be brief, with no controversial matters coming to the floor. Thus, members would be able to meet their obligations for Friday evening and the remainder of the weekend.

Several members came to the floor to discuss the amendments they had planned to offer, but as part of the leadership agreement to move debate on the passage of the supplemental along, they had agreed not to offer at this time. In brief speeches, they in effect outlined projects or concerns to themselves and constituents which they would again bring before the Senate at a later point in time. By so doing, especially under the watchful eyes of the C-SPAN camera, they were keeping their constituents back home informed of their Washington activity. By explaining how that activity benefits the state, they were building political support with the people back home. Explaining Washington activity is interrelated with what Fenno has identified as a member's "presentation of self," in which a member works to win the trust of constituents by letting them know he or she is aware of their needs, is working to solve their problems, and will be able to help them in the future.[22]

The two floor managers—Senator Byrd and Senator Hatfield—brought several additional amendments to the Senate floor. All were noncontroversial and had received clearances from both the Democratic and Republican leadership of the respective Appropriations subcommittee.

QUICK PASSAGE?

As we watched the progress of the bill, it became apparent that if the Kohl dropout amendment could be cleared on both sides of the aisle, it could be easily dispensed with that afternoon by the floor managers.

We would need the clearances of Senator Harkin, chair of the Subcommittee on Labor-HHS-Education; Senator Byrd, chair of the Appropriations Committee; Senator Specter, ranking Republican member on the Subcommittee on Labor-HHS-Education; and Senator Hatfield, ranking Republican member on the Appropriations Committee. Getting these clearances and quickly bringing the amendment to the floor was an approach Senator Kohl readily approved.

A division of responsibility was made, with Sherry Hayes on Senator Kohl's staff checking for clearance on the Democratic side and Karen Strickland on Senator Wilson's staff seeking the clearance on the Republican side. Meanwhile, I accompanied Amanda Broun and Ann Young to the floor of the Senate to await word from Sherry and Karen as to whether the respective senators with jurisdiction over this legislation had given the clearances. A call to Sherry revealed that Senator Harkin had given approval since we had identified an acceptable offset. Amanda, Ann, and I briefly talked with James English, Senator Byrd's staff director for the Appropriations Committee (and were even allowed to venture into the Cloakroom for a brief moment). We were assured that if we could get the clearances, Senator Byrd would permit the floor leaders to offer the Kohl amendment for quick approval by voice vote. If clearances from the other relevant senators were received, Senator Byrd would also give his approval.

The minutes went by quickly. The day's session was nearing an end, and we still did not have the necessary approvals. It appeared that the session would soon go into recess and this approach would fail. We awaited word from Sherry, and when she and Karen appeared outside the entrance to the Senate floor, it looked like we just might make it. However, while Harkin had given his go-ahead, the Republican side had not given its clearance. Since Senator Hatfield had indicated he would be a cosponsor, Karen had assumed that no phone call to his office was necessary.

As James English approached us and asked if the clearances had been received, we looked at each other and then had to say, "No." In all likelihood if we had said "Yes," Senator Byrd would have quickly brought the amendment to the floor for passage. But the norms of courtesy and reciprocity that operate in the Senate and the respect for Senator Byrd and the institution were overwhelming deterrents to such a rash action and deliberate lie. And in looking up to English (who was taller than any of us), one sensed that by virtue of his position and through his own work and style he commands a similar type of respect as that accorded his boss.

As I stood there, I recalled Donald Matthews's discussion of the longstanding Senate norm of reciprocity. According to Matthews, "a single senator could sneak almost any piece of legislation through the Chamber by acting when floor attendance is sparse and by taking advantage of the looseness of the chamber rules. . . . [However] If a senator *does* push his formal powers to the limit, he has broken the implicit bargain and can expect, not cooperation from his colleagues, but only retaliation in kind."[23]

Several years ago, a reporter described Byrd's "voluminous memory" that extends beyond just the Senate rules and parliamentary procedures: "He routinely recites poetry from memory during debate. Offering a revealing glimpse of his leisure time, Byrd said on the Senate floor last fall that, while he had never played golf, he had read all of Shakespeare's plays within the past year and the entire Old Testament during the August recess; he was in the middle of his second reading of the dictionary."[24] That memory would keep Senator Kohl and any other senator from pushing ahead without proper clearances. We never regretted our choice.

And so our hopes for quick passage came to an end as Senator Hatfield, the acting minority leader, and Majority Leader George Mitchell concluded the business of the Senate a little after 6 P.M. As the lights of the Senate chamber were turned down and we sat in the back of the chamber watching the two leaders leave the floor, I reflected on all that had happened that day and how close we had come to our legislative objective. Now we would have to wait until Monday, April 30, to try again.

SUCCESS IN THE SENATE

As a way of facilitating legislative activity on the floor of the Senate while accommodating to as great an extent as possible the individual needs of members, the leadership works out a unanimous consent agreement. Once the Democratic and Republican leadership have hammered out an agreement after extensive consultation with committee and subcommittee chairs, the agreement is offered in the form of a motion on the floor. There it is modified to accommodate interests that were overlooked. Once agreed to, the unanimous consent agreement will set forth the upcoming floor schedule, often listing the order of amendments, as well as the time allowed for debate, and the scheduled time for floor roll call votes. This helps the senators to plan their own day-to-day schedule, given the conflicting demands on members for their time.

According to the unanimous consent agreement reached Friday afternoon, consideration of the supplemental appropriations bill would resume at noon on Monday, April 30, with amendments to be offered by Senator John Danforth (R-Mo.) on court taxation, Tim Wirth (D-Colo.) and Don Riegle (R-Mich.) on S & Ls, Kent Conrad (D-N.D.) on drought disaster relief, Alan Dixon (D-Ill.) on the Air Force, and then Kohl on dropouts, to be followed with amendments by several other senators. In addition, approximate times were indicated for consideration of each of these amendments to give the senators an indication of when their amendment would be up (i.e., when they would need to be on the floor) and how long debate would last. In this schedule, the Kohl amendment was set for consideration at 5 P.M.

The effort to line up support continued throughout the day as information was hand-delivered, faxed, or communicated over the phone to Senate offices by constituents, interest groups, and the sponsors of the legislation. The Council of the Great City Schools went after the senators who had some of the largest school districts in the country as constituents. As soon as we had the support of one senator from a state, we gave a courtesy call to the office of the other senator of the state, reporting his or her colleague's co-sponsorship. By the time the Kohl amendment was brought to the floor, the support garnered for the amendment had become quite impressive. There were now twenty-one sponsors.[25] As Senator Kohl read the names of his colleagues who had joined him in sponsoring the amendment, a staff member sitting in the back of the chamber commented, "they seem to have enough support. . . . How many sponsors do they need?"

This time the dropout coalition was determined not to fail. Accordingly, sponsors were lined up right up until the moment Senator Kohl brought his amendment to the floor. Even then additional co-sponsors signed on.

After all the work of the last few months and the intensity of the effort in the past week, the final debate on the floor was rather anticlimactic. It lasted only minutes. Senator Kohl explained the purpose of the amendment, how the offset to pay for the program was derived, and also "express[ed] . . . appreciation to Senators McConnell, Wilson, Nickles, Kasten, Hatfield, Roth, and Heinz, who . . . joined in this truly bipartisan effort"; as well as the "staff on the Senate Labor Committee, particularly Amanda Broun and Ann Young, who have been very helpful in the development of this amendment."[26] In addition, Senator Kohl also thanked the respective chairs and ranking minority members of the Appropriations Committee and its Subcommittee on Labor-Health and Human Services-Education, Senators Byrd, Hatfield, Harkin, and Specter.

Senator Byrd, the floor manager for the Dire Emergency Supplemental Appropriations bill, indicated that

this amendment has been cleared on this side. I do not believe it will require a roll call vote. Senator Harkin, Chairman of the Labor-HHS-Education Subcommittee, supports the amendment, and has no objection to it. Senator Hatfield is here, and he will speak to the wishes of Mr. Specter, the ranking member.

The amendment does have an offset and it is deficit neutral. As Senator Kohl has explained, this amendment extends 1989 dropout demonstrations that now exist in 31 States and the District of Columbia. These demonstrations expire on August 31, 1990, and the amendment will extend them until September 30, 1991.

As the Dropout Demonstration Program receives no funding in fiscal year 1990, this amendment is necessary to extend these demonstrations for 1 year, when we expect the fiscal year 1991 funds will be available against which they can compete. The offset comes from surplus funds available from the teacher cancellation payment under the Perkins Loan Program.

I commend the distinguished Senator and his fellow cosponsors in offering the amendment on my side. I am prepared to accept the amendment, and hope that the Senate will adopt it.[27]

With Byrd's acceptance of the amendment, along with Hatfield's support, there was no question that the amendment would now be passed.

Republican senators Specter and Hatfield, both representing states with demonstration dropout projects, joined in as co-sponsors. Senator Hatfield even took to the floor of the Senate to express his support for the amendment and to describe the two dropout demonstration projects in Oregon. In talking about the program at West Valley Academy in Sheridan, Oregon, he described the "almost unbelievable phenomenal success in returning to the classroom and . . . graduating 482 out of 484 students over a 5-year period."[28] Senator Wilson also came to the floor to speak on behalf of the amendment. He mentioned that without continued funding California would "lose close to $2 million in dropout assistance in six separate school districts."[29]

During the brief debate, Senator Alan Simpson was added as a co-sponsor. He had heard from Native Americans in his state, a group that rarely called about such issues. By the end of the day, Senators Riegle (D-Mich.), Sasser (D-Tenn.), and Chafee (R-R.I.) had also joined in as co-sponsors.

The amendment was agreed to by voice vote so fast that I nearly missed the moment. On May 1 the Senate voted approval of the entire supplemental package.

Fenno has observed that "Members particularly like to be able to claim credit for bringing tangible benefits to their constituents, because it proves their concern for others as well as their effectiveness."[30] Credit claiming can take many different forms. For example, Senator Wilson sought to take the lead away from Senator Kohl by introducing his own amendment to the supplemental to fund the dropout program. A more frequently used method is for the member to co-sponsor legislation, and yet present his or her role as far more important than it really was—that is, signing on as a co-sponsor when there is little political risk, yet taking full credit for a role that suggests the member was a major player (see Box 10-1).

Box 10-1 Credit Claiming

"Is not a Patron, my Lord, one who looks with unconcern on a man struggling for life in the water, and when he has reached ground, encumbers him with help?"

Samuel Johnson

One of the unusual twists in the quest for funding the dropout program came from Senator Kasten's office. Senator Kasten, a Republican and the senior senator from Wisconsin, was a member of the Appropriations Committee and could have used his position on that committee to help secure funding. However, while Wisconsin constituents had been asking for help in funding this program for months, it was only in the final days that the senator joined Senator Kohl in co-sponsoring his amendment. And then Senator Kasten jumped on the bandwagon of support once the amendment had achieved the momentum that would assure its passage. He inserted a statement into the *Congressional Record* briefly mentioning the three Wisconsin programs and indicating his support for the program.

To add to this brief saga, I received a phone call the next morning from Senator Kasten's office in which I was informed that one of the Wisconsin projects had called *Kasten's* office to find out if the amendment had passed, and Kasten's office told them the good news. I thought it odd at the moment that the call had gone to Kasten's office instead of to Kohl's office where the work had been done on the amendment. However, I soon learned that, in fact, once the amendment was passed, Kasten's staff immediately called at least one of the Wisconsin demonstration projects to let them know the amendment had passed, thereby claiming credit for funding a program for which he had done little to help when that help was especially needed.

Given the national rhetoric on reducing the dropout rate, the lack of apparent opposition, and a good deal of support from colleagues, this was an amendment that would have few, if any, political costs. However, it could give a member who signed on as a co-sponsor a certain amount of political capital. And so what had once seemed a nearly impossible task, facing insurmountable odds, had become a foregone conclusion.

CHAPTER 11

A Conference with the House

At long last the amendment had passed in the Senate. The "easy" part was now done. The remaining obstacle—agreement by the House to go along with the Senate—loomed large on the horizon. This task would not be easy, even with a newfound confidence that this legislation just might become law.

Action quickly turned to the House side of the Hill. Now that the Senate had passed the Dire Emergency Supplemental Appropriations bill, a conference committee would be formed of members of the House and Senate appropriations committees in order to reconcile disagreements between the versions passed by the House and Senate.[1] The House version had only approved $2.4 billion in spending, whereas the Senate bill contained an additional billion for expenditures.[2] These differences would have to be resolved before the bills could be reported back to the House and Senate and passed again in identical form.

As Longley and Oleszek have noted, "congressional conference committees are the central element of bicameralism and conference politics the essence of bicameral politics."[3] The House and Senate would have to engage in a bargaining process that would test the resolve of each chamber to protect the interests of its respective members, and yet reach an agreement that would be supported by a majority in both chambers. With the House and the Senate controlled by the Democrats, partisan politics would not be as important a factor as in the case of split-party control of the House and Senate. However, the power of committee and subcommittee chairs would come into play, as would factional interests that had formed around particular items.

One difference between the House and Senate bills was the dropout program funding. The Senate had approved funding, but the House had not. Since it had been such a long shot that funding for the program would even be approved on the supplemental, thus far the energy of both constituents and lobbyists had been focused only on the Senate. Given "underlying . . . structural and functional characteristics that set it apart from the

134

House," the Senate had a reputation for allowing more add-ons. Thus, if there was to be any chance of success, it would probably begin on the Senate side.[4] Moreover, interest groups do not like approaching House members to support a cause with a high probability of failure. They would rather keep their political capital in reserve to draw on at a later time when the odds may be more favorable.

The key to securing the funding in the conference agreement would be to get the House to go along with the Senate language on the dropout program spending. An underlying assumption was that the Senate conferees would fight to keep the dropout spending in the final conference language. In this fight the support of Senator Harkin would be extremely useful. He was the chair of the relevant subcommittee, and the House and Senate subcommittee chairs, along with their staffs, were meeting privately to negotiate differences in their respective sections of the supplemental before the full conference committee met. Unfortunately, the dropout spending never won Senator Harkin's support, in spite of the efforts of his constituents from the Des Moines Public Schools. The approval for funding remained an uphill struggle.

STRENGTHENING THE SENATE'S BARGAINING POSITION

The dropout coalition quickly moved into action. There wasn't a moment to waste, since the conferees would soon be named, and the conference would begin immediately since the president had been urging Congress to move quickly on the foreign aid package to assist the new governments of Panama and Nicaragua.

While Senator Harkin was a key player in the conference committee (for the dropout spending came under his subcommittee's jurisdiction), even without his commitment to back this program in conference with the House, it had potential support in the conference meeting room. Six senators who had co-sponsored the amendment were named as conferees—Senators Hatfield, Hollings, Sasser, Kasten, Specter, and Nickles. Senator Kasten's staff had indicated he would "lead the fight" in the conference committee. In addition, a number of conferees—Senators Johnston (D-La.), Mikulski (D-Md.), Adams (D-Wash.), Fowler (D-Ga.), Garn (R-Utah), Cochran, (R-Miss.), D'Amato, (R-N.Y.), Grassley (R-Iowa), and Harkin (D-Iowa)—had not co-sponsored the amendment but had dropout prevention projects in their states. Therefore, they might be supportive.

Senator Kohl sent a letter to each of the twenty-four co-sponsors of the Kohl amendment thanking them for their support and explaining the current situation—that is, "the House passed bill does not contain any provision for the School Dropout Prevention Program."[5] At the same time, co-sponsors were asked to sign a letter in which the conferees were urged to keep the Senate provision funding the dropout program in the supplemental. Once signatures on this letter were obtained, the letter would be hand delivered to the four principal conferees—Senators Byrd and Hatfield, and Representatives Whitten (D-Miss.) and Conte (R-Mass.). In order to expedite this process, the office fax number of each of the twenty-four co-sponsors was obtained by a quick phone call to each office. (Congressional offices are hesitant to publicize these numbers for fear of the volume of material that might flood the office.) Since time was of the essence, drafts of the letter were faxed, while the original letters to each senator were printed and signed. As soon as the letters were ready for delivery, they were sorted by rooms within the three Senate office buildings—Hart, Dirksen, and Russell—for hand delivery that afternoon.

Meanwhile, the Council of the Great City Schools was in contact with its member schools, as well as schools with federally funded dropout prevention projects. They were urged to contact their respective senators and generate phone calls from constituents as needed in order to get their senators to sign on to the letter being circulated on the Hill by Senator Kohl's staff. This letter, which was to be sent to the respective chairs and ranking members of the appropriations committees, asked that the funding be kept for the dropout programs. (See Box 11-1.)

In addition to Senator Kohl, thirty-five senators agreed to sign the letter. Again, Mike McCarthy, the legislative correspondent in Senator Kohl's office, was given the task of physically obtaining the signatures from each of the thirty-five senators. Each senator had to sign four original copies of the letter—one to Senator Byrd, one to Senator Hatfield, one to Representative Whitten, and one to Representative Conte. Commitments were received from the thirty-five senators throughout the day, and so Mike would keep calling back to Senator Kohl's office as he made his way through the Russell and Dirksen Senate Office buildings to see if another signature could be gotten from a nearby office before he went to

---

Box 11-1   Letter Requesting Dropout Program Support

May 2, 1990

Dear _____:

We urge your support in the Emergency Supplemental Appropriations conference for the School Improvement Program language co-sponsored by Senators Kohl, Pell, Kennedy, McConnell, Wilson, Levin, Nickles, Shelby, Lieberman, Biden, Simon, Kasten, Dodd, Hollings, Roth, Hatfield, Specter, Boren, Ford, Heinz, Bentsen, Riegle, Sasser, Chafee, and Simpson. The provision would provide $19.45 million for the School Dropout Assistance projects now operating in 31 states. Without this supplemental appropriation, these projects will lose all federal funds this summer and be forced to close their doors.

The Nation's dropout rate is alarmingly high. Given the growing demands for a functionally literate workforce, this trend threatens to undermine the economic competitiveness of the United States. The School Dropout Assistance Program is the only federal program with the sole objective of reducing the Nation's dropout rate. The Department of Education has evaluations of these projects underway, and early reports indicate that the program is accomplishing its goals.

Earlier this year the Nation's Governors joined the President in declaring a reduction in the high school's dropout rate to be one of the Nation's top goals. Congress now has the responsibility and opportunity to continue funding for a program that is meeting this goal.

Please lend your support to this worthwhile provision.

Sincerely,

Claiborne Pell	Herb Kohl
John H. Chafee	Edward M. Kennedy
Wendell H. Ford	Joseph R. Biden
Carl Levin	Mitch McConnell
Christopher J. Dodd	Paul Simon
John Heinz	Donald W. Riegle
Jim Sasser	Pete Wilson
Alan K. Simpson	Don Nickles
David L. Boren	Joseph I. Lieberman
Lloyd Bentsen	William V. Roth
Richard C. Shelby	Wyche Fowler, Jr.
Howard M. Metzenbaum	Terry Sanford
Paul Sarbanes	John Glenn
Albert Gore	Alan Cranston
Brock Adams	Timothy E. Wirth
Alfonse M. D'Amato	Jeff Bingaman
Bob Graham	Howell T. Heflin
John F. Kerry	Daniel Patrick Moynihan

the next building. Mike did an outstanding job in getting the signatures and was even able to get the support of Senator Jeff Bingaman (D-N. Mex.). Although not one of the eighty-nine dropout prevention projects was located in New Mexico, Mike thought that perhaps Senator Bingaman would be interested in signing the letter since he had just been assigned to the Senate Labor and Human Resources Committee and its education subcommittee to fill the vacancy created by the death of Senator Spark M. Matsunaga (D-Hawaii), earlier in the year. This would give Bingaman an opportunity to join Senator Kennedy, the committee chair, and Senator Pell, the subcommittee chair, in their support for the program. After Bingaman's staff was filled in on the details of the legislation, he was soon added to the growing list of supporters. Again, efforts were made to insure that if one senator from a state had signed on, the office of the other senator would be promptly contacted in order to share that information. For example, as soon as Senator Pete Wilson had signed the letter, a call to Senator Alan Cranston's office was made, and in the end both California senators supported the initiative. Senator Kohl and his staff received a lot of thanks from senators whose states had projects for giving them a "head's up" on the amendment and also on the followup letter to the Appropriations Committee. Some offices appreciated receiving information on projects in their state that they had known little about.

While senators, staff, interest groups, and constituents conducted an intensive lobbying campaign on the Senate side, a totally different approach was used on the House side.

"THE COLLEGE OF CARDINALS"

With 435 members, the House is a large institution, and so the needs of individual members cannot be accommodated to the extent they are in the Senate, where, for example, a filibuster, or unlimited debate, is still allowed. Because of the large size of committees, power tends to become more centralized within the leadership of a House committee than within that of a Senate committee. In addition, most substantive legislation must come through the appropriate committee in the House. In the Senate, where less restrictive rules of procedure are in place, substantive issues may reach the floor via amendments, since nongermane amendments are allowed.[6]

The House Appropriations Committee is one of the most powerful committees in Congress because it controls spending. In the spring of 1990, the committee was headed by Jamie Whitten (D-Miss.), the dean of the House of Representatives, who has served since 1941, longer than any other member. Whitten has stated that no one can run a committee of fifty-nine; rather, "you have to lead a committee. . . . If you're right, temperate, you can influence the group."[7] With the budget ceilings capping spending limits, however, even the Appropriations Committee and its chair are confronted by external limits on what the committee can do. Yet Whitten worked through the "College of Cardinals"—a term used to refer to the thirteen subcommittee chairs in Appropriations with nearly absolute control over the flow of spending under their respective jurisdictions.

The term *College of Cardinals* has been applied because each chair can "operate somewhat autonomously within the full committee."[8] However, owing to their years of service on the same committee, their deference to each other, and the need to unite as a committee to withstand pressures from elsewhere in Congress, there is a special camaraderie among the "cardinals." For an illustration of the "Cardinals' " style of operation and the contrast between the approach of representatives and senators, Box 11-2 provides a brief excerpt of an exchange that occurred in the 1991 House-Senate conference committee to resolve differences in the Agriculture appropriations bill. (In 1992, due to ill health resulting from a stroke, Whitten turned over the day-to-day running of the Appropriations Committee to his friend Representative William Natcher. In December 1992, Natcher replaced Whitten as Chair of the Appropriations Committee, although Whitten continues to serve on the committee. Whitten also lost his role as chair of the Agriculture subcommittee.)

The chairs of the thirteen subcommittees are extremely powerful, and their power derives from several different sources. For one, the Appropriations Committee is large (with fifty-seven members in the One Hundred and First Congress). The work of the committee must be done in its subcommittees. The subcommittee chairs are also among the most senior members in the House. This is one of the most highly desired committees,

---

Box 11-2   The 1991 House-Senate Conference Committee: A Sample Exchange

Agriculture politics are the original politics of place. Unlike the defense bill, through which the Pentagon spreads vast projects such as building bombers to subcontractors in every state, the agriculture bill gains its momentum from many self-contained projects individual members promote.

Although such interests may appear parochial and almost trivial to outsiders, it is difficult to overestimate their importance in crafting the agriculture appropriations bill. Whitten has been known to bring powerful senators to their knees over a seemingly inconsequential attempt to earmark funds for a local project.

The tensest moment of this year's conference came when Sen. Bob Kasten, R.-Wis., who is facing a tough re-election bid, squared off against a united front of hostile House conferees. In the course of a 15-minute discussion, it became clear how much a project can mean to a politician and how much power the House chairman wields.

Kasten, a member of the Senate Appropriations Committee but not on the Agriculture Subcommittee, rushed in near the end of the conference to ask for $1.5 million for a rural health-care project to be run through the Medical College of Wisconsin in Milwaukee. It is a fine project, Kasten said; a needed project that was also supported by Rep. David R. Obey, a Wisconsin Democrat. Kasten was "hopeful" the conference committee would see fit to fund it.

Whitten waited for Kasten to finish before turning to Cochran and Burdick. "We cannot make exceptions," he said, explaining that he had made a rule that no hospital or medical school projects could be funded through the agriculture bill. "What excuse did they give for not taking it up with the proper subcommittee?" Whitten asked.

Kasten quickly volunteered. "We presented it to the Health and Human Services Subcommittee on our side and they said—" he began, but Rep. William H. Natcher, D-Ky., a wizened appropriator as canny as Whitten, interrupted. "This has never been presented to the House subcommittee," Natcher, chairman of the Labor-HHS panel, said in a slightly outraged tone.

Suddenly—out of thin air, it seemed—fellow appropriator Obey materialized at the conference table. "The senator has said that I am supportive of the project," he began. "I certainly want this to proceed, but not if it takes away from other items in the bill for Wisconsin and for the area I represent. I don't want it squeezing the biotech lab at the University of Wisconsin."

That lab, a $13 million project, has been in the works for four years, Obey said, and he hoped to finish it this year. Kasten pleaded: "It's $1.5 million. It doesn't seem to me we are asking for too much."

There was a cold silence from the House side. No Senators came to Kasten's aid.

Burdick, ceding to Whitten, ended the discussion abruptly. "Next issue," he said, leaving Kasten with not a penny.

From: Alissa J. Rubin, " 'Permanent Secretary.' " in *Congressional Quarterly Special Report*, "Where the Money Goes," December 7, 1991, p. 33. Reprinted by permission.

and vacant seats will often go to members who are willing to move from another committee assignment to one of the coveted seats on Appropriations.[9] Once members are on the committee, they stay on, especially given the size of the committee and the fact that it may take many years of service on the committee before a subcommittee chair position opens up. The individual power base of each of the thirteen subcommittee chairs is so great that in 1974, when the Democratic Caucus initiated a series of reforms that contributed to greater decentralization and dispersal of power in the House, included in the reforms was the requirement that all thirteen subcommittee chairs of the Appropriations Committee be elected by the Democratic Caucus. Of over 100 subcommittee chairs, these are the only ones subject to this rule.[10] The average seniority of the thirteen subcommittee chairs was over twenty-three years in 1990. In addition, owing to the long-time service on this committee and on a particular subcommittee, each subcommittee chair has developed an expertise due to specialization in the work of that subcommittee. The full committee tends to defer to the work and recommendations of its subcommittees (as is true for most committees in Congress[11]). Finally, by virtue of its control over the federal purse strings, the agenda of the Appropriations Committee makes it both a desirable and a powerful committee.

The work of several members on the House Appropriations Committee, assisted by colleagues on the House Education and Labor Committee, led to the overall acceptance by the House conferees of the Senate language.

One of several members of the House who was particularly concerned over the threatened loss of funding was Representative Carl C. (Chris) Perkins. Perkins, a Democrat, inherited his seat from his father, the highly respected Carl Perkins, who represented the Seventh District of Kentucky from 1948 until his death in 1984. The senior Perkins was chair of the House Education and Labor Committee for seventeen years, and his son followed him on to that committee.[12] One of the eighty-nine federal drop-out prevention programs was located in the Seventh District. This district, located in the Appalachians in the eastern part of Kentucky, has been described as "one of the poorest parts of the nation since it was first settled" in the 1700s.[13]

Threatened with the loss of federal funding to his economically depressed district, Representative Perkins approached fellow Kentuckian William H. Natcher for assistance. Natcher, elected in 1953 and ranked second in seniority on the Appropriations Committee behind Chair Jamie Whitten of Mississippi, was chair of the Appropriations Subcommittee on Labor-HHS-Education. He has been described as "one of the House's most hard-working and conscientious members. . . . He is one of a kind—

one of the men and women who makes the House work, and work much better than its detractors think. He is above all meticulous and attentive to detail, . . . he is appalled by anything that smacks of corruption." And unlike some members, he "resists relying on staff; he does his own reading and research and prides himself on being well prepared."[14] Natcher also objects to earmarking funds for special projects. This would prove to be a stumbling block in the effort to continue funding for existing projects.

Everyone was vividly aware that Natcher's support would be essential when the House conferees met with the Senate conferees. Perkins carefully explained to Natcher that the Senate bill had included funding that would allow the dropout prevention program to continue and that he had a project in his district which would be able to continue for one more year. As the dropout network began to call their representatives on the House side and Perkins began to receive calls from constituents, he went back to Natcher to reinforce the concern among his constituents that the program be continued.

Perkins probably had a better chance than most junior members (he was only first elected in 1984) to make a case for funding the program with Natcher. Not only was he a fellow Kentuckian, but more importantly, his father had had a close relationship with Chairman Natcher. The two senior Kentuckians had worked as colleagues in the House for years, especially on education policy, with Perkins chairing the authorizing committee and Natcher chairing the education appropriations subcommittee.[15] Although Natcher indicated he would try to help, it was not clear whether he had made a commitment to help continue the funding for the *existing* projects.

Over the course of the next few days, a number of representatives with funded projects in their districts approached Natcher, including Sidney Yates (D-Ill.), Butler Derrick, (D-S.C.), Neal Smith, (D-Iowa), Charles Hayes (D-Ill.), J. J. (Jake) Pickle (D-Tex.), and Augustus Hawkins (D-Calif.). Several of these representatives were Natcher's colleagues on the Appropriations Committee, including Smith and Yates. All would work to sensitize Natcher to the issue by concentrating on what impact losing the program would have in their respective congressional districts. Natcher appeared to have made a general commitment of support in that he would see what he could do, but no one felt that he had made an absolute commitment to continue the funding for the dropout program.

Jeff Simering, who has worked with members of Congress in the area of education policy for a number of years, noted that "With Representative Natcher you don't necessarily get a direct commitment, but you get a sense of what he's willing to do, and if he is anything, he is a man of his word. You get a commitment—if he says he's willing to help, he's going to help. He'll do everything he can. If he says he's going to do it he's damned sure going to do it."[16]

After a few days several members seemed to feel that Natcher supported funding for the program. Owing to his distaste for earmarking (i.e., targeting funds for specific projects), however, they thought he would not agree to language that would continue existing projects. Rather, he would probably allow language to set up a new round of competition among school districts for demonstration dropout grants.

Even when a program has support, endless obstacles may exist and derail efforts to build a supportive coalition. The continuation of demonstration projects may be particularly vulnerable since many members do not have a project in their district and therefore will find little incentive to support the program. Others, such as Natcher, may object on principle to earmarking funds for specific projects. The crafting of any legislative proposal is a difficult and time-consuming process, and regardless of the final language, some aspect or other will generate opposition. The fact that Natcher would agree to any continued funding led Simering to observe at the time that "Well, we're at least halfway there."[17]

Whereas on the Senate side the staff played an important role in lining up support needed to get the Kohl amendment passed, on the House side the members did their own lobbying to win Natcher's support. The system harkened back to the days before the staff explosion and increased complexity of workload lessened the members' direct involvement in the legislative process.

Representative Dale E. Kildee (D-Mich.) in a private conversation with Natcher on the floor of the House during debate on another matter, finally asked him whether he would support the dropout prevention funding passed by the Senate. Natcher replied, "Yes." Kildee went one step further, asking, "Does that mean you are going to support continued funding for existing grants?" Natcher again replied, "Yes." At that point, the commitment was finally made, and with Natcher a man of his word, the House would probably agree to keep the language passed by the Senate.[18]

Even though the fate of the language was now in the hands of the actual House and Senate conferees, the work of the dropout coalition was not yet finished. However, any grass-roots effort to generate support in the House as was done on the Senate side was quickly abandoned once Natcher made the commitment. With his word pledged, nothing else was needed. A "Dear Colleague" letter that was circulating among House offices and that had already gotten a number of signatures was pulled when it became clear that this action might work at cross purposes. If the petition had continued to circulate, it would have implied that Natcher could not be trusted to keep his word. According to Simering, "You don't deal with the Cardinals from the grass roots."[19]

As the conference drew near, those friends and colleagues who had approached Natcher personally for his support followed up these conversations with personal letters of thanks once the commitment had been made. While the letters were used to reinforce the commitment, they were also part of the norms and folkways of the House which expected members to treat each other with courtesy and respect. However, as the week of the conference neared, some uncertainty still remained.

For one thing, before the conference with all the House and Senate conferees met, a mini-conference of the chairs and ranking members and top staff of each subcommittee would meet to go over differences in their section of the supplemental bill. Among these conferees would be Representatives Natcher and Conte and Senators Harkin and Specter. While Specter and his staff had been supportive all along, Harkin's staff aide had never been, and Natcher had just indicated his commitment days before. For his part, Conte, who did not have a project in his district, was now pushing for continued funding of the program but with a new round of competition. With new competition, schools in his district would be eligible to compete for those funds.

Conte maintained that the Department of Education would be able to run a new competition for grants within a 90-day period. As soon as the coalition of lobbyists and Senate congressional staff members learned of this new obstacle, they quickly obtained a copy of the Department of Education's assessment of provisions in the supplemental, including the Senate dropout funding amendment. Upon closer reading of the assessment, it became clear that the awarding of grants within approximately a three-month period was based on the assumption the grants would be going to *existing* grantees.[20] Otherwise, a new round of competition would take approximately six months, after the next academic year was well under way. Thus, any awards would not be able to be used in the 1990–91 academic school year. Efforts were made to contact the key conferees who would be meeting with Conte to be sure they understood that the three-month timetable applied only if existing projects were continued.

But Representative Conte had been unhappy with much of the Senate's action from the very beginning. On May 3, 1990, when the House conferees were named, he offered a motion to instruct the conferees to "(1) agree to those Senate amendments that respond to budget requests and reestimates of cost submitted by the President . . . and (2) . . . insist upon its disagreement to all Senate amendments that provide funding for programs, projects or activities which are not dire emergencies."[21] Conte explained to his colleagues:

. . . my motion to instruct the conferees on the supplemental appropriations bill is simple. It directs the conferees to agree to Senate amendments on food stamps, veterans, and census, sums that were recently requested by the President, but it directs our conferees to strip from the bill all Senate amendments which are not dire emergencies. It will be like shooting fish in a rain barrel.

Mr. Speaker, the Senate, in its unmatchable wisdom, added 180 amendments to the House-passed bill. They had a ball. They spent the better part of 5 days on the floor, and they added some real beauties.

Listen to these so-called dire emergencies:

One Samoan ferry boat.

Further design of the Franklin Delano Roosevelt Memorial.

Capitol Police protection for 467 Senate parking spaces in the Union Station garage, spaces which cost $135 each per month, for a total cost of $756,000 per year.

Paying Senate consultants at a rate of $95,715 per year. That's Senate consultants, mind you.

A procurement for the Stuttgart, AR Fish Farm Laboratory.

Recycling New Jersey's batteries.

. . . .

The $185 million for moving the FBI's fingerprint facility to that hotbed of crime, West Virginia. And talk about a smoking gun—$238 million for an ammunition plant in Louisiana.

Mr. Speaker, while we have kept our nose to the grindstone over here, the Senate had theirs in the cookie jar; or in the catnip.

Mr. Speaker, it is time to clean up the Senate's excesses. Vote for my motion to instruct conferees to do just that.[22]

The motion passed by a vote of 388 to 8.[23]

While the House voted to instruct its conferees to reject these Senate add-ons, this motion would not be binding on the conferees. Rather, "this places additional political and moral pressure on the conferees and normally hardens their position in conference committee bargaining."[24] However, the full House would need to approve the conference agreement, and Senate conferees would be well aware of the need for final approval in the House.

The concern remained: would Natcher agree with Conte, and the interests of the House, and refuse to allow the Senate add-on regarding the school dropout program? Natcher would be torn between protecting the interests of the House and his position as a negotiator vis-à-vis the Senate in future conferences, and the promise of support to several of his colleagues since this program could be viewed as a "dire emergency."

To help insure Natcher's understanding of the two separate issues—continued funding of the program and of the existing projects—the chair of the authorizing committee (House Committee on Education and Labor), Augustus Hawkins, sent a carefully worded letter to Natcher. Hawkins expressed his appreciation of Natcher's "sensitivity to respecting the rights of the authorizing Committee in considering amendments to that bill adopted by the Senate," by consulting with him on the matter. He added: "After discussing with you the Senate amendment to fund the school dropout program, I checked the law and consulted with my counsel. I can tell you on behalf of the authorizing committee that the law is silent as regards the third year of funding. Therefore, I see no impediment in the law to continuing a grant for a third year."[25]

In other words Hawkins would approve of adding authorizing language in this case to the appropriations bill, in order to continue the funding of this program. He was putting his full weight as chair of the House Committee on Education and Labor behind the Senate amendment and the continuation of funding for existing projects. He wrote: "Now that the Congress has finally enacted an extension of the national program, and the Senate has provided funding for it, we have an opportunity to continue a Federal effort to prevent school dropouts. I am very pleased that you are willing to consider the Senate amendment in order to fund that effort."[26]

Without language allowing the continuation of existing programs, no federal dropout program would be in place in 1990–91, even though both Congress and the president had agreed to the authorization of the program for 1990–91. Given the lag time the Department of Education needed to set up a grants competition, by the time the department announced a new competition for funds, reviewed grant applications, and awarded grants to school districts, the 1990–91 academic year would be well under way. Therefore, the language that continued existing programs had to be kept intact. The Council of the Great City Schools, representing a number of school districts with dropout programs, again worked to make constituents aware of the potential loss of this valuable program, contacting member schools as well as non-member schools that had projects. For example, the West Valley Academy in Oregon organized its administrators, teachers, parents, and even students to call in to congressional offices.

As constituents contacted their representatives about the Kohl amendment, Senator Kohl's office began to receive a lot of phone calls from the House side asking for more information on the program and the amendment. Copies of the amendment, along with explanatory material on the offset, were faxed from one side of Capitol Hill to the other. One of the most frequent questions asked was, "Is there a project in my district?" While we had a list of projects by state and cities, we did not have a breakdown by congressional district. Therefore, we did the best we could to relay information as to the schools involved and the size of federal grant received, as well as to provide a name and phone number of the project director. The calls continued right up to the beginning of the conference.

THE CONFERENCE BEGINS—OR DOES IT?

The conference convened on May 9. However, the House's displeasure with the Senate additions to the bill was clear. As reported in *Congressional Quarterly,* Whitten told his Senate counterparts: " 'I realize your rules are somewhat different, if you have any rules—sometimes I wonder.' " Whitten then went on to say that "his staff needed more time to study the Senate's amendments."[27] Observers of the situation who were "familiar with his approach agreed [that] he was jerking the Senate's chain."[28] As one House Republican member noted, Whitten is "angry 'that they got so much and he got so little, . . . He said, 'We got taken.' "[29]

Whitten had done what he could to move the bill quickly through the House, and the House had approved it on April 3. "Bowing to pressure from House leaders, Whitten—who has long believed that every emergency is an opportunity—uncharacteristically rejected many members' attempts to pile on projects."[30] Characteristically, the Senate was not so restrained in adding projects and programs, and did not complete its work on the bill until May 1.

On May 9, at the conference meeting, the senators tried to find out when Whitten would be ready and willing to begin work on an agreement. Senator Mark Hatfield observed: " 'The House staff followed the process of the Senate bill, . . . I would only like to ask . . . how much time the House feels would be required to reacquaint itself with these amendments.' "[31]

Whitten would not budge, at least not on this day. He did state that "he would reassess the situation on May 14. 'I don't know that we need to meet . . . we have no desire or purpose in delaying.' "[32] Byrd tried to get Whitten to move forward and asked whether he should " 'expect a call? . . . I would be happy to come by your office.' "[33] And so the meeting adjourned, with Whitten and his House conferees making a point with the Senate but accomplishing little else.

It thus appeared that the conference might begin on Monday, May 14, following this preliminary meeting of the week before. However, on May 14, the conference was postponed until the next day. A call to the staff of the Senate Appropriations Committee revealed that "no meeting would take place today, and none is scheduled!" Given the urgent need to respond to the president's request for aid to Nicaragua and Panama, along with the other "dire emergencies" included in the spending package, I found this behavior rather odd.

It soon became clear, however, that the House Appropriations Committee remained upset with the bill passed by the Senate. The Senate had added on several projects—for example, the FBI fingerprint identification facility to be built in West Virginia at Senator Byrd's request and $238 million for a new ammunition plant to be built in Louisiana, as requested by Senator J. Bennett Johnston (D-La.)—while killing a $90 million appropriation for ammunition produced at a plant in Mississippi (the home state of Chairman Whitten).[34]

The House Appropriations Committee's bad mood was reinforced when it was reported that Chairman Whitten had instructed the committee's staff not to talk to the Senate Appropriations Committee staff. A Senate staff member reported that the staff from the two sides of the Hill bypassed this directive by using the following approach: "We're not speaking, but if we were . . . here's what we would want to discuss."

As Fox and Hammond have observed, "activist or entrepreneurial staff are often the norm on Capitol Hill."[35] Staff members had vested a good deal of their energy in getting to this point and, therefore, would do what they could to keep the negotiations moving forward. They were aware that the political battle between the House and Senate could be worked out and that symbolic differences were more important than substantive disagreements. Moreover, staff aides often serve as "negotiators," by meeting before the conference begins to discuss the agenda, "set meeting times and places, [and] prepare working documents."[36] They may even be called on to work through disagreements.[37]

Finally, on Wednesday, May 16, the conference committee met in a room on the Senate side of the Capitol. Only staff working for members of the Appropriations Committee were allowed in the room. Other staff had to remain outside the door, barely able to hear what was being said inside. Lobbyists were at first allowed to wait in the lobby outside the conference meeting room and were soon ushered down the hall and around the corner to the Senate Reception Room.

While waiting outside the conference room, I briefly gained access to one of two copies of the supplemental Whitten had brought to the conference. In this version, the funding for the dropout programs was continued but required a new round of competition for the grants. It also contained some changes in the Senate language which suggested that the House was demonstrating its disapproval of the Senate's addition of so many programs to fund by cutting programs or adding restrictive language to them. However, as the conference got under way, it was clear that a second version was in use. In this version, the House "receded and concurred with the Senate in Amendment No. 101," which provided continued funding for the school dropout demonstration programs. After all the efforts leading up to this moment, resolution came very quickly, with no discussion. Just a few brief words conveyed the information that the House would go along with the Senate.

Many of the areas of disagreement on other issues were worked out by staff and members before the official conference meeting and thus were quickly dispensed with at the conference meeting. The process speeded up as the House conferees added another $100 million to the spending bill to meet the needs of their constituents. Among other items, it included flood-relief money for southeastern states and $5 million for communities with a large number of Cuban and Haitian refugees, which would benefit Miami, represented by Appropriations Committee member William Lehman.[38]

Bettilou Taylor of Senator Specter's staff was allowed in the conference room and would be present when the staff put the final language of the House-Senate agreement into a new bill and conference report. She added a sentence to fully express the Congress's intent that the existing projects should be assured continued funding for the 1990–91 academic year. Since the funding had not been requested in the president's fiscal year 1991 budget, concern was voiced that an effort might be made to delay spending in the area. The conference report read as follows: "The agreement provides the full $19,945,000 for dropout demonstration grants as proposed by the Senate and provides that these funds shall be allocated by the Secretary as continuation awards to grantees funded in 1989. The conferees expect these funds to be awarded by September 1, 1990."[39]

Negotiations on other parts of the appropriations bill continued, and it was unclear whether both the House and Senate could reach agreement before the Memorial Day recess scheduled to begin May 25.[40]

FINAL PASSAGE

The bill was finally sent to the floor of the House on May 24 and approved by a vote of 308–108, but not before conservative Republicans launched a battle to delete some of the "home-state favors inserted by influential members."[41] However, any change in the conference agreement reached with the Senate had the potential of derailing the entire agreement, and so the leadership worked to block any attempts to modify the agreement.

One of my most satisfying moments had come earlier that day when Jamie Whitten, in introducing the bill as the debate on the floor began, included "dropouts" in his listing of "dire emergencies" included in his spending bill.

Later that evening, after the action was completed in the House, the bill came over to the Senate where it was nearly derailed by the actions of Senators Sam Nunn (D-Ga.) and Kent Conrad (D-N.D.). Senator Nunn had concerns over planned personnel cuts in the armed forces that were the result of cuts in defense spending made the previous year in order to meet Gramm-Rudman-Hollings deficit requirements. Nunn agreed to postpone consideration of the matter to a later date, after Secretary of Defense Dick Cheney agreed to delay the cuts a few weeks to give more time for an agreement to be worked out.[42]

Senator Conrad, trying to add an amendment to help the drought-stricken farmers in his home state of North Dakota, presented a more serious problem. It was nearing midnight and few senators were still in their offices to vote. Also, an addition of this sort would force the bill to be sent back to the House, whose members had already departed for the Memorial Day weekend recess. Senate Byrd patiently explained in a frustrated tone that

> If we are going to have amendments called up to an appropriations bill and the amendments are defeated, and then the conference report comes back to the body with amendments in disagreement and those same amendments are offered again—the process has been very slow already— if we are going to start doing that, there will be other Senators who will want to offer their amendment, which had been offered and not agreed to, feeling that this is an opportunity in which somehow or other a miracle will work, and I just have to oppose the amendment.[43]

If Conrad ever hoped to get appropriations for his constituents in North Dakota, he would need Byrd's support, or at minimum, no opposition from Byrd. To thwart the will of both the Senate and the House, and especially the leadership and chair of the Appropriations Committee, could cost Conrad the goodwill and support of other members he would need at a later date. Upon the not so gentle urging of colleagues, including Senator Byrd and the Democratic leadership, Conrad was persuaded to give up on a roll call vote. A standing vote was requested, and his amendment was defeated shortly after midnight.[44] In a few brief moments, the Senate passed the Conference Report with a voice vote.[45]

Since President Bush was already at his family home in Kennebunkport for the Memorial Day weekend, the bill was flown up to Maine for his signature.[46] And so, on May 25, 1990, the continued funding for the school dropout prevention program was at last signed into law.[47]

AFTERMATH: CREDIT CLAIMING

Although most lawmakers readily take credit for work they have done, especially when it helps their constituents, as Fenno has observed, not all members care as much about credit claiming as we would expect. Perhaps credit claiming comes later in a member's career, especially as they gain more legislative experience and confidence. Both members and staff may find that constituents' judgments center on how well the job of "effective legislator" is being done.[48] As noted earlier, Senator Herb Kohl had just been elected in 1988 and had never held elective office earlier. When the funding became law, his office did not even send out a press release to that effect, despite the senator's major role in getting approval for the funding. The office decided against issuing a press release because in February of that year, a press release had been issued explaining the Senate's reauthorization of funding. Perhaps that announcement had been a bit premature since without appropriations the authorization really would do nothing to keep the program running.

However, in March 1991 Senator Kohl was recognized for his work on the bill. He received an award from the Council of the Great City Schools at a reception on the Hill attended by many representatives of the schools receiving the federal funds. Clearly, they knew of the work of the junior senator from Wisconsin.

CHAPTER 12

Conclusion

Congress in the 1990s may not be the exact institution the framers of the Constitution had envisioned, but in many ways it adheres to their original conception. Over the years it has been a remarkably adaptive institution, accommodating the interests of political parties and groups while at the same time dealing with a pervasive media presence.

A COMPLEX INSTITUTION

The United States Congress has always been a complex institution; it is at once collegial, responsive, representative, with both decentralized and centralized power, and with its own set of rules, both formal and informal. It shares policymaking power with the president, and this shared power both strengthens support for policy initiatives (as in 1991 when the president asked Congress for authorization to use force in the Persian Gulf) and frustrates policy initiatives (as reflected in President Bush's vetoes of a number of congressional initiatives that Congress was not able to override).

As we saw in Chapter 3, the effort to create a federal program that would address the needs of school dropouts quickly became entangled in several other legislative proposals, including the massive omnibus education and trade bills. In addition, at various points in time the language of the dropout legislation, in particular the reference to counseling services for pregnant minors, became linked to the abortion debate.

The same scenario applied to the struggle to obtain continued funding for the program. The search for $20 million to continue funding was of extreme urgency to hundreds of students and school administrators but only a minor issue on the congressional agenda. In fact, the only press attention it received was in hometown newspapers that made use of press releases from senators after the amendment was passed. That spring the dropout issue was subsumed by a host of other matters before the Congress.

This situation is typical of much of the work of Congress: it is done with little, if any, notice by the press. The American public, though now given a seat in the House and Senate chambers through C-SPAN's gavel-to-gavel coverage, does not have access to most hearings held by committees and subcommittees throughout the Hill, or to the many meetings members hold with their staffs, constituents, interest group lobbyists, and executive branch personnel. While the issue of continued funding for the dropout program consumed many hours of work on the part of senators and their staffs, the actual floor debate, the congressional activity most accessible to the public, lasted only a few minutes, unnoticed by most. In addition, larger bills involving billions of dollars and affecting many Americans, often determine the fate of smaller provisions attached to them. Unrelated but very controversial items (e.g., abortion) can also have an impact on legislative outcomes.

The story of the school dropout program, from the struggle to create the program to the subsequent efforts to keep the program running, is a story that could be told about any number of programs that Congress has considered. The cast of characters may differ, but the basic parameters remain the same. In any Congress, many more legislative proposals will be introduced than will be passed. In the One Hundredth Congress, S. 320, the School Dropout Demonstration Assistance Act, was but one of 3325 bills introduced.[1] Only 1002 bills, or 30 percent of all bills introduced, passed that year. (In the House of Representatives, 6263 bills were introduced in that same Congress, with only 1061, or 17 percent passing.)[2]

A RESPONSIVE INSTITUTION

Congress may appear to be slow in responding, but it is nonetheless a responsive institution. The response often comes after consensus has been reached. This is another aspect of Congress that has endured for over 200 years. The inherent tension created in a system of separation of powers with a bicameral legislature was designed to guarantee that the national government's actions would be deliberative and well thought out. The dropout issue had been on the congressional agenda since at least the Ninety-eighth Congress. Over the course of several years, the issue began to capture the attention of many members of Congress, including key subcommittee and committee chairs. This new interest paralleled a growing public realization that the dropout problem was serious, having long-term economic consequences for the United States, and therefore a matter demanding national attention.

Not all issues on the congressional agenda will be redefined as the dropout program was when it became part of the Omnibus Trade and Competitiveness Act of 1988. However, "the recent practice of relying on megabills to process much of Congress's annual workload is a product in large measure of legislative-executive, House-Senate conflict."[3] This is especially true in the case of split-party control of the White House and Congress that dominated much of the last twenty years. These omnibus bills give Congress a weapon to wield in the face of presidential veto threats. In fact, the program was originally authorized through a continuing resolution, a technique used when appropriations bills have not been passed in time for the start of the new fiscal year.[4] In this case, the continuing resolution did not continue funding for the program. Rather, it authorized spending for the program as well as providing funds, since the authorizing language was still caught up in conference.

Congress remains a bicameral institution. Before being sent to the president for signature, any legislation must receive the approval of both houses in the same form in the same Congress.[5] However, originally the Senate was intended to be the more "stable institution," given its longer term of service (six years) than that of the House (two years) which would be constantly held sway to the fleeting whims of the masses.[6] The senators' longer terms would theoretically guard against decisions based on the wild swings in public opinion. On the other hand, James Madison, in describing the House of Representatives, wrote: "As it is essential to liberty that the government in general should have a common interest with the people, so it is particularly essential that the branch of it under consideration should have an immediate dependence on, and an intimate sympathy with, the people."[7]

Yet both the House and the Senate are driven by the demands of their constituents, as Senator Conrad's actions so clearly demonstrated. In the last twenty-five years, incumbents in the House have actually been more successful in retaining their seats then Senate incumbents, thereby providing more of the continuity originally intended of the Senate as expressed by John Jay:

> It was wise, therefore, in the convention to provide, not only that the power of making treaties should be committed to able and honest men, but also that they should continue in place a sufficient time to become perfectly acquainted with our national concerns, and to form and introduce a system for the management of them. The duration prescribed is such as will give them an opportunity of greatly extending their political information, and of rendering their accumulating experience more and more beneficial to their country. Nor has the convention discovered less prudence in providing for the frequent elections of senators in such a way as to obviate the inconvenience of periodically transferring those great

affairs entirely to new men; for by leaving a considerable residue of the old ones in place, uniformity and order, as well as a constant succession of official information, will be preserved.[8]

In the case of the dropout funding, the House and Senate used different strategies. The differences may actually reflect the nature of the difference between the two chambers. One factor that influences the strategy is the composition of each chamber and the nature of the membership. As stated above, in recent years incumbents have generally done better in the House than in the Senate. And so with the "Cardinals" in control of the House Appropriations Committee, the strategy used to secure the dropout funding was based on an understanding of the norms of that institution. Rather than attempt a grass-roots pressure approach, the senior members worked to get the support of fellow members, outside of public view.

In both the House and the Senate, however, incumbency rather than party affiliation has proven critical to electoral success. Recent studies have shown that voters are more likely to defect to incumbents than vote for a member of their own party.[9] When voting, people need information, and if people know nothing about a candidate, then they will be inclined to vote for the other candidate. Name recognition leads to votes. Senate challengers tend to be better known than House challengers, and so a Senate incumbent's political advantages of name recognition are lessened.[10]

In the House, seats are usually challenged by an unknown who spends little money on the campaign. This is typically not the case in Senate races.[11] This situation reflects the different nature of congressional districts from statewide races. States are usually

> more heterogeneous in their economic and social structure and therefore more likely to contain opposing groups which constitute the base for challenges. Partly as a result of this diversity, Senate challengers are better able to raise the large sums of money necessary to mount a serious campaign; they also attract a good deal of attention from the press, giving them much more free media time than is available to House challengers. In addition, the prestige of the Senate—and the six year term—attracts a higher caliber of candidate, including a number of House members who have already achieved a substantial public following.[12]

As a result, vulnerable senators may need to be more in tune with district concerns than is the case for deeply ensconced representatives. Overall, in terms of the House and Senate membership, and especially given the staying power of House incumbents, the result is:

> something of a self-fulfilling prophecy here. House incumbents are increasingly strong at the polls because potentially strong opponents, per-

ceiving that strength, do not run, thus ensuring a wide margin of victory. In the Senate, the pattern is just the reverse. The recent success of many challengers in defeating incumbents or at least in reducing their margins of victory has made all senators appear potentially vulnerable, which in turn has encouraged more vigorous opposition, making the appearance a reality.[13]

As we have seen, in the House the "Cardinals," the long-time members of the Appropriations Committee, controlled the fate of the funding for the school dropout projects and operated in a style reminiscent of the House of thirty years ago. In contrast, in the Senate, a grass-roots lobbying campaign throughout the country, coupled with leadership from one of the most junior members of the Senate, resulted in success.

SUCCESS OF THE DROPOUT FUNDING EFFORT

In looking back at the effort to continue the funding for the dropout program, I asked Jeff Simering to reflect on why this effort succeeded when so many factors were working against it. Simering replied as follows:

This was a very targeted grass roots effort and very limited in scope . . . it did work effectively. . . . It was not a case of . . . just calling an office, not knowing who to talk with, not knowing what to tell them, not knowing what the status of the thing was.

There was a lot of orchestration to the key calls, as well as people like Maureen Coffey and Jan Davidson getting on the phone to everybody that had a grant, as well as Mike Casserly's staff assistant Isabel Salinas calling them, and just telling them to call in and raise hell and get five, at least five more people to call in and raise hell from your areas.

A lot of them could tell the staff person what they were doing with the money and why it was doing some good things for dropouts. . . . I heard some real neat stories in talking with some of these project directors. I was impressed.[14]

The success of our effort was the result of many factors: these were good projects, they were in key districts, it was an election year and perhaps members would be more responsive to constituent needs, the public was involved, people working in the dropout coalition were knowledgeable (or quickly learned what was needed), and all had credibility. As Simering observed, "Individuals on the Hill operate in good faith, and as human beings. That doesn't necessarily happen in the business world. Credibility is a cornerstone of power—i.e., the credibility of Members, their staffs, and lobbyists."[15]

John Fiegel, the program administrator, observed that "if people are willing to take a stand, things can happen. Those who participated knew the system can work, and it did."[16]

Throughout the attempt to secure the funding, the lobbyists and congressional staffs involved repeatedly assured both representatives and senators that this was not an effort to continue the same demonstration projects year after year. Rather, the effort was made to ensure that a federal commitment to reducing the dropout rate would continue. The only means available at this point in time was to extend two-year projects for a third year, which would allow evaluations to be concluded, and keep up a federal effort. If this program were allowed to die, many thought it would be a difficult fight to start again, given the years it takes to get a federal program started.

The grass-roots support, the overwhelming support given by the Senate, and Whitten's labeling of school dropouts as a "dire emergency" led to a quick and easy passage of the next reauthorization in the summer of 1991. The program was modified slightly, but it retained provisions for a new round of competition for dropout prevention grants. In addition, the House Appropriations Education Subcommittee gave overwhelming support for the program, increasing the funding over the president's budget request, and noted in the committee report that "while progress has been made in improving overall dropout rates, in certain communities this remains a critical problem. Given the importance of school completion to economic self-sufficiency, the Committee has supported a significant expansion of this grant program."[17]

Finally, in the new round of competition, less than a third of the originally funded projects received a grant in this new competition, providing evidence that the program was functioning as a "demonstration" program and not as an endless "sink-hole." The system was working.

SOME FINAL THOUGHTS: CONGRESS AND ITS FUTURE

"I used to think about running for Congress, but I no longer want to."

"There are no sincere politicians."

As media attention focused on the Clarence Thomas confirmation hearings in the fall of 1991, followed by stories of the House banking scandal in the spring of 1992, the public's distrust of elected officials and the growth in cynicism in government was also being recorded by the press. These negative perceptions came to a head during the 1992 presidential election campaign. In November 1992, the political outsider, Ross Perot, captured 19 percent of the popular vote after he had spent months berating nationally elected officials for their role in a system characterized by gridlock that left urgent national problems unresolved. The two statements above came from my students in Maine during the fall of 1992. If these statements reflect popular sentiment, and I think they may, it is a harsh indictment of a system of government based on the principles of representative democracy.

Perhaps political scientists, in their writings on Congress and their teachings on the American political process, have tried to be too objective and too critical of the system. Perhaps the press, in its eagerness to take on a greater investigative role, has failed to report on the nuts and bolts of what Congress is doing. It may be that this cynicism was a product of the 1980s, when the president and Congress were in the hands of opposite parties and for most people "gridlock" characterized government. It may also reflect the serious problems created by the growing deficit and realization that the government cannot solve all problems.

At a time when Eastern Europe is turning to the U.S. system of government as a model that works and the Asia Foundation is sponsoring Asian government officials to be participant-observers of the U.S. Congress, perhaps more needs to be done to explain what it is about this system that works.

The rules and procedures may be designed to preserve the status quo, but change is possible. The growth in support for the dropout program paralleled the growth in society's perception that dropouts were a national concern. By 1991 dropouts were clearly on the nation's agenda. The dropout program was kept alive by groups who believed the system could work and was responsive.

Some contend that the members of Congress themselves have inadvertently distanced the institution of Congress from the American public. In 1987, near the end of his tenure in the Senate, Senator William Proxmire (D-Wis.), in an impassioned speech before his colleagues, talked about "what's right about the Congress." Proxmire recounted the historic role of the Iran Contra hearings which revealed "lies, deceptions, and fraudulent misuse of congressionally appropriated money" within the executive branch.[18] In noting the public response to the hearings, Proxmire observed that

The administration suffered a minor drop in popularity. The prime agent advancing the administration's deception—and hypocrisy—Lt. Col. Oliver North, became a national hero. And Congress—the agency that brought the administration to account, that fought the good fight for a responsible democracy got little or no credit by administration critics and a torrent of criticism from administration supporters.[19]

According to Proxmire, "nobody ever defends the Congress." For this he put the blame squarely on the shoulders of the members of Congress: "The people of this country think the Congress is the pits because we in the Congress tell them we are the pits. I have listened to many Members of this body who have made a career out of attacking Congress. Every time they make a speech on the floor, in committee, to constituents, the Congress is the one sure, predictable object of their scorn, their ridicule, their derision."[20] The public, listening to these attacks, responds accordingly, and the institution of Congress suffers in their minds. The norm of "institutional patriotism" means little to members when they are outside of Washington. Senator Byrd joined Proxmire in a defense of Congress, imploring members and the American public to

> look at whatever legislation you want—veterans legislation, Social Security, Medicare, health care, education funding, whatever legislation it is— highway funding, safety laws—it comes from this place here. And while we all may find at times that we are not happy with the work of the Senate or the work of the House, we have to remember that without this institution we would cease to be a republic.[21]

With members of Congress doing little to explain, let alone defend the institution of Congress, the public is left with an enigma—an unknown and unfamiliar institution, yet an institution where individual members continue to have public support.

This work has presented a case study of a very small program affecting the lives of many people. Although the dropout issue was not a major policy issue, it symbolizes a lot of what Congress is all about, every day in a wide range of policy areas. It demonstrates Congress learning and educating itself and the American public, assessing tradeoffs, making judgments and difficult choices (and not always with complete information), and explaining actions. Congress is held accountable because its members face reelection every two or six years; if the current movement to legislate term limits is successful, they will no longer be subject to this kind of accountability.

As the president turns to advisers and policy specialists (witness the December 1992 economic summit of hundreds of advisers called together to give President-elect Clinton input on budget priorities, economic planning, and deficit reduction), so too does Congress turn to staff, constituents, interest groups, and experts in the executive branch. On most issues before Congress, however, a number of members have gained expertise owing to years of service on the Hill. Colleagues can also look to these experts for guidance. Presidents even draw upon the experience and expertise of members of Congress in filling top posts in their administration. For example, Clinton selected Senator Lloyd Bentsen to head the Treasury Department, Representative Les Aspin as Secretary of Defense, and Representative Leon Panetta to direct the Office of Management and Budget.

As we saw in this case study, several members of Congress were most involved in the dropout issue. Senator Kohl benefited from the years of experience offered by Senators Pell and Kennedy and their respective staffs, as did Representative Hayes in gaining the support of Representatives Augustus Hawkins and William Natcher. But the success in gaining continued funding for the program also owed a great deal to *informed* constituents who brought the issue to Senator Kohl's attention, reinforced by supportive material from program administrators in the Department of Education and from interest groups. The story of the school dropout program is indeed the story of much of the day-to-day work in Congress—unseen, unreported, and generally unknown.

I presented this case study primarily to convey the hard work, optimism, complexity of the legislative process, and spirit of cooperation that I witnessed in my year on the Hill. I hope this story can give the reader a better sense of the institution of Congress—that is, Congress at work as well as a sense of optimism about the political process that may set the 1990s apart from the 1980s—a sense that government can work.

Appendix A

Chronology

1983

National Commission on Excellence in Education releases report, "A Nation at Risk."

1984

(January) Senate Children's Caucus holds forum in New York City on causes of high dropout rates.

1985

(July) H.R. 3042, The Dropout Prevention and Reentry Act, creating a four-year demonstration dropout prevention program, is introduced in the House of Representatives by Representative Charles Hayes (D-Ill.).

(July) S. 1525, the companion bill to H.R. 3042, is introduced in the Senate by Senator Arlen Specter (R-Penn.).

(December) Gramm-Rudman-Hollings deficit reduction plan is passed by Congress.

1986

(August) H.R. 3042 passes in the House; S. 1525 fails in the Senate.

99th Congress adjourns without the dropout prevention program passing in both the House and Senate.

1987

As 100th Congress begins, Democrats regain control of Senate and maintain control of House.

(January) H.R. 5, The School Improvement Act, an omnibus education bill, is introduced in the House (with no dropout prevention program provisions).

(January) S. 320, The School Dropout Demonstration Assistance Act, creating a demonstration dropout program, is introduced in the Senate by Senator Pell (D-R.I.).

(April) The House passes its omnibus trade bill (with no dropout prevention program provisions).

(May) The House passes its omnibus education bill, H.R. 5, with no dropout prevention program provisions.

(June) S. 320 becomes part of S. 406, the Education for a Competitive America Act, which is added to the Senate's Omnibus Trade and Competitiveness Act.

(July) The Senate passes its omnibus trade bill (with dropout prevention program provisions).

(December) S. 320 becomes part of S. 373, the Senate omnibus education bill; the Senate passes its omnibus education bill.

House and Senate conference committees meet to resolve differences in omnibus trade and education bills.

(December) Continuing resolution authorizing and appropriating funds for the demonstration dropout prevention program in fiscal year 1988 is passed by both the House and Senate and signed into law.

1988

House and Senate conference committees continue to meet to resolve differences in trade and education bills.

(April) The Augustus F. Hawkins-Robert T. Stafford Elementary and Secondary School Improvement Amendments of 1988 is passed and signed into law authorizing the demonstration dropout prevention program for fiscal year 1989.

(August) The Omnibus Trade and Competitiveness Act of 1988 is passed and signed into law authorizing the demonstration dropout prevention program for fiscal year 1988.

1989

(April) President Bush sends education package to Congress; introduced as S. 695 in the Senate and as H.R. 1675 in the House.

(June) House passes H.R. 2281, extending authorization for school demonstration dropout programs for fiscal years 1990 and 1991.

(July) The Senate Labor and Human Resources Committee adds provision to extend authorization for school demonstration dropout programs for fiscal years 1990 and 1991 to S. 695.

(September) President Bush and nation's governors hold education summit at the University of Virginia; set national goal of a 90 percent high school graduation rate by the year 2000.

(November) Senate passes reauthorization of dropout program but as a rider to the Taft Institute reauthorization.

1990

(January) Congress begins consideration of the Dire Emergency Supplemental Appropriations bill, eventually including President Bush's requests for aid for Panama and Nicaragua, and disaster relief for victims of Hurricane Hugo and the 1989 San Francisco earthquake.

(February) S. 695, President Bush's Educational Excellence Act package of education programs passes in the Senate, including a reauthorization of the dropout prevention program.

(February) H.R. 2281, reauthorizing the dropout prevention program, passes in the Senate.

(March) H.R. 2281 is signed into law by President Bush.

(April) The supplemental appropriations bill, with no funding for the dropout prevention program, is passed in the House.

(April) The Kohl amendment adding appropriations for fiscal year 1990 for the school dropout prevention program is approved by the Senate.

(May) The Dire Emergency Supplemental Appropriations bill, with funding for the dropout prevention program, is passed in the Senate.

(May) House and Senate conferees meet to resolve differences in the supplemental appropriations bills passed by the House and Senate and agree to keep the Kohl amendment, funding the dropout prevention program, in the final supplemental appropriations bill.

(May) The House and Senate each approve compromises agreed to by the conference committee.

(May) President Bush signs the supplemental appropriations bill into law, continuing funding for the school dropout prevention programs.

OKLAHOMA

Cushing Public Schools
Indianola Public Schools
Lawton Public Schools
Tulsa Area Vocational-Technical
  School District

OREGON

School District #1, Portland
West Valley Academy, Sheridan

PENNSYLVANIA

Philadelphia School District
Pittsburgh School District
Washington County Alternative
  Schools, Claysville
Wattsburg Area School District

RHODE ISLAND

Providence School Department

SOUTH CAROLINA

Anderson School District No. 1,
  Williamston
Aiken County Consolidated School
  District

TENNESSEE

Memphis City Schools

TEXAS

Austin Independent School District

Coleman Independent School District
Dallas Independent School District
Grayson County Cooperative, Pottsboro
Houston Independent School District
North East Independent School District, San Antonio
Pampa Independent School District
Southwest Texas State University,
  San Marcos

UTAH

San Juan School District, Monticello

VIRGINIA

Fairfax County Public Schools

WASHINGTON

Career Path Services, Spokane
Center for At-Risk Education, Seattle
Seattle School District No. 1

WISCONSIN

Lac du Flambeau Band of Lake
  Superior Chippewa Indians
Milwaukee Area Technical College
Milwaukee Public Schools

WYOMING

School District No. L4, Wyoming
  Indian School, Ethete

Appendix C

School Dropout Demonstration Assistance Program Recipients
(1991)

ARIZONA

Chicanos Por La Causa, Inc.
Phoenix Union High School District

CALIFORNIA

San Juan Unified School District
Sweetwater Unified High School
    District
Long Beach Unified School District
Los Angeles Unified School District
Butte County Office of Education
Santa Ana 2000

DELAWARE

Colonial School District

DISTRICT OF COLUMBIA

ASPIRA Association, Inc.

FLORIDA

Volusia/Lake/Flagler Private Indus-
    try Council
School Board of Broward County
Cities in Schools of Miami

GEORGIA

Georgia Cities in Schools

ILLINOIS

Community High School 165
Board of Governors of State Col-
    leges and Universities
Rockford Public Schools No. 205

KANSAS

Wichita Public Schools

LOUISIANA

New Orleans Public Schools

MARYLAND

Anne Arundel County Public
    Schools
Baltimore City Public Schools

MASSACHUSETTS

Jobs For Youth-Boston, Inc.
New Bedford Public Schools

MICHIGAN

School District/City of Detroit
School District/City of Flint
Grand Rapids Public Schools
Onaway Area Community School

MISSISSIPPI

Jackson County School District

MISSOURI

Economic Opportunity Corporation
  of Greater St. Joseph
Human Development Corporation
  of Metropolitan St. Louis

MONTANA

Browning Elementary and High
  School District No. 9

NEVADA

Clark County School District

NEW JERSEY

Newark Board of Education

NEW MEXICO

Youth Development, Inc.

NEW YORK

SUNY Research Foundation
Community School District No. 18,
  Brooklyn
New York City Public Schools,
  Brooklyn
Flowers with Care
Community School District No. 3,
  New York

Good Shepherd Services
New York City Public Schools, New
  York

OHIO

Cincinnati Public Schools

OKLAHOMA

Cushing Public Schools
Indianola Public Schools
Central Area Vocational/Technical
  School
Tulsa County Area Vocational/Tech-
  nical School

OREGON

Umatilla Education Service District

PENNSYLVANIA

School District of Philadelphia

RHODE ISLAND

Providence Public School System

SOUTH CAROLINA

Centerville Elementary/Anderson
  School District No. 5
School District of Williamsburg
  County
McCormick County School District

TENNESSEE

Jackson County Board of Education

TEXAS

Houston Independent School District

San Antonio 70001
Intercultural Development Research Association (IDRA)
Southwest Texas State University

UTAH

San Juan School District

VIRGINIA

Hampton City Schools

WASHINGTON

Seattle School District No. 1
University of Washington
Career Path Services
Tacoma-Pierce County Employment and Training Consortium

WISCONSIN

Milwaukee Area Technical College
Milwaukee Public Schools

Appendix D

S.1525

99TH CONGRESS
1ST SESSION

To amend the Elementary and Secondary Education Act of 1965 to provide grants to local educational agencies for dropout prevention demonstration projects.

IN THE SENATE OF THE UNITED STATES

July 30 (legislative day, JULY 16), 1985

Mr. SPECTER (for himself, Mr. PELL, Mr. CHAFEE, Mr. STAFFORD, Mr. KENNEDY, and Mr. BRADLEY) introduced the following bill; which was read twice and referred to the Committee on Labor and Human Resources

---

A Bill

To amend the Elementary and Secondary Education Act of 1965 to provide grants to local educational agencies for dropout prevention demonstration projects.

Be it enacted by the Senate and House of Representatives of the United States of America in Congress assembled, That the Elementary and Secondary Education Act of 1965 is amended by redesignating title X as title XI, by redesignating the sections of such title as sections 1101 to 1106, and by inserting the following new title after title IX:

"TITLE X—THE DROPOUT PREVENTION AND REENTRY ACT OF 1985

"SEC. 1001. SHORT TITLE.

"This title may be cited as the 'Dropout Prevention and Reentry Act of 1985'.

"SEC. 1002. PURPOSE.

"The purpose of this title is to reduce the number of children who do not complete their elementary and secondary education by providing grants to local educational agencies to establish and demonstrate—

"(1) effective programs to identify potential drop-outs and prevent them from dropping out;

"(2) effective programs to identify and encourage children who have already dropped out to reenter school and complete their elementary and secondary education; and

"(3) model systems for collecting and reporting information to local school officials on the number, ages, and grade levels of the children not completing their elementary and secondary education and the reasons why such children have dropped out of school.

"SEC. 1003. AUTHORIZATION OF APPROPRIATIONS.

"There are authorized to be appropriated to carry out this title $50,000,000 for fiscal year 1987 and such sums as may be necessary for fiscal years 1988, 1989, and 1990.

"SEC. 1004. GRANTS TO LOCAL EDUCATIONAL AGENCIES.

"(a) ALLOTMENT TO CATEGORIES OF LOCAL EDUCATIONAL AGENCIES.—From the amount appropriated under section 1003 for any fiscal year, the Secretary shall allot 20 percent to each of the following categories of local educational agencies:

"(1) Local educational agencies containing schools with an enrollment of 250,000 or more elementary and secondary school students.

"(2) Local educational agencies containing schools with an enrollment of at least 100,000 but fewer than 250,000 such students.

"(3) Local educational agencies containing schools with an enrollment of at least 50,000 but fewer than 100,000 such students.

"(4) Local educational agencies containing schools

with an enrollment of at least 20,000 but fewer than 50,000 such students.

"(5) Local educational agencies containing schools with an enrollment of fewer than 20,000 such students.

"(b) AWARD OF GRANT.—From the amount allotted for any fiscal year to a category of local educational agencies under subsection (a), the Secretary shall award as many grants as practicable within each such category to local educational agencies whose applications have been approved by the Secretary for such fiscal year under section 1005 and whose applications propose a program of sufficient size and scope to be of value as a demonstration. The grants shall be made under such terms and conditions as the Secretary shall prescribe.

"(c) MAXIMUM NUMBER OF GRANTS.—A local educational agency may receive no more than one grant in each of three fiscal years under this title.

"(d) AMOUNT.—The amount of a grant awarded under this section to a local educational agency for any fiscal year, to the extent practicable, shall be proportionate to the extent and severity of the local dropout problem, except that the amount of the grant shall not exceed 90 percent of the total cost of a project during the project's first fiscal year, 80 percent of such cost during the project's second fiscal year, and 70 percent of such cost during the project's third fiscal year.

"SEC. 1005. APPLICATION.

"(a) IN GENERAL.—A grant under this title may be made only to a local educational agency which submits an application to the Secretary containing such information as may be required by the Secretary by regulation. Such application shall—

"(1) provide documentation of (A) the number of children formerly enrolled in the applicant's schools who have not completed their elementary or secondary education, and (B) the percentage that such number of children is of the total school-age population in the applicant's schools;

"(2) include a plan for the development and implementation of a dropout information collection and reporting system for documenting the extent and nature of the dropout problem, in accordance with standards established by the national school dropout study under section 1008;

"(3) include a plan for the development and implementation of a project which will—

"(A) implement comprehensive identification, prevention, outreach, and reentry programs for dropouts and potential dropouts,

"(B) address the special needs of pregnant minors and school-age parents,

"(C) disseminate information to students, parents, and the community related to the dropout problem,

"(D) include coordinated activities involving at least one high school and its feeder junior or middle schools and elementary schools for those local educational agencies having such feeder systems,

"(E) establish annual procedures for (i) evaluating the effectiveness of the project, and (ii) where possible, determining the cost-effectiveness of the particular dropout prevention and reentry methods used and the potential for reproducing such methods in other areas of the country,

"(F) establish an advisory council which is broadly representative of the entire community and the dropout populations to be served, and

"(G) use the resources of the community and parents to help develop and implement solutions to the local dropout problem; and

"(4) contain such other information as the Secretary considers necessary to determine the nature of the local needs, the quality of the proposed project, and the capability of the applicant to carry out the project.

"(b) SPECIAL CONSIDERATIONS.—For the purpose of approving applications under this section, the Secretary shall give first priority within each category under section 1004(a) to applicants that have either very high numbers or very high percentages of school dropouts.

"(c) REVIEW OF PROJECTS.—In any application from a local educational agency for a grant to continue a project for the second or third fiscal year following the first fiscal year in which a grant was awarded to such local educational agency, the Secretary shall review the progress being made toward meeting the objectives of the project. The Secretary may refuse to award a grant if he finds that sufficient progress has not been made toward meeting such objectives, but only after affording the applicant notice and an opportunity for a hearing.

"SEC. **1006.** AUTHORIZED ACTIVITIES.

"Grants under this title shall be used to carry out plans in applications approved under section 1005. In addition, grants may be used for the following activities:

"(1) to establish systemwide or school-level policies, procedures, and plans for dropout prevention and school reentry;

"(2) to provide guidance and counseling services, including peer interaction activities;

"(3) to provide ombudsman or mentor services;

"(4) to develop and implement activities, including extended day or summer programs, to address poor achievement, language deficiencies, or course failures, in order to assist students at risk of dropping out of school and students reentering school;

"(5) to establish or expand work-study, apprentice, or internship programs;

"(6) to use the resources of the community, including contracting with public or private entities or community-based organizations, to provide services to the grant recipient or the target population;

"(7) to evaluate and revise program placement of students at risk;

"(8) to review curriculum relevancy;

"(9) to implement activities which will improve student motivation and the school learning environment;

"(10) to provide training for school staff on strategies and techniques to identify children at risk of dropping out, to intervene in the instructional program with support and remedial services, to develop realistic expectations for student performance, and to improve student-staff interactions; and

"(11) to provide other services and implement other activities which directly relate to the purpose of this title.

"SEC. **1007.** PROGRAM LIMITATIONS.

"Not less than 30 percent of each grant shall be used for activities related to dropout prevention, and not less than 30 percent of each grant shall be used for activities related to persuading dropouts to return to school and assisting former dropouts with specialized services once they return to school.

"SEC. 1008. NATIONAL SCHOOL DROPOUT STUDY.

"(a) IN GENERAL.—From amounts appropriated to the Secretary for fiscal year 1986, the Secretary shall use not more than $500,000 to conduct a one-year study of the nature and extent of the dropout problem in the United States. In conducting the study, the Secretary shall—

"(1) establish a standard definition of a school dropout;

"(2) develop a standard list of reasons why children are dropping out of school, including major factors that contribute to children dropping out;

"(3) develop a model dropout information collection and reporting system;

"(4) develop minimum reporting system requirements;

"(5) identify the numbers of children and the general reasons for their dropping out of school among population groups with particularly high dropout rates;

"(6) identify the characteristics of children who appear to be at risk of dropping out of school;

"(7) identify the factors or policies which may attract children who have dropped out to reenter school and complete their elementary and secondary education;

"(8) identify methods and techniques being used successfully to reduce the number of school dropouts; and

"(9) provide recommendations for activities and policies which can be implemented at each level of government and in communities to ameliorate the dropout problem.

"(b) OTHER REQUIREMENTS.—Recipients of grants under this title shall cooperate with the Secretary in carrying out the study under subsection (a) by providing data and information on the nature and extent of the dropout problem and the effectiveness of techniques used to address the problem.

"SEC. 1009. GENERAL PROVISIONS.

"(a) WITHHOLDING PAYMENTS.—Whenever the Secretary, after reasonable notice and opportunity for a hearing to any local educational agency, finds that the local educational agency has failed to comply substantially with the provisions set forth in its application approved under section 1005, the Secretary shall withhold payments under this title until the Secretary is satisfied that there is no longer any failure to comply.

"(b) ANNUAL REPORT.—The Secretary shall prepare and submit to Congress an annual report on January 1 on the activities assisted under this title during the preceding fiscal year.

"(c) AUDIT.—The Comptroller General shall have access for the purpose of audit and examination to any books, documents, papers, and records of any local educational agency receiving assistance under this title that are pertinent to the sums received and disbursed under this title.

"(d) GRANTS MUST SUPPLEMENT OTHER FUNDS.—A local educational agency receiving funds under this title shall use the Federal funds only to supplement the funds that would, in the absence of such Federal funds, be made available from non-Federal sources for activities to prevent students from dropping out of elementary and secondary school and to persuade dropouts to reenter school and complete their education.

"SEC. 1010. DEFINITIONS.

"As used in this title—

"(1) the term 'community-based organization' means a private nonprofit organization which is representative of a community or significant segments of a community and which provides educational or related services to individuals in the community;

"(2) the term 'Secretary' means the Secretary of Education; and

"(3) the terms 'State educational agency', 'local educational agency', 'elementary school', and 'secondary school' have the same meanings given those terms in section 198 of the Elementary and Secondary Education Act of 1965 (20 U.S.C. 3381)."

Notes

INTRODUCTION

1. Monica West, C-SPAN, phone interview, July 23, 1992.

2. Richard Morin and Helen Dewar, "Approval of Congress Hits All-time Low, Poll Finds," *Washington Post* (March 20, 1992), p. A16.

3. *CQ Almanac 1989* (Washington, D.C.: Congressional Quarterly, 1990), p. 67.

4. Senator Herb Kohl (D-Wis.), Floor Speech, *Congressional Record,* April 26, 1990, p. S5142.

5. Entitlement programs are programs that provide a certain set of benefits to all individuals who meet eligibility requirements as set forth in law. Such programs include Medicare, Medicaid, food stamps, and unemployment compensation.

6. Michael J. Malbin, *Unelected Representatives* (New York: Basic Books, 1980), ch. 10.

7. For example, see Malbin, *Unelected Representatives,* ch. 10.

CHAPTER 1

1. The latter category includes Dick Cheney, who stayed in Washington following his year on the Hill, eventually serving as chief of staff in the Ford White House and as secretary of defense in the Bush administration.

2. These include such works as *Congress: The Electoral Connection,* by David Mayhew; *Majority Leadership in the U.S. House,* by Barbara Sinclair; *The New Congress,* edited by Thomas E. Mann and Norman Ornstein; *The Politics of Finance: The House Ways and Means Committee* by John F. Manley; *Congress Reconsidered,* edited by Lawrence C. Dodd and Bruce Oppenheimer; and *Committees in Congress* by Steven S. Smith and Christopher J. Deering.

3. "Congressional Fellows: Helping Congress Help America," *Exxon USA* (Second Quarter 1984): 24. Duggan, a former congressional fellow, was the vice president for taxation at the Association of American Railroads in 1984.

4. "A Report on the Congressional Fellowship Program, 1989–90 and 1990–91," *PS* (March 1991): 125.

5. The list of speakers in the 1989 orientation program (who gave us off-the-record insights, anecdotes, and helpful information) reads like a "Who's Who in Washington": Norm Ornstein of the American Enterprise Institute; Al Hunt, Washington Bureau chief of the *Wall Street Journal;* David Gergen, editor-at-large for *U.S. News and World Report;* Thomas Mann, director of Governmental Studies at the Brookings Institution; Richard A. Baker, historian of the United States Senate; Roger Porter, assistant to President Bush for Economic and Domestic Policy; David Broder of *The Washington Post;* Terry Eastland, of the National Legal Center for the

Public Interest; and Rudolph G. Penner, former director of the Congressional Budget Office.

6. Other structures on Capitol Hill include the Library of Congress housed in several buildings, as well as several annex buildings for additional staff of the House of Representatives.

7. This book focuses on the legislative role in the policy process; therefore, this discussion is limited primarily to the staff serving in these roles. Many of the thousands of staffers in the Hill have jobs that are not directly related to legislation—including those primarily doing constituent casework, press jobs, computer work, and general office assistance. For further discussion, see Michael J. Malbin, *Unelected Representatives* (New York: Basic Books, 1979), p. 10.

8. Ross K. Baker, *House and Senate* (New York: W. W. Norton, 1989), p. 54.

9. There are also staff who work back in the district primarily on constituent casework, as well as in coordinating the schedule of the members when they are back home.

10. Malbin, *Unelected Representatives,* pp. 11–14; Harrison W. Fox, Jr., and Susan Webb Hammond, *Congressional Staffs* (New York: Free Press, 1977), ch. 4.

11. Thomas W. Still, "Is the Only Good Senator a Poor Senator," *Wisconsin State Journal* (January 21, 1990), p. 19a.

12. Michael Barone and Grant Ujifusa, *The Almanac of American Politics, 1990* (Washington, D.C.: National Journal), pp. 1315–1318.

13. Senator Herb Kohl, phone interview, July 24, 1992.

14. What Is Herb Kohl Up To?" *Fort Atkinson Jefferson County Union* (January 15, 1990).

15. Randall B. Ripley and Grace A. Franklin, *Congress, the Bureaucracy, and Public Policy,* 4th ed. (Chicago: Dorsey Press, 1987), p. 8.

CHAPTER 2

1. *Making America Work,* Governor Bill Clinton, Chair (Washington, D.C.: National Governors' Association, 1987), p. 48.

2. Charles O. Jones, *An Introduction to the Study of Public Policy,* 2nd ed. (North Scituate, Mass.: Duxbury Press, 1977), p. 42.

3. Roger W. Cobb and Charles D. Elder, *Participation in American Politics: The Dynamics of Agenda-Building,* 2nd ed. (Baltimore, Md.: Johns Hopkins University Press, 1983), p. 116.

4. E. E. Schattschneider, *The Semisovereign People* (New York: Holt, Rinehart and Winston, 1960), p. 11.

5. Denis P. Doyle and Terry W. Hartle, *Excellence in Education* (Washington, D.C.: American Enterprise Institute, 1985), pp. 1–7.

6. Ibid., p. 13.

7. The governors were Bob Graham (D-Fla.), Chuck Robb (D-Va.), William Winter (D-Miss.), Bill Clinton (D-Ark.), James B. Hunt (D-N.C.), Richard Riley (D-S.C.), and Lamar Alexander (R-Tenn.).

8. Doyle and Hartle, *Excellence in Education,* pp. 13–14; William E. Schmidt, "Southern States Moving to Improve Schools," *New York Times* (January 11, 1984), p. A1.

9. Doyle and Hartle, *Excellence in Education,* p. 14.

10. Schmidt, "Southern States Moving to Improve Schools," p. A4.

11. Ibid., p. A4.

12. Barbara Vobejda, "Reforms May Increase Dropout Rate," *Washington Post* (October 16, 1985), p. A7.

13. Roger H. Davidson and Walter J. Oleszek, *Congress and Its Members,* 3rd ed, (Washington, D.C.: CQ Press, 1990), p. 368.

14. Ibid., p. 368.

15. Ibid., p. 298.

16. Interview, Marsha Renwanz, Washington, D.C., March 1992.

17. *Congressional Record,* October 11, 1984, p. S14421.

18. Ibid.

19. Edward B. Fiske, "Commission on Education Warns 'Tide of Mediocrity' Imperils U.S.," *New York Times* (April 27, 1983), p. A1:4.

20. Joyce Purnick, "Senators Seek Answers at Forum on High School Dropout Problem," *New York Times* (January 24, 1984), p. B8.

21. "Wanted: Dropout Solution" *New York Times* (January 23, 1984), p. B3.

22. Gerald M. Boyd, "Dropout Rate Is up Sharply in U.S. Schools, Survey Says," *New York Times* (January 6, 1984), p. D13.

23. Gene I. Maeroff, "Study Finds Hispanic Students Are 'Wasted,' " *New York Times* (December 13, 1984), p. A25.

24. U.S. Congress, House Subcommittee on Elementary, Secondary, and Vocational Education of the Committee on Education and Labor, "H.R. 3042, The Dropout Prevention and Reentry Act," Hearings, 99th Cong., 2nd sess., May 20, 1986, pp. 20–21.

25. *School Dropouts: Survey of Local Programs* (Washington, D.C.: General Accounting Office, July 1987), p. 4 [GAO/HRD–87–108].

In fact, problems in definition continue. In 1988 Congress asked the National Center for Education Statistics "for an annual report on the dropout rate with an eventual state-by-state breakdown." For two years the National Center for Education Statistics conducted a pilot program with twenty-nine states and territories in order "to monitor dropouts in the same way across district and state lines. The sampling wasn't representative, but early indications lead some to conclude there may be fewer dropouts than the number frequently cited (one in four)." Still, the need for standardization in data collection methods for all states remains, with most agreeing that tracking students is the best way to determine true graduation rates, whether by degree or GED. As of the summer of 1991, forty states had agreed to cooperate in the Department of Education study. As one observer has noted, "It's up to the federal government and the governors to cajole the reluctant state education departments." ["How Many Dropouts," *Washington Post National Weekly Edition* (June 17–23, 1991), p. 26].

26. "New Breed of School Dropouts Is Seen Emerging," *New York Times* (February 16, 1987), p. A11.

27. Ibid.

28. "Coca-Cola to Aid Fight on Dropouts," *New York Times* (May 15, 1984), p. B3.

29. Doron P. Levin, "$2 Million Awards Program Aids to Cut School Dropouts," *New York Times* (May 18, 1989), p. A18; "Coca-Cola to Aid Fight on Dropouts."

30. Harold L. Hodgkinson, "All One System: Demographics of Education— Kindergarten through Graduate School" (Washington, D.C.: Institute for Educational Leadership, 1985).

31. Ibid., p. 11.

32. Ibid., pp. 11–12.

33. Joyce Purnick, "Job Project Gets Dropouts to Return to City Schools," *New York Times* (June 19, 1984), p. B1.

34. "ARC Workshop Showcases Practical Programs for Dropout Prevention." *Appalachia,* Fall 1985, p. 1.

35. Winifred A. Pizzano, Appalachian Regional Commission Co-Chairman, quoted in "The Workshop Panels," *Appalachia,* Fall 1985, p. 4.

36. Sally Reed, "Students Make Tough Graders," *New York Times* (September 22, 1985), section 4, p. 22.

37. Gene I. Maeroff, "Teacher Group to Open Drive on the Dropout," *New York Times* (June 29, 1985), p. 6; Judy Hodgson, National Education Association, interview, March 5, 1993.

38. Maeroff. "Teacher Group to Open Drive on the Dropout."

39. For example, *The Way Out: Student Exclusion Practices in Boston Middle Schools* (a report by the Massachusetts Advocacy Center, November 1986) focused on the middle schools as the target population for keeping children in school. It identifies "two of the practices in the Boston middle schools . . . [which put] children at risk of dropping out—attendance rules and retention at grade level . . . [as having been] widely marketed as reforms which would restore excellence to the school system. These practices were adopted with virtually no consultation with those affected: parents and students" (Foreword).

In addition, Jan Novak and Barbara Dougherty's two-phase study and report became an important resource tool for those working on dropout prevention programs. Their report, published by the Wisconsin Vocational Studies Center at the University of Wisconsin, included statistical data on dropouts, along with detailed suggestions for those setting up dropout prevention programs on such topics as the use and preparation of staff, facilities needed, program evaluation mechanisms, and the creation and use of advisory committees ("Dropout Prevention in Wisconsin, Vol. I: A Review of Programs and Activities, Vol. II: Staying In . . . A Dropout Prevention Handbook, K–12").

40. For example, see the report of the Business Advisory Commission of the Education Commission of the States, chaired at the time by Governor Charles Robb of Virginia. Representatives from major corporations and labor unions, as well as public officials served on the Commission. Jonathan Friendly, "Schools Cited as Helping Dropouts Succeed," *New York Times* (November 2, 1985), p. 26:1.

41. Kathleen Teltsch, "$1 Million Set for 21 Cities to Cut Dropout Rates" *New York Times* (November 30, 1986), p. 33.

42. "A High School Paradox," Editorial, *Washington Post* (November 17, 1985), p. B6.

43. Nancy Rubin, "How They're Wooing the Potential Dropout," *New York Times* (August 2, 1987), section 12, p. 48.

44. Testimony inserted in the *Congressional Record,* October 11, 1984, Vol. 130–Part 23, p. 32013.

45. Bob Lyke, "High School Dropouts: Current Federal Programs," CRS Report for Congress, 90–144 EPW, March 14, 1990.

46. Ibid.

47. Richard A. Lacey, "Revitalizing the Ninth Grade in Boston's Public Schools: Compact Ventures 1984–1985," in U.S. Congress, Senate Committee on Labor and Human Resources Subcommittee on Education, Arts and Humanities, Hearings, October 17, 1985, 99th Cong., 1st sess., S. 1525, pp. 50–57.

48. *Congressional Record,* September 17, 1985, p. H7477.

49. *Congressional Record,* March 13, 1984, pp. S2616–S2617.

50. Ibid., p. S2629.

51. Phone interview, Deb Stipek, August 5, 1992.

52. "Federal Abortion Alternatives Cut by Reagan," pp. 465–469; "Senate Action," p. 490, in *1984 CQ Almanac.*

53. See Davidson and Oleszek, *Congress and Its Members,* 3rd ed., p. 368 for a discussion of policy formulation.

54. "Hearings on Secondary Schools Basic Skills Act" (H.R. 5749), Subcommittee

on Elementary, Secondary, and Vocational Education of the House Committee on Education and Labor, 98th Cong., 2nd sess., Washington, D.C., June 12 and 13, 1984, p. 46.

55. Ibid., p. 46.

56. Ibid., p. 49.

57. Ibid., pp. 45–55.

58. Among those providing supplemental material and letters of support were Ted J. Comstock, president of the National School Boards Association, and Robert Hanley, representing the National Association of Secondary School Principals. Both of these associations would be included in the earliest meetings in 1985 of the emerging National Dropout Prevention Network.

59. Bob Lyke, "High School Dropouts: New Federal Legislation and Current Programs," CRS Report for Congress, December 30, 1991, 92–23 EPW.

60. U.S. Congress, Senate Subcommittee on Education, Arts and Humanities of the Committee on Labor and Human Resources, S. 373 (Elementary and Secondary Education Amendments of 1987), Hearings, 100th Cong., 1st sess., June 26, 1987, p. 418.

61. U.S. Congress, Senate Subcommittee on Education, Arts and Humanities of the Committee on Labor and Human Resources, S. 1525 (Dropout Prevention and Reentry Act of 1985), Hearings, 99th Cong., 1st sess., October 17, 1985, p. 78.

62. The few witnesses who emphasized this point included Richard Heckert and John T. Casteen III. Heckert, vice chair and chief of operations of E. I. DuPont Company, had been the chair of a panel sponsored by the National Academy of Sciences, the National Academy of Engineering, and the Institute of Medicine, which looked at the nation's future workforce and issued a report, "High Schools and the Changing Workplace: An Employer's View." Casteen, secretary of education, state of Virginia, served on the panel. Both noted employers' concerns about a workforce lacking basic academic skills—for example, "the ability to read, comprehend, and interpret written materials," or "the ability to understand and apply basic mathematics, at least through elementary algebra," in both high school graduates and dropouts. See "Hearings on Secondary Schools Basic Skills Act," H.R. 5749, Subcommittee on Elementary, Secondary, and Vocational Education of the House Committee on Education and Labor, 98th Cong., 2nd sess., Washington, D.C., June 12 and 13, 1984, pp. 71–73.

63. Ibid., especially pp. 68–80.

64. U.S. Congress, Senate Subcommittee on Education, Arts and Humanities of the Committee on Labor and Human Resources, S. 1525 (Dropout Prevention and Reentry Act of 1985), Hearings, 99th Cong., 1st sess., October 17, 1985, p. 2.

65. Ibid., p. 17.

66. Alec M. Gallup, "The 18th Annual Gallup Poll of the Public's Attitudes toward the Public Schools," *Phi Delta Kappan,* September 1986, p. 53.

67. S. 1525 (Dropout Prevention and Reentry Act of 1985), Hearings, October 17, 1985, p. 100.

68. "GAO's Best Sellers," *New York Times* (February 12, 1988), p. B6.

69. *Making America Work, Bringing down the Barriers,* Governor Bill Clinton, Chair (Washington, D.C.: National Governors' Association, 1987).

70. Kenneth J. Cooper, "Governors Adopt Goals for Educational Reform," *Washington Post* (February 26, 1990, p. A6).

CHAPTER 3

1. U.S. Congress, House Committee on Education and Labor, Report 99–706 on H.R. 3042 (Dropout Prevention and Reentry Act of 1986), 99th Cong., 2nd sess., p. 5.

2. Ibid., p. 6.

3. Hayes represented Chicago's First District from 1983 until 1993. A victim of the congressional check bouncing scandal, he was defeated in a close primary contest in the spring of 1992. His primary election defeat came just days after the names of the top check bouncers were leaked to the media. Hayes had continued a tradition of black representation in the First District which began in 1928.

4. Michael Barone and Grant Ujifusa, *The Almanac of American Politics 1990* (Washington, D.C.: National Journal, 1989), p. 350.

5. Ibid., pp. 350–351.

6. Ibid., p. 351.

7. Interview, Jeff Simering, Washington, D.C., March 20, 1992.

8. Interview, Michael Casserly, Washington, D.C., January 9, 1992.

9. U.S. Congress, House Subcommittee on Elementary, Secondary, and Vocational Education of the House Committee on Education and Labor, H.R. 3042 (Dropout Prevention and Reentry Act), Hearings, 99th Cong., 2nd sess., May 20, 1986, June 23, 1986, p. 2.

10. Ibid., p. 2.

11. Simering Interview.

12. In fact, his Democratic opponent in the November election, Representative Bob Edgar, did win the backing of the Pennsylvania state education association later that year. "PA—Senate: Specter Against Geography," *Congressional Quarterly Weekly Report* (October 11, 1986), p. 2477.

13. Simering Interview.

14. In recent years a far greater number of bills have been introduced in each Congress than have been passed, with less than a third of all Senate bills and less than a fifth of all House bills introduced passing. Norman J. Ornstein, Thomas E. Mann, and Michael J. Malbin, *Vital Statistics on Congress 1989–90* (Washington, D.C.: CQ Press, 1990), pp. 155–159.

15. H.R. 3042, Hearings, May 20, 1986, p. 11.

16. Legi-Slate Report on H.R. 3042.

17. Barone and Ujifusa, *The Almanac of American Politics 1990,* pp. 149–151, 350–351. When Hawkins retired at the end of the One Hundred and First Congress, the House lost one of its strongest defenders of the poor and middle class. As a representative, he demonstrated through his legislative activity his firm belief "that government programs can help, and have helped the poor and the middle class; [and] that aid to education has strengthened the nation and helped to make more equal the opportunities open to each child" (Barone and Ujifusa, *The Almanac of American Politics 1990,* p. 150).

18. *Congressional Record,* July 30, 1985, p. S10423.

19. H.R. 3042, Hearings, May 20, 1986, p. 140.

20. Walter J. Oleszek, *Congressional Procedures and the Policy Process,* 3rd ed. (Washington, D.C.: CQ Press, 1989), p. 147.

21. Ibid.

22. Ibid.

23. Ibid., p. 121.

24. Barone and Ujifusa, *The Almanac of American Politics, 1990,* p. 1069.

25. Sequestration is an across-the-board cutting mechanism begun under the Gramm-Rudman-Hollings Balanced Budget Act, which allows the president to withhold funds from being spent in order to meet deficit reduction targets.

26. Chapter 1 of the Elementary and Secondary Education Act provides financial assistance to states and local school districts to help in the education of economically disadvantaged children by providing such needs as funding for reading specialists.

Head Start, a program administered by the Department of Health and Human Services, funds a comprehensive preschool experience for economically and education- ally disadvantaged children, including health, nutrition, social services, and early edu- cation programs. Head Start served over 500,000 children in 1991, less than half of the preschool children eligible for the program (*CQ Almanac 1991,* p. 510).

27. *Congressional Record,* August 7, 1986, pp. H5621–H5622.

28. Ibid., p. H5622.

29. Ibid., p. H5625.

30. Ibid., p. H5629.

31. Ibid., pp. H5621–H5629. By volume, most measures passed by Congress are noncontroversial and are passed by voice vote. More controversial measures are usu- ally decided by a roll call vote, where each individual member's vote is known.

32. U.S. Congress, Senate Subcommittee on Education, Arts and Humanities of the Committee on Labor and Human Resources, S. 1525 (Dropout Prevention and Reentry Act of 1985), Hearings, 99th Cong., 1st sess., October 17, 1985.

33. H.R. 3042, Hearings, May 20, 1986, p. 12.

34. *CQ Almanac, 1985* (Washington, D.C.: Congressional Quarterly, 1986), p. 285.

35. H.R. 3042, Hearings, May 20, 1986, p. 135.

36. Ibid.

37. Ibid., p. 134.

38. Senators Phil Gramm (R-Tex.), Warren Rudman (R-N.H.), and Ernest Hollings (D-S.C.).

39. Alan Ehrenhalt, "86 Still a Puzzle," *Congressional Quarterly Weekly Report* (October 11, 1986), p. 2395.

40. "Pennsylvania," *Congressional Quarterly Weekly Report* (October 11, 1986), p. 2477.

41. *Congressional Record,* September 8, 1986, p. S12045.

42. *Congressional Record,* August 11, 1986, p. S11251.

43. *Congressional Record,* July 30, 1985, p. S10423.

44. David Rapp, "Education to Receive a Boost in New Democratic Congress," *Congressional Quarterly Weekly Report* (December 20, 1986), p. 3128.

45. Michael Barone and Grant Ujifusa, *The Almanac of American Politics 1986* (Washington, D.C.: National Journal, 1985), p. 820.

46. First elected to the Senate in 1960 and the chair of the Senate Foreign Rela- tions Committee, Pell has probably made a stronger mark in education than in foreign policy. A long-time member of the Subcommittee on Education, Arts and Humanities, Pell is perhaps best identified for his work in setting up a federal grant program for economically needy college and university students that now bears his name—the well- known Pell Grants.

47. Two-thirds vote in both the House and Senate is required for Congress to override the president's veto. In 1987 the Democrats had a 55–45 seat majority in the Senate and a 258–177 majority in the House.

48. Rapp, "Education to Receive a Boost in New Democratic Congress," p. 3127.

49. *Congressional Record,* January 16, 1987, p. S861.

50. Ibid.

51. Ibid., p. S862.

52. *CQ Almanac, 1987,* p. 527.

53. Ibid.

54. Ibid.

55. Ibid.

56. U.S. Congress, Senate Committee on Labor and Human Resources, S. 406

(Education for a Competitive America Act), Committee Report 100–73, 100th Cong., 1st sess., June 16, 1987, p. 9.

57. Oleszek, *Congressional Procedures and the Policy Process,* p. 75.

58. *Congressional Quarterly Almanac 1987,* pp. 641–650.

59. S. 406, Committee Report 100–73, June 16, 1987, p. 3.

60. In addition to concerns over the cost of the programs, given the budget deficit, Senator Quayle also objected to the expedited consideration of the programs by linking them to issues of trade and competitiveness. Some of the programs were already on the agenda for reauthorization in this session, and he felt the programs should be reviewed under the regular reauthorization process. S. 406, Committee Report 100–73, p. 41.

61. *CQ Almanac, 1987,* p. 640.

62. The Star Schools program is designed to provide grants for telecommunications networks in order to make instruction available in the areas of the sciences, math, and foreign languages. (See U.S. Congress, Senate, Committee on Labor and Human Resources, S. 406, Education for a Competitive America Act, Committee Report 100–73, 100th Cong., 1st sess., June 16, 1987, pp. 1–12.

63. *Congressional Record,* December 1, 1987, p. S16777.

64. Ann Young, interview, January, 1992, Washington, D.C.

65. U.S. Congress, Senate Committee on Labor and Human Resources, S. 373 (Robert T. Stafford Elementary and Secondary Education Improvement Act of 1987), Committee Report 100–222, 100th Cong., 1st sess., November 19, 1987, p. 85.

66. For example, Senator Hatch has worked with Senator Kennedy on such bills as AIDS education and treatment. See Barone, *The Almanac of American Politics, 1990,* p. 1225.

67. *Congressional Record,* December 1, 1987, p. S16818.

68. *Congressional Record,* May 21, 1987, p. H3827.

69. *CQ Almanac, 1987,* p. 521.

70. Ibid., pp. 531, 641.

71. Ibid., p. 640.

72. Ibid., p. 640.

73. Ibid., p. 640.

74. Public Law 100–202, December 22, 1987, p. 101 STAT. 1329–278 and 101 STAT. 1329–442.

75. Oleszek, *Congressional Procedures and the Policy Process,* 3rd ed., p. 74.

76. Public Law 100–297, April 28, 1988, p. 102 STAT. 265. *United States Statutes at Large* (Washington, D.C.: U.S. Government Printing Office, 1990).

77. Public Law 100–297, p. 102 STAT. 265 to p. 102 STAT. 274.

78. *Congressional Record,* June 13, 1989, p. H2490–H2491.

CHAPTER 4

1. Material in this section is drawn from interviews with June Moore, Maureen Coffey, Ron Fancher, and Joe Pellegrin, May 14, 1992, Milwaukee, Wisconsin.

2. Kenneth J. Cooper, "Financial Penalties Prove No Easy Solution to Dropout Problem," *Washington Post* (February 16, 1990), p. A3.

3. Vincent M. Mallozzi, "Tying Welfare to School Attendance," *New York Times* (January 3, 1988), Section 12, p. 7.

4. Maureen Coffey, interview, Milwaukee, Wisconsin, May 14, 1992.

5. Cooper, "Financial Penalties Prove No Easy Solution to Dropout Problem," p. A3.

6. Material on West Valley Academy, Inc. is taken from a "Program Description of West Valley Academy," prepared by William G. Savard, p. 1.

7. Ibid., p. 3.
8. Ibid., pp. 3–4.
9. Ibid., p. 4.
10. Ibid., p. 8.
11. Ibid., pp. 8–9.
12. John Fiegel, Department of Education, phone conversation, January 1990.

CHAPTER 5

1. E. J. Dionne, Jr., "President Stresses Schools and Drugs in His Courting of Governors," *New York Times* (August 1, 1989), p. 14.

2. Edward B. Fiske, "Will President Bush Pass the Test at His Education Summit Conference?" *New York Times* (September 13, 1989), p. B10, and Edward B. Fiske, "Meeting on Education Starts Today in Virginia," *New York Times* (September 27, 1989), Section II, p. 8.

3. "The Statement by the President and Governors," *New York Times* (October 1, 1989), Section IV, p. 22.

4. Edward B. Fiske, "Paying Attention to the Schools Is a National Mission Now," *New York Times* (October 1, 1989), Section IV, p. 1.

5. "Address before a Joint Session of the Congress on the State of the Union," *Public Papers of the Presidents,* January 31, 1990, p. 131.

6. "The Statement by the President and Governors," p. 22.

7. Denis P. Doyle and Terry W. Hartle, *Excellence in Education: The States Take Charge* (Washington, D.C.: AEI, 1985), p. 1.

8. "Department of Education," in *Congressional Quarterly Weekly Report,* Special Report, "Where the Money Goes" (December 7, 1991, Supplement to Vol. 49, No. 49), p. 108.

9. Doyle and Hartle, *Excellence in Education,* p. viii.

10. Michael Casserly, interview, Washington, D.C., January 9, 1992.

11. Michael Casserly, interview; Jeff Simering, interview, Washington, D.C., March 20, 1992.

12. U.S. Congress, House Committee on Education and Labor, H.R. 5 (School Improvement Act of 1987), Report 100–95, 100th Cong., 1st sess., May 15, 1987, p. 15.

13. Ibid., p. 16.
14. Ibid., p. 19.

15. U.S. Congress, House, Conference Report 100–567 to accompany H.R. 5 (Elementary and Secondary Education), 100th Cong., 2nd sess., April 13, 1988, pp. 330–334.

16. *Congressional Record,* May 9, 1989, p. H1791.

17. *Congressional Record,* June 13, 1989, p. H2491.

18. Suspension of the rules allows business to be expedited through a two-thirds vote; *Congressional Record,* June 13, 1989, pp. H2490–H2491.

19. *Congressional Record,* November 20, 1989, p. S16319.

20. "Oh, Yes—the Taft Institute," *Congressional Quarterly Weekly Report* (November 25, 1989), p. 3245.

21. *CQ Almanac, 1988* (Washington, D.C.: Congressional Quarterly, 1989), p. 348.

22. Projects included "$10 million for the Massachusetts Corporation for Educational Telecommunications; $7.5 million for a university library consortium in the Washington, D.C. area; $6.5 million for a Biotechnology Research Center at the University of Kansas; $5 million for a clinical law center at Seton Hall University in Newark, N.J." *CQ Almanac, 1988,* p. 348.

23. Ibid.

CHAPTER 6

1. Joseph Pellegrin, interview, Milwaukee, Wisconsin, May 14, 1992.

2. Ibid.

3. In order to receive a grant, each educational agency had submitted an application outlining the specifics of its dropout prevention program. The Department of Education reviewed proposals and awarded grants based on an assessment of each proposal in accordance with criteria set by Congress in creating the program. With additional funding, there would be several options, including the extension of programs receiving funds or the establishing of a new series of grants to be awarded to local educational agencies based on a new round of applications open to existing programs and those not yet funded.

4. See Michael J. Malbin, *Unelected Representatives* (New York: Basic Books, 1980); Harrison W. Fox, Jr., and Susan Webb Hammond, *Congressional Staffs* (New York: Free Press, 1977), ch. 4.

5. *1991/2 Congressional Staff Directory* (Mount Vernon, Va.: Staff Directories, Ltd., 1991), p. 798.

6. *1991/2 Congressional Staff Directory*, p. 872.

7. Malbin, *Unelected Representatives*, p. 28.

8. Hugh Heclo, "Issue Networks and the Executive Establishment," in Anthony King, ed., *The New American Political System* (Washington, D.C.: American Enterprise Institute, 1978), p. 117.

9. John Fiegel, Department of Education, interview, Washington, D.C., March 17, 1992.

10. Randall B. Ripley, *Congress, Process and Policy*, 2nd ed. (New York: W. W. Norton, 1978), p. 350.

11. *CQ Almanac 1990* (Washington, D.C.: Congressional Quarterly, 1991), p. 610.

12. U.S. Congress, Senate Committee on Labor and Human Resources, Report 101–136 to accompany S. 695 (Educational Excellence Act of 1989), 101st Cong., 1st sess.

13. The House companion measure to S. 695 failed to win approval; a partisan battle erupted, with the Democratic leadership introducing legislation to address the educational goals set earlier in the year by the president and the nation's governors, but with a price tag too high given the nation's deficit (*CQ Almanac, 1990*, pp. 610–615).

14. *CQ Almanac, 1990*, p. 610.

15. *Congressional Record*, February 20, 1990, p. S1206.

16. Ibid.

17. Ibid., p. S1207.

18. Walter J. Oleszek, *Congressional Procedures and the Policy Process*, 3rd ed. (Washington, D.C.: CQ Press, 1989), p. 290.

19. Ibid., p. 75.

20. Ibid., p. 66.

21. Allen Schick, *The Capacity to Budget* (Washington, D.C.: Urban Institute Press, 1990), p. 1.

22. Ibid., p. 2.

23. Ibid., pp. 5.

24. Ibid., pp. 4–5.

25. Joseph White and Aaron Wildavsky, *The Deficit and the Public Interest* (Berkeley: University of California Press, 1989), pp. xviii–xix.

26. Michael Oreskes, "Deficit Pact Blurs Party Boundaries," *New York Times* (October 4, 1990), p. D22.

27. Anne Wexler, "Son of Gramm-Rudman," *New York Times* (October 28, 1990), p. C7.

28. *CQ Almanac, 1989* (Washington, D.C.: Congressional Quarterly, 1990), p. 67.

29. "The Annual Appropriations Cycle . . . From President to Congress," *Congressional Quarterly Weekly Report,* Special Report, "Where the Money Goes," (December 7, 1991, Supplement to Vol. 49, No. 49), pp. 14–15.

30. Lance T. LeLoup, *Budgetary Politics,* 4th ed. (Brunswick, Ohio: King's Court Communications, 1988), p. 220.

31. This has become even truer since the budget agreement between the president and the Congress in late 1990, which set spending caps for discretionary spending in each of the categories of domestic, defense, and international spending. There has been some talk of modifying this agreement to allow sizable cutbacks in defense spending (beyond those set in the 1990 budget agreement), so that money can be used for domestic program needs, especially jobs and health care.

32. "Hill Readying to Raid Pentagon for 'Emerging Democracies,' " *Congressional Quarterly Weekly Report* (March 3, 1990), p. 680.

33. Allen Schick, "The Three-Ring Budget Process: The Appropriations, Tax and Budget Committees in Congress," in Thomas E. Mann and Norman J. Ornstein, eds., *The New Congress* (Washington, D.C.: American Enterprise Institute, 1981), p. 316.

34. I owe a great deal to Senator Kohl's budget legislative assistant at the time, Tom Stubbs, who in many conversations would carefully (and very patiently) explain the rules of the budget process.

CHAPTER 7

1. Donald R. Matthews, *U.S. Senators and Their World* (New York: Vintage Books, 1960).

2. Ibid., p. 92.

3. Ibid., p. 93.

4. Ibid., p. 95.

5. Ibid., p. 97.

6. Ibid., pp. 101–102. Matthews refers to this as "institutional patriotism."

7. Ibid., p. 99.

8. Ibid., pp. 100–101.

9. *CQ Almanac, 1990* (Washington, D.C.: Congressional Quarterly, 1991), p. 229.

10. Michael Barone and Grant Ujifusa, *The Almanac of American Politics 1990* (Washington, D.C.: National Journal, 1989), pp. 516–520.

11. Eleanor Clift, "The Prince of Pork," *Newsweek* (April 15, 1991), p. 35.

12. Barone and Ujifusa, *The Almanac of American Politics, 1990,* p. 1298.

13. Janet Hook, "The Byrd Years," *Congressional Quarterly Weekly Report* (April 16, 1988), p. 976.

14. Ibid.

15. *CQ Almanac, 1990,* p. 236.

16. See Senate floor debate, *Congressional Record,* March 29, 1990.

17. *CQ Almanac 1990.* p. 237.

18. Only Senator Strom Thurmond (R-S.C.) has more seniority than Byrd.

19. *CQ Almanac, 1990,* p. 237.

20. *Congressional Record,* March 29, 1990, p. S3490.

21. *CQ Almanac, 1990,* 237.

22. *Congressional Record,* March 29, 1990, p. S3491.

23. Ibid.

24. Bob Williams, *"Dare to Dream* Conference a Success!" *National Dropout Prevention Newsletter* (Summer 1989), Vol. 2, No. 3.

25. Maureen Coffey, phone interview, Milwaukee, Wisconsin, April 22, 1992.

26. Michael Casserly, telephone interview, January 9, 1992.

27. It remained unclear whether the lack of support was due to the pressures coming from other members of the Appropriations Committee seeking a means for protecting their programs, or whether there were real objections to the program. Whether Senator Harkin personally objected to the funding was not known, but it was clear that Michael Hall, his top staff aide, did object.

28. Maureen Coffey, interview, Milwaukee, Wisconsin, May 14, 1992.

29. Jeff Simering, interview, Washington, D.C., March 20, 1992.

30. Roger H. Davidson and Walter J. Oleszek, *Congress and Its Members* (Washington, D.C.: Congressional Quarterly, 1990), pp. 292–294.

CHAPTER 8

1. Senator Claiborne Pell to Senator Robert Byrd, letter, April 17, 1990.

2. Almost any letter sent from a congressional office will go through a number of revisions, reflecting input from the members as well as various staff assistants. For this reason, it may take several days before a final copy of a letter can be circulated among colleagues.

3. Isabel Salinas Almendarez, interview, Washington, D.C., March 19, 1992.

4. Ibid.

5. Michael Barone and Grant Ujifusa, *The Almanac of American Politics 1990* (Washington, D.C.: National Journal, 1989), pp. 79–83.

6. See Donald R. Matthews and James A. Stimson, *Yeas and Nays* (New York: John Wiley and Sons, 1975), especially chs. 3 and 4, on the need for cue-taking by members and on cue-giving sources.

7. Jeff Simering, interview, Washington, D.C., March 20, 1992.

8. Ross K. Baker, *House and Senate* (New York: W. W. Norton, 1989), pp. 28–31.

9. Simering, interview.

10. Joseph White and Aaron Wildavsky, *The Deficit and the Public Interest* (Berkeley: University of California Press, 1989), p. 2.

11. *Congressional Record,* April 26, 1990, p. S5141.

12. Simering Interview.

13. *Congressional Record,* April 26, 1990, p. S5142.

14. Kenneth B. Noble, "Federal Workers Get Unexpected Holiday," *New York Times,* October 18, 1986, p. 33:5.

15. The Perkins Loan program provides long-term, low-interest loans to financially needy students attending a postsecondary institution. Part or all of the loan can be canceled in exchange for public service in the following areas: teaching of the handicapped; teaching in schools with high concentrations of low-income students; or work in the Head Start, Peace Corps, or Vista programs.

16. Budget Information Sheet, "Perkins Loans, 1991 Budget Proposal" Department of Education.

17. *Congressional Record,* April 30, 1990, p. S5323.

CHAPTER 9

1. Norman J. Ornstein, Thomas E. Mann, and Michael J. Malbin, eds., *Vital Statistics on Congress, 1991–92* (Washington, D.C.: Congressional Quarterly, 1992), p. 113.

2. Jackie Calmes, "Bush Dealing from Strength as Budget Season Opens," *Congressional Quarterly Weekly Report* (February 3, 1990), p. 300.

3. Ibid., p. 299.

4. Ibid., p. 300.

5. *CQ Almanac, 1990* (Washington, D.C.: Congressional Quarterly, 1991), p. 111.

6. Ibid.

7. Ibid.

8. *Congressional Record,* April 26, 1990, p. S5044.

9. *CQ Almanac, 1990,* p. 844.

10. Jackie Calmes, "Line Begins for Ride on Spending Bill," *Congressional Quarterly Weekly Report* (March 10, 1990), p. 735.

11. John Felton, "Power of the Ballot Box Gives U.S. Policy a Fresh Start," *Congressional Quarterly Weekly Report* (March 3, 1990), p. 677.

12. Dinah Wisenberg, "Bush's $300 Million in Aid Faces Complications," *Congressional Quarterly Weekly Report* (March 17, 1990), p. 844.

13. Ibid.

14. Pat Towell, "Tapping the 'Peace Dividend," *Congressional Quarterly Weekly Report* (March 17, 1990), p. 845.

15. Ibid.

16. John Felton, "Battle Over Aid, Round Two: Issues of Scope, Control", *Congressional Quarterly Weekly Report* (March 10, 1990), pp. 756–758.

17. John Felton, "Panama-Nicaragua Money Bill Tangled in Other Issues," *Congressional Quarterly Weekly Report* (March 24, 1990), p. 928.

18. Pat Towell, "Supplemental Bill to Give Bush What He Asked, and More," *Congressional Quarterly Weekly Report* (March 31, 1990), pp. 1011–1012.

19. Brian Nutting, "Supplemental Spending Bill Stuck on Senate Floor," *Congressional Quarterly Weekly Report* (April 28, 1990), p. 1244.

20. Ibid.; Phil Kuntz, "Bush Has Add-Ons, Too," *Congressional Quarterly Weekly Report* (May 19, 1990), p. 1533.

21. John Felton, "Carrots-and-Sticks Policy Yields Possible Truce on the Hill," *Congressional Quarterly Weekly Report* (May 5, 1990), p. 1368.

22. John Felton, "Hill Group Paints Dark Picture of Rights in El Salvador," *Congressional Quarterly Weekly Report* (May 5, 1990), p. 1370.

23. Ibid., p. 1371.

24. Julie Rovner, "Abortion Fight Resumes," *Congressional Quarterly Weekly Report* (April 28, 1990), p. 1243.

25. Helen Dewar, "D.C. Death-Penalty Clause Stalls Senate Bill," *Washington Post* (April 28, 1990), p. A4.

26. Phil Kuntz, "Deal Near on Supplemental as House Lards the Bill," *Congressional Quarterly Weekly Report* (May 19, 1990), p. 1532.

27. *Congressional Record,* April 27, 1990, p. S5185.

28. Ibid., p. S5281.

29. Ibid., p. S5283.

CHAPTER 10

1. *Congressional Record,* April 25, 1990, p. S4991.

2. Ibid., p. S4972.

3. Ibid., p. S4991.

4. Ibid., p. S4999.

5. *Congressional Record,* April 26, 1990, p. S5141.

6. *Congressional Record,* April 30, 1990, p. S5323.

7. *Congressional Record,* April 26, 1990, p. S5105.

8. Ibid.

9. Ibid., p. S5106.

10. Walter J. Oleszek, *Congressional Procedures and the Policy Process,* 3rd ed. (Washington, D.C.: CQ Press, 1989), pp. 210–215.

11. See *Congressional Record,* July 31, 1989, p. S9134; *Congressional Record,* August 1, 1989, pp. S9319–S9323; U.S. Congress, Senate Committee on Governmental Affairs (Missing Links: Coordinating Federal Drug Policy for Women, Infants, and Children), Hearing, 101st Congress, 1st session, July 31, 1989.

12. Richard F. Fenno, Jr., *The Making of a Senator: Dan Quayle* (Washington, D.C.: CQ Press, 1989), p. 122.

13. R. H. Davidson and W. J. Oleszek, *Congress and Its Members* (Washington, D.C.: CQ Press, 1990), p. 184.

14. Senator Phil Gramm, *Congressional Record,* April 27, 1990, p. S5188.

15. Michael J. Barone and Grant Ujifusa, *The Almanac of American Politics 1990* (Washington, D.C.: National Journal, 1989), p. 1003.

16. *Congressional Record,* April 27, 1990, p. S5191.

17. The rules of the Senate require that all members address the president of the Senate, or the individual presiding in the absence of the president, rather than speak directly to each other. If Senator Hatfield had yielded his right to the floor, he might not have regained it, depending on who is recognized first by the presiding officer, and the filibuster would be over.

18. *Congressional Record,* April 27, 1990, p. S5191.

19. Ibid.

20. Ibid., p. S5194.

21. Ibid., p. S5195.

22. See Richard F. Fenno, Jr., *Home Style: House Members in their Districts* (Boston: Little, Brown and Co., 1978), especially chs. 3, 4, and 5.

23. Donald R. Matthews, *U.S. Senators and Their World* (New York: Vintage Books, 1960), pp. 100–101.

24. Janet Hook, "The Byrd Years," *Congressional Quarterly Weekly Report* (April 16, 1988), p. 976.

25. In addition to Senator Kohl, the co-sponsors were Senators Pell, Kennedy, McConnell, Wilson, Levin, Nickles, and Shelby, Lieberman, Biden, Simon, Kasten, Dodd, Hollings, Roth, Hatfield, Specter, Boren, Ford, Heinz, and Bentsen (*Congressional Record,* April 30, 1990, p. S5323).

26. *Congressional Record,* April 30, 1990, p. S5323.

27. Ibid., p. S5325.

28. Ibid.

29. Ibid., p. S5326.

30. Fenno, *Home Style,* p. 140.

CHAPTER 11

1. The conferees included the thirteen Democratic subcommittee chairs of the House Appropriations Committee, eight of the thirteen ranking Republicans of the subcommittees, and all twenty-nine members of the Senate Appropriations Committee (*Congressional Record,* May 3, 1990, p. D540; May 1, 1990, p. S5444).

2. Helen Dewar, "Aid Voted to Panama, Nicaragua," *Washington Post* (May 2, 1990), p. A4.

3. Lawrence D. Longley and Walter J. Oleszek, *Bicameral Politics* (New Haven, Conn.: Yale University Press, 1989), p. 3. Longley and Oleszek's exhaustive study of

conference committees is a useful source for those seeking more information on a device that is essential in the United States' bicameral legislative system.

4. Ross K. Baker, *House and Senate* (New York: W. W. Norton, 1989), p. 29.

5. Letter, Senator Kohl to colleagues, May 2, 1990.

6. Steven S. Smith and Christopher J. Deering, *Committees in Congress*, 2nd ed. (Washington, D.C.: CQ Press, 1990), p. 121.

7. Life and Career of Jamie Whitten," C-SPAN interview, November 28, 1991.

8. "F. Michael Hugo," in John L. Zorack, *The Lobbying Handbook* (Washington, D.C.: Professional Lobbying and Consulting Center, 1990), p. 506.

9. See the case of Representative Joseph P. Kennedy II, who in his second term, unsuccessfully challenged a fellow Massachusetts Democrat, Chester G. Atkins, who was in his third term, to fill a vacant seat on the House Appropriations Committee. Janet Hook, "Kennedy Muscle No Match for House Seniority," *Congressional Quarterly Weekly Report* (December 10, 1988), p. 3477, cited in Smith and Deering, *Committees in Congress*, pp. 72–73.

10. Smith and Deering, *Committees in Congress*, p. 51.

11. Allen Schick, "The Three-Ring Budget Process: The Appropriations, Tax, and Budget Committees in Congress," in Thomas E. Mann and Norman J. Ornstein, eds., *The New Congress* (Washington, D.C.: AEI, 1981), pp. 295–300.

12. Michael Barone and Grant Ujifusa, *The Almanac of American Politics 1990* (Washington, D.C.: National Journal, Inc., 1989), pp. 484–485.

13. Ibid., p. 484.

14. Barone and Ujifusa, *The Almanac of American Politics 1990,* p. 474.

15. Jeff Simering, interview, Washington, D.C., March 20, 1992; Michael Casserly, interview, Washington, D.C., January 9, 1992.

16. Simering Interview.

17. Ibid.

18. Simering and Casserly interviews.

19. Simering Interview.

20. Department of Education, "Effect of Senate Action, Fiscal Year 1990 Supplemental," "School Improvement Programs."

21. *Congressional Record,* May 3, 1990, p. H2020.

22. Ibid., pp. H2020–2021.

23. Ibid., p. H2020.

24. Walter J. Oleszek, *Congressional Procedures and the Policy Process,* 3rd ed. (Washington, D.C.: CQ Press, 1989), p. 248.

25. Letter, Augustus F. Hawkins to William H. Natcher, May 10, 1990.

26. Ibid.

27. Phil Kuntz, "Add-Ons Hold Up Conferees on Supplemental Spending," *Congressional Quarterly Weekly Report* (May 12, 1990), p. 1466.

28. Ibid.

29. Ibid.

30. Ibid.

31. Ibid., p. 1467.

32. Ibid.

33. Ibid.

34. Dan Morgan, "Of Swords, Plowshares, and . . . Pork," *Washington Post* (May 2, 1990), p. A21.

35. Harrison W. Fox, Jr., and Susan Webb Hammond, *Congressional Staffs* (New York: Free Press, 1977), p. 158.

36. Longley and Oleszek, *Bicameral Politics,* p. 140.

37. Ibid., pp. 140–141.

38. Phil Kuntz, "Deal Near on Supplemental as House Lards the Bill," *Congressional Quarterly Weekly Report* (May 19, 1990), pp. 1532–1534.

39. *Congressional Record*, May 22, 1990, p. H2742; U.S. Congress, House Conference Report 101–493 to accompany H.R. 4404 (Dire Emergency Supplemental), 101st Congress, 2nd session, May 22, 1990, p. 66.

40. Phil Kuntz, "Deal Near on Supplemental as House Lards the Bill," *Congressional Quarterly Weekly Report,* May 19, 1990, p. 1532.

41. Phil Kuntz, "A Pork-Heavy Supplemental Is Belatedly Sent to Bush," *Congressional Quarterly Weekly Report* (May 26, 1990), p. 1630.

42. Ibid., pp. 1630–1633.

43. *Congressional Record,* May 24, 1990, p. S6986.

44. Ibid., p. S6989.

45. Ibid.

46. "Bush Signs Aid Package for Panama, Nicaragua," *The Washington Post* (May 27, 1990), p. A13.

47. Ibid.

48. See Richard F. Fenno, Jr., *The Making of a Senator: Dan Quayle* (Washington, D.C.: CQ Press, 1989), for a more extended discussion of credit claiming based on observations of Senator Dan Quayle over a number of years.

CHAPTER 12

1. Norman J. Ornstein, Thomas E. Mann, and Michael J. Malbin, *Vital Statistics on Congress 1991–92* (Washington, D.C.: Congressional Quarterly, 1992), p. 153.

2. Ibid., pp. 151–153.

3. Walter J. Oleszek, *Congressional Procedures and the Policy Process,* 3rd ed. (Washington, D.C.: Congressional Quarterly, 1989), p. 284.

4. Ibid., p. 53.

5. A Congress lasts two years, beginning in the odd-numbered years.

6. James Madison, "The Federalist No. 62," reprinted in Roy P. Fairfield, ed., *The Federalist Papers,* 2nd ed. (Baltimore, Md.: Johns Hopkins University Press, 1981), p. 185.

7. James Madison, "The Federalist No. 52," in *The Federalist Papers,* p. 165.

8. John Jay, "The Federalist No. 64," in *The Federalist Papers,* p. 188.

9. Gary C. Jacobson, *The Politics of Congressional Elections,* 2nd ed. (Boston: Little, Brown and Co., 1987), p. 109.

10. Thomas E. Mann, "Elections and Change in Congress," in Thomas E. Mann and Norman J. Ornstein, eds., *The New Congress* (Washington, D.C.: American Enterprise Institute for Public Policy Research, 1981).

11. Based on receipts through October 17, 1990, for the November 1990 congressional elections, the approximate average amount spent in House races was $390,000 by Democratic incumbents and $83,900 by Republican challengers; and by Republican incumbents, $378,000 and Democratic challengers, $82,300. In Senate races, the approximate average amount spent by Democratic incumbents was $3.4 million and Republican challengers, $1.6 million; the total by incumbent Republicans was $3.2 million and by Democratic challengers $1.1 million. See *CQ Weekly Report* (November 3, 1990), p. 3757.

12. Mann, "Elections and Change in Congress," pp. 42–43.

13. Ibid., p. 43.

14. Jeff Simering, interview, Washington, D.C., March 20, 1992.

15. Ibid.

16. John Fiegel, interview, Washington, D.C., March 17, 1992.

17. U.S. Congress, House Committee on Appropriations, H.R. 2707 (Depart-

ments of Labor, HHS, and Education, and Related Agencies Appropriations Bill, 1992), Report 102–121, June 20, 1991, p. 156.

18. *Congressional Record,* September 10, 1987, p. S11918.
19. Ibid.
20. Ibid.
21. Ibid., pp. S11919–S11920.

INDEX

ABOUT THE AUTHOR

Janet M. Martin is associate professor of government at Bowdoin College. She previously taught at Gettysburg College. Professor Martin spent her sabbatical year in 1989–1990 as an APSA congressional fellow, working in the offices of Senator Herb Kohl and Majority Leader George Mitchell. Articles focusing on her interest in presidential appointments have appeared in *Western Political Quarterly* and *Presidential Studies Quarterly*. She is currently working on a project that discusses recruitment and governance by women in the executive branch since the Kennedy administration. Professor Martin remains an observer of events on the Hill (mostly through C-SPAN), watching with interest those issues that deal with education policy and congressional reform.